The War of 1812 in the Champlain Valley

A New York State Study

The War of 1812
in the Champlain Valley

ALLAN S. EVEREST

Syracuse University Press • 1981

ALLAN S. EVEREST is the author of *Moses Hazen and the Canadian Refugees in the American Revolution, Our North Country Heritage,* and *Rum Across the Border: The Prohibition Era in Northern New York.* He has also written articles for *New York History* and *Vermont History.*

First Paperback Edition 2010
10 11 12 13 14 15   6 5 4 3 2 1

∞ The paper used in this publication meets the minimum requirements
of the American National Standard for Information Sciences—Permanence
of Paper for Printed Library Materials, ANSI Z39.48-1992.

For a listing of books published and distributed by Syracuse University Press,
visit our Web site at SyracuseUniversityPress.syr.edu.

ISBN (paper): 978-0-8156-3258-0
ISBN (cloth): 978-0-8156-2240-6

Library of Congress Cataloging in Publication Data

The Library of Congress has cataloged the hardcover edition as follows:

Everest, Allan Seymour.
The War of 1812 in the Champlain Valley.

(A New York State study)
Bibliography: p.
Includes index.
1. Champlain Valley—History—War of 1812.
I. Title.   II. Series: New York State Study.
E355.1.C48E93   973.5'23   81-5659
ISBN 0-8156-2240-6   AACR2

Manufactured in the United States of America

CONTENTS

ILLUSTRATIONS

MAPS

PREFACE

Before the construction of the canal connecting Lake Champlain with the Hudson River, the economic development of the Champlain Valley was inextricably linked to its markets in Canada. Its inhabitants used the Richelieu River, outlet of the lake, to send their timber products, potash, and foodstuffs to consumers in Quebec and Great Britain. They imported by the same route many of the manufactured goods which, coming from the British Isles, were of better quality and lower price than any readily available to them in the United States. A nicely balanced economy was the result.

This happy state of affairs received its first jolt in 1807 with the enactment of the Embargo Act. The Jefferson administration attempted through economic coercion to persuade the British to terminate impressment of American citizens and violation of neutral rights on the seas. Since these were not problems on Lake Champlain, the people of the valley saw no reason to obey either the embargo or subsequent navigation laws designed to stop all commerce with the British, whether in Canada or elsewhere. Illegal trade flourished in the years before the war, and its importance and the impetus it had gained made it impossible to stop during the war itself.

This book presents the impact of the War of 1812 upon the people and governments of Lower Canada, Vermont, and New York. As in wars past, and for similar reasons, Lake Champlain became one of the major theatres of military operations. For two and a half years its people saw armies raised, defeated, and disbanded. They saw their own militia repeatedly called out to protect the border areas and to serve as adjuncts to regular army units. They knew that large diversions of energy were made to combat illicit trade, including Americans' willingness to help equip British warships.

Through a series of disheartening military reverses, loss of life, and de-

vii

struction of property, civilians maintained a remarkable degree of aplomb. They fled if battle threatened but soon returned to pick up the threads of their lives. This book is the story of their sufferings, of marching men and clashing ships, and of occasional heroic deeds.

For much of the military and naval material, I had the generous help of staff members at the National Archives in Washington and the Public Archives in Ottawa. For the local scene I am indebted to Charles W. McLellan of Champlain for the use of the Pliny Moore papers, and to Dennis Lewis, who shared the research he is doing for the Lake Champlain Archaeological Association. The staff at the library at the College of State University in Plattsburgh unearthed numerous sources from other institutions.

Special Collections at the College contain largely unused materials such as the Bailey and Kent-Delord manuscripts. The director, Dr. Bruce Stark, not only encouraged and aided me in my efforts, but made invaluable suggestions about the manuscript, for which I am deeply grateful.

Plattsburgh, New York   Allan S. Everest
Spring 1981

The War of 1812 in the Champlain Valley

1

SETTLEMENT OF THE CHAMPLAIN VALLEY

The Champlain Valley at the beginning of the nineteenth century, though still a youthful frontier area, was undergoing a peaceful and prosperous period of rapid growth. Although only thirty-five years earlier the valley had been an unsettled wilderness, already thousands had rushed in on both sides of the lake to establish towns and a complex network of economic relationships among themselves and, more particularly, with Canada.

It had not always been so. Beginning with the discovery of the lake by Samuel de Champlain in 1609, the French who ruled Canada also claimed the Champlain Valley. Not for many years were they able to establish a presence there, but the Dutch and later the English of New York were even less ready to stake a claim. The most the French could do by the 1640s was to try to Christianize the Mohawks on the Mohawk River. Father Isaac Jogues, discoverer and namer of Lake George (Lac du St. Sacrement), was the first martyr when he lost his life among the Indians.

As English and French population and ambitions increased, their settlements expanded toward each other, rivalries increased, and the Champlain Valley lay at the heart of their conflict over land and furs. With the outbreak of the wars of Louis XIV in Europe, military clashes spread to North America. Between 1689 and 1763, four intercolonial wars were fought between the French with their Indian allies and the English, supported by the Iroquois. Lake Champlain became a warpath between the contending forces, and during the eighteenth century it was continuously controlled by the French. They carved the entire shoreline on both sides into huge land grants, or seigneuries, after the Canadian pattern. However, few of these grants were ever settled or developed because of the scarcity of available French settlers.

Regardless of their inability to people the valley, the French were able to

1

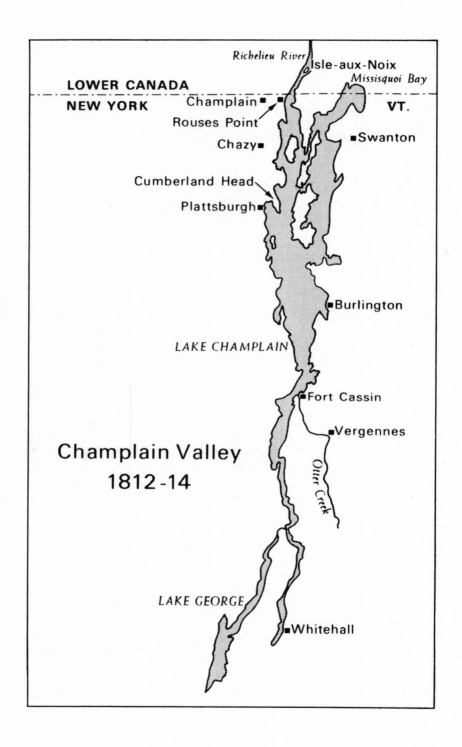

Richelieu River
Isle-aux-Noix
Missisquoi Bay

LOWER CANADA

NEW YORK

Champlain ■
Rouses Point

Chazy ■

Cumberland Head
Plattsburgh ■

VT.

■ Swanton

■ Burlington

LAKE CHAMPLAIN

■ Fort Cassin

■ Vergennes

Champlain Valley
1812-14

Otter Creek

LAKE GEORGE

■ Whitehall

strengthen their claims by constructing fortresses. In 1731 they erected a stockaded fort at Chimney Point which they subsequently moved to Crown Point, where Fort St. Frédèric was built of stone. From there they were able to dominate the lake and negate British claims which were backed only by a fort on the upper Hudson River. In 1755 the French further affirmed their dominion by starting the construction of Fort Carillon (Ticonderoga), which commanded the carrying place from Lake Champlain to Lake George.

The last of the great French-British wars (1754–63) was waged intensively in the Champlain Valley. The struggle involved such notable personalities as Montcalm for the French and Robert Rogers and General Jeffrey Amherst for the British. In 1759 Amherst succeeded in driving the French from both Forts Carillon and St. Frédèric. Although he could repair the partial French destruction at Carillon, the more complete demolition at St. Frédèric persuaded Amherst to build a new fort at Crown Point. He also ordered the construction of the military Crown Point Road across the Green Mountains to the lower Connecticut Valley. Montreal fell to the British in 1760, and the war in North America came to a close, although fighting elsewhere and protracted peace negotiations postponed a treaty of peace until 1763. One of its major terms was the British acquisition of all of Canada, together with French claims to the Champlain Valley.

Even before the signing of the treaty, but after the collapse of French Canada, Governor Benning Wentworth of New Hampshire resumed a practice he had started before the war of granting townships on the east side of what is now Vermont. He believed that the entire area between the Connecticut River and Lake Champlain belonged to New Hampshire by the none-too-clear terms of its original charter. Encouraged by the pressure for new lands for the overflowing farm population of southern New England, whose appetite had been whetted by the accounts their veterans brought back from the war, and driven by his own cupidity for the lands he could reserve to himself with each grant, he started handing out townships with a free hand. Between 1761 and 1764, he dispensed 114 of them, some along Lake Champlain, to groups of speculating proprietors in southern New England. For example, in 1761 he chartered the towns of Addison, Bridport, Middlebury, New Haven, Salisbury, and Shoreham. He continued the next year with Charlotte and Ferrisburg. In 1763 it was Burlington, Colchester, Orwell, and Shelburne.

Few of the proprietors came to their lands. Instead, they peddled them to jobbers who passed them on to retailers, who advertised and created markets for hundreds of family-sized farms. By the mid-1760s, trickles of settlers had begun to arrive along the east shore of the lake.

Meanwhile, the Wentworth pretensions were challenged by the colony of New York, which likewise thought its original charter to the duke of York included all the area which was becoming known as the "New Hampshire Grants." Referring its claim to London, New York was gratified with the royal decision of 1764, which declared the lands east to the Connecticut River "to be" a part of New York. Immediately the governors of the two colonies engaged in an acrimonious dispute over the meaning of "to be," New Hampshire declaring that it meant "henceforth" while New York insisted that it was retroactive.

Acting on this conviction, the successive governors of New York demanded that "Grants" farmers either reregister their land with New York and pay the appropriate fees, or else lose their property to new proprietors from New York. The ensuing turmoil gave rise to a vigilante group, the Green Mountain Boys led by Ethan Allen, whose original purpose in organizing was to resist New York sheriffs and to evict New York claimants to the lands of their friends and neighbors. Only the American Revolution temporarily put an end to this clash of wills between stubborn settlers and New York authorities.

Meanwhile, the west side of the lake had also begun to be opened to settlement. New York granted much of the land along the lake in small parcels to veterans of the French war. Most of the veterans did not choose to occupy their grants, but they were quite willing to sell to speculators. In this way Philip Skene laid the groundwork for his baronial estate at Skenesborough (Whitehall), and William Gilliland his large holdings at the mouth of the Bouquet River. Captain Charles de Fredenburgh received thirty thousand acres at the mouth of the Saranac River (later Plattsburgh) directly from the king in 1766. All three locations became centers of considerable agricultural and industrial production before the Revolution, while smaller beginnings were made at Chazy and Peru.

The two sides of the lake offer sharp contrasts in method of settlement. The people on the east side, individual owners of their farms, emulated the pattern of townships which they had known in southern New England. This included town governments for which they elected their own officials. On the New York side, on the other hand, the big owners (Skene, Gilliland, de Fredenburgh) established patriarchal domains of tenant farmers which duplicated the land-holding system of the great manor lords of the Hudson Valley.

The valley of the Richelieu River also began to be occupied more intensively than before the war. The new British rulers were willing to continue the French seigneurial pattern of settlement by recognizing the old French holdings all over Quebec and by granting many new ones, often to British or American petitioners. And so the lands along the Richelieu became taken up with seigneuries whose proprietors established extensive agricultural operations as well as a variety of industrial and commercial enterprises. One of the most profitable was the preparation of masts and staves for the export market, and this led to the exploitation of the virgin forests on the shores of Lake Champlain. Adolphus Benzel, assistant surveyor of the king's woods, toured the lake in 1772 and reported in alarm the fast-dwindling supply of mast-sized pine, and of huge white oaks being wastefully cut into staves. He surmised that much of this cutting on unsettled lands was being directed by entrepreneurs in Canada.[1]

A separate colony at the south end of Lake Champlain almost came into existence just before the Revolution. Fretting over their isolation and neglect by the government of New York, proprietors Skene and Gilliland, joined by Ethan Allen, plotted a new colonial entity under their own leadership. Skene took the plans to London, but the outbreak of the Revolution put an end to their project—henceforth, it was every man for himself.

The Revolution, although not originating in the Champlain Valley, nevertheless affected every one of its residents. It was the first war to rampage through the area after it had been settled. Skene and de Fredenburgh, for remaining loyal to the crown, forfeited their lands to New York State. Gilliland lost much of his property as well because of the mistaken notion that he too was a Loyalist. Across the lake the more numerous settlers abandoned their farms and went back to their place of origin or retreated behind a line of forts at Rutland and Pittsford.

At the start, in 1775, the American war effort was rewarded by dazzling victories. Green Mountain Boys seized Fort Ticonderoga and Crown Point, surprising small and unprepared garrisons. Benedict Arnold raided St. Jean on the Richelieu and made off with a much-needed schooner. In the fall of the year, an ambitious campaign was launched in the valley for the conquest of Canada before it could be reinforced from Great Britain. Led at first by General Philip Schuyler and later by General Richard Montgomery, the invasion succeeded after long delays in capturing the forts at Chambly and St. Jean. In November, the Americans took control of Montreal, then hastened to join Colonel Benedict Arnold, who had led another force northward from Maine. Their joint attack on Quebec City at the end of the year failed, Montgomery was killed and Arnold wounded.

Although the American army besieged the city for the rest of the winter, the men were dispirited and disease-ridden by smallpox. In May, strong British reinforcements appeared in the St. Lawrence, and the Americans retreated upriver in great confusion. By June, they were debouching into Lake Champlain in a race for survival. But smallpox accompanied them, and for a time during the summer Fort Ticonderoga was a pest house. The effort to drive the British out of Canada had failed because too few French residents had been persuaded of the chances of American success to join them; the army had no hard money with which to purchase supplies (the Canadians distrusted the paper promises they were offered and sometimes forced to accept); and the Americans were too few in number for the magnitude of the undertaking.

Governor General Guy Carleton believed that the Champlain Valley was now wide open to British conquest. Until October, he constructed a fleet of warships and troop carriers, then started south in search of the Americans. Alert to the danger, Arnold had also spent the summer creating a navy at Skenesborough. The two fleets clashed on October 11, 1776, in the channel behind Valcour Island. In a battle which need never have been fought, and which Arnold had been ordered to avoid if his opponent were stronger than he, Arnold lost almost his entire fleet on the 11th and the two days' pursuit that followed. The victorious Carleton contented himself with briefly occupying Crown Point before he pulled his entire force back to Canada for the winter.

His destruction of Arnold's fleet gave General John "Gentleman Johnny" Burgoyne control of the lake when he invaded the valley in 1777. Capturing Fort Ticonderoga early in July, he pushed on to the Hudson River by way of Skenesborough. But after crossing the Hudson he found himself in deep trouble, and after two hard engagements at Saratoga, he surrendered his entire army. For the rest of the war the Champlain Valley remained under British control for most of the time. British and Indian troops launched destructive raids deep into the river valleys on both sides of the lake, driving out or capturing the few hardy souls who were trying to keep their farms in operation.[2]

During the war, the people of the New Hampshire Grants, having resisted New York's efforts to assimilate them, formed their own state government and wrote a constitution declaring their separation from both Great Britain and New York. Choosing the name of Vermont for their little republic, they sought to enter Congress as an equal partner to the other thirteen states, only to be blocked at one time or another by both New Hampshire and New York.

Left to their own devices, the state's leaders decided to seek an accommodation with the British, especially after their destructive raids in 1779. Talks began between British and Vermonters in 1780 and were protracted through the next year. The Vermont delegation, usually including Ira Allen, met British representatives of Governor General Frederick Haldimand, hence the name of the "Haldimand Negotiations." The Vermonters dangled the prospect that at some "propitious" time they would rejoin the British Empire, in return for which the British agreed to suspend their raids in the valley. The propitious time was always made to appear just over the horizon, but it never arrived. Yet for two years the Vermonters warded off attacks from Canada.

The traditional view of the Haldimand Negotiations has always been that Vermonters really wanted to join the Union, that they used the negotiations as a lever to open the doors of Congress to them, at the same time keeping their frontiers safe. The biographer of Ethan Allen, on the other hand, has decided that Vermont's activities bordered on treason. The most recent scholar on the subject believes that Vermont's leaders wanted to protect their frontiers, that they probably primarily wanted to join the Union but that they kept the British option open as long as possible.[3]

Even before the peace treaty was concluded, Vermonters began to return to their valley farms, and a wave of new settlers also moved in. They came mostly from southern Vermont and southern New England. By 1790, their numbers in the valley were some twenty-nine-thousand people. The process of county-making continued during the 1780s and 1790s: Rutland County was created in 1781 and included the entire west side of the state to the Canadian border; Addison was set off in 1785, Chittenden in 1787, Franklin in 1792, and Grand Isle in 1802.

Vermont, operating as an independent republic because still denied membership in the Union, created its own coinage and paper money, operated a post office and built post roads as well as other internal improvements. In 1785 Ira Allen and others went to Canada in search of a trade agreement. They failed to get one but they obtained free trade in most of their produce on a year-by-year basis. Allen also negotiated with British officials for a ship canal on the Richelieu, again without success. Nevertheless, Vermont's farm and forest products had a ready market in Montreal and Quebec City. The only blight on its complete freedom of action was a British garrison left at Dutchman's Point on North Hero, in clear violation of the peace treaty. The British also stayed on at Point au Fer on the west side of the lake.

Meanwhile, the New York side became a somewhat later frontier. Few of the prewar proprietors and settlers returned; instead, state patents to new proprietors opened vast tracts for settlement by New Yorkers and New Englanders. One of the earliest was the regranting of the old de Fredenburgh patent to a group of proprietors, several of them Platts, from Dutchess County, New York, in 1784. Most of these new owners came to settle on their lands, establishing the village of Plattsburgh in 1785. In the following year the state solved the problem of the several hundred refugees and their families from Quebec and Nova Scotia who had fled their homelands, the men to fight for the American cause in the Revolution. The state's largess created a large land grant, the Canadian and Nova Scotia Refugee Tract, which occupied the northern third of the present Clinton County. The grant brought settlers, mostly French Canadian, to the area; it also provided a field day for American land speculators who bought up Canadian rights and disposed of their holdings to American settlers.

In 1787 the Moorsfield Patent was granted to a group led by Pliny Moore, who came to establish the town of Champlain. In a few years the entire west shore of the lake had been granted—several other large sections to Zephaniah Platt—and vigorous promotion brought a steady stream of settlers. In 1790 the population of the New York side of the lake was 15,600, about half the number on the Vermont shore. One significant difference in the make-up stemmed from the legal existence of slavery in New York. Consequently, the New York settlements included sixty-four slaves, whereas Vermont had abolished the institution in its Constitution of 1777. Typical of a frontier area, the census showed a preponderance of males over females—in Plattsburgh a ratio of 59 to 41, and in Champlain 56 to 44.

As on the Vermont side, county building progressed from south to north. Washington County existed from 1784. Clinton, consisting of all of northern New York, was formed in 1788. Essex was set apart in 1799, and Franklin in 1808. On the New York shores a more important role for county government developed than in Vermont, but townships were still significant, suggesting a blending of the New England and the southern New York patterns. In 1790 there were only four organized towns in northern New York: Champlain, Plattsburgh, Willsboro, and Crown Point.

On both sides of the lake, obtaining the land was for many a financial strain. In New York the first step was buying from the patent-holders; similarly, in Vermont the purchase was made from the town proprietors or their agents. Both groups offered inducements to locate settlers, although Vermonters engaged in fewer giveaway schemes. The Plattsburgh proprietors, on the contrary, offered gift and cheap lots to the first comers, and even promised 100 acres to the first male child born in town. After the flow of settlers had been primed, the proprietors were happy to charge all the traffic would bear.

The success stories on the frontier have traditionally concealed the fact that there were failures as well. Most settlers, in order to buy their land, needed financial help, usually from moneylenders or mortgages on their property. Many an unpublicized tragedy, discoverable only by a search of old deed and mortgage records, resulted from the premature death of the head of the family, a fire that destroyed his barn, a loss in the Canadian market, or other unforeseen reversals. The defeated family had the choice of either returning to their place of origin or, more often, going to work for someone else.

The frontier experience, except for the few who arrived with the financial reserves to develop the water power and other natural resources of the area, required superhuman effort on the part of all who survived it. A log cabin was the first priority and clearing the land was nearly as urgent. A skilled woodsman could clear an acre of forest land in seven to ten days; he could clear and sow ten acres in his first year if he had nothing else to do. For a while, the lack of markets limited the size of the space he cleared for crops. On the average, three to four acres were cleared in a year, meaning that a life-time was required to bring a modest farm under cultivation.

The many travel accounts of the period contain vivid descriptions of the dehumanizing effect of frontier conditions upon many settlers. The Reverend Nathan Perkins, who toured western Vermont in 1789, and the Reverend Timothy Dwight, who travelled through parts of New England and New York in 1805, were aghast at what they saw.[4] Not surprisingly, both of these ministers found the frontier an ungodly place where religion and education were neglected. But they also reported abysmal poverty and weakness in newly settled areas. Primitive living conditions were unavoidable because of the lack of minimum quantities of clothing and food; people were often ragged, dirty, buggy, and coarse but, unaccountable to the prim Mr. Perkins, contented and joyous at the prospects for their future.

The account of one young settlement illustrates the difficult first years on a typical frontier. Grand Isle was settled in 1783. For the first several years food was scarce, and many people subsisted on what they could obtain from hunting and fishing. The lucky ones with wheat had to travel to Whitehall or Granville, New York, the nearest gristmills at the time. One resident made several trips on horseback to Whitehall, carrying only two or three bushels per trip. During the winter of 1784–85, food was so scarce that some families were reduced to one or two small meals a day. In the fall of 1785, the settlers pooled all their money and sent one of their number to Bennington on horseback to buy shoes and clothing. He returned in mid-December with frozen feet.[5]

But the settlements *did* persist and most people *did* succeed in establishing themselves in farming, milling, or shipping. A modest prosperity had developed by the turn of the century throughout the valley, based largely upon the marketing of produce in Canada. Meanwhile, two irritants were removed: in 1790 New York finally gave up its claim to Vermont in return for a small cash payment to satisfy some of its claimants; this opened the way for Vermont to join the Union in 1791. The other improvement in the atmosphere occurred in 1796, when the British relinquished their outposts on Dutchman's Point and Point au Fer.

From almost the beginning of settlement, the Champlain Valley had exportable surpluses which found their natural outlet in Canada. An all-water route to the Hudson River was not developed for several decades, and the poor roads discouraged large-scale shipments by land. On the other hand, the outlet of Lake Champlain was the Richelieu River, which flowed into the St. Lawrence at Sorel. Unfortunately, the ten-mile stretch between St. Jean and Chambly was a series of unnavigable rapids. American shippers had their choice of unloading their cargo at St. Jean and hauling it overland to Montreal; unloading at St. Jean for carting around the rapids, or shooting the rapids during the period of high water in the spring. Most of the produce was headed for either Montreal or Quebec City for reexport to Great Britain. This was true of all the potash, most of the timber products and much of the wheat that flowed out of the valley. Ingenious shippers discovered that huge timber rafts could be constructed to survive the rapids and to carry super-cargoes of other goods as well.

Alongside the Canadian trade, the traffic in passengers and cargo developed between the shores of the lake itself. Numerous sailing ships and ferries were launched which helped to tie the valley into a single economic unit. In 1809 the world's second successful steamboat began to share this lively commerce. Small industries, from textiles to cast iron, proliferated on both sides of the lake, although the preponderance was on the Vermont side. The mills processed the exports of farm and timber products to Canada. In exchange, Americans imported quantities of furs, British manufactures, and other goods. Gradually, as Professor Muller points out, there developed "a closely-knit community of interests, which in future years would transcend tariffs, international tensions, and even war."[6]

Largely as a result of the liberal interpretation of Section III of Jay's Treaty of 1795, this international commerce underwent a rapid increase. Its annual value at the St. Jean customshouse jumped from a mere £17,300 before the treaty to £50,200 in 1797, and to more than £200,000 by 1807, the last year of uninterrupted trade before the imposition of the Embargo Act.[7] Thus a powerful economic interest tied the Champlain and St. Lawrence valleys together until it was challenged by the exigencies of the nation's foreign policy.

2

A POSTPONED WAR

Into this peaceful scene a long-festering international discord exploded. On June 18, 1812, the Senate of the United States completed action on a troublesome measure which, with the president's signature, committed the nation to war with Great Britain. Two days previously, the government in London announced its intention of repealing the Orders in Council. The actions of each might have been quite different if they could have had up-to-date information on the activities of the other. The decisions of each had been long delayed. Belatedly the British took steps to remove a major cause of friction, while the Americans passed over their periods of genuine war feeling and finally forced the issue when internal dissension was at its height.

The final plunge came not only after weeks of debate, but also following seven years of British arrogance in their treatment of neutrals, and of American protests and weak diplomacy to avoid a showdown. In one sense the war was an anticlimax; it might as logically have been declared three, twelve, or sixty months earlier. But when it came many Americans opposed it, while the British were incredulous and bitter over what they considered perfidious behavior.

Since 1803, Great Britain had been trying uninterruptedly to bring about the downfall of Napoleon Bonaparte. In spite of every weapon the British and their European partners could bring to bear, Napoleon had remained supreme and apparently unbeatable on the continent. They believed that they were fighting for the survival of western civilization.

For this struggle the British had long had difficulty in manning their great navy. Because of its low pay, harsh discipline, and long stays away from home ports, volunteers never came forward in sufficient numbers. Thus by necessity and usage since the Middle Ages, the press gang had become a distasteful fact of British life. Citizens, when they could be caught off guard, were kidnapped into duty on His Majesty's ships. To combat the tendency to desert, seamen were denied shore leave, sometimes for years on end.

During the Napoleonic wars, the British navy never had its full complement of one hundred and fifty thousand men. The press gangs were busy despite continuous complaints from all over the British Isles. The admiralty also revived an internationally accepted practice of recapturing deserters wherever they could be found. This policy embroiled Britain in a major dispute with the United States. British seamen were well trained and eager to work for even the lowest American wages, which averaged $24 per month, whereas the British pay was about $7. British seamen were notoriously eager to escape from the hardships of the British navy for the somewhat milder and more egalitarian practices of the American navy and merchant marine.

Impressment from American ships had been carried on since before 1800, with little American opposition as long as the British held to the general rule of reclaiming only their own citizens. As time went on, however, conflict arose over two practices—the impressment of former British nationals who now claimed American citizenship, and the too-frequent seizure of undeniably American nationals. American law allowed citizenship after five years' residence, but Great Britain maintained that all British-born persons remained British and that in an emergency such as the war against Napoleon their services could be claimed for their mother country.

Impressment alone provides an insufficient explanation for the outbreak of war; the conflict resulted from its continuation over many years, complicated by other kinds of British restrictions on neutral trade, such as blockade, and search and seizure. Toward the end of the prewar period these practices were so onerous that impressment was only one of several American grievances.

The death in 1806 of Tory leader William Pitt offered some prospect of checking the deterioration of British-American relations. Although distinct party lines on all issues were not yet established in British politics, a wide difference of opinion existed between Tories and Whigs on policies involving the United States. The Tories, who were to rule with only a brief interruption between 1803 and 1812, were devoted to the shipping interests and determined to maintain the navigation system intact. Their leaders believed in the strict enforcement of the trade acts and the prohibition of neutral commerce in the foreign West Indies. Their program was motivated by a determination to deny Napoleon any outside help, to preserve Britain's commercial supremacy, and to minimize the growing rivalry of the American merchant marine.

The Whigs, on the other hand, contained a sprinkling of the old "friends of America" from the days of the American Revolution. They reflected the interests of Britain's fast-growing manufacturers, to whom the

American market was of great importance. Exports of British products to the United States increased from 30.5 percent of the total in 1805, to 33.4 percent in 1807.[1] Thus an interruption in the American trade would cost them one-third of their export business. Unfortunately for them, their period of rule lasted only a year and was followed by the return of the Tories to power.

In the fall of 1806, Napoleon opened the "war of edicts" with the Berlin Decree, which placed Great Britain under blockade and prohibited all trade in British goods with the north of Europe. In January 1807, the Whig ministry responded with the first of a series of Orders in Council which forbade neutral trade *between* ports held by Napoleon. Both sides thus adopted policies harmful to neutral, especially American, commerce.

In June 1807, a case of flagrant British impressment almost brought open conflict. Three deserters from a British ship were known to have enlisted on the American warship, the *Chesapeake*. The American government refused to return them after first learning that they were American-born subjects who had been impressed by the British. As the unfinished *Chesapeake* sailed for the Mediterranean, she was challenged by a British ship of fifty-six guns, the *Leopard,* just outside the Virginia Capes. When Commodore James Barron refused to surrender the British "deserters," his ship was fired on, resulting in the death of three men and the wounding of eighteen more. Unable to return the fire, the *Chesapeake* struck her colors. A British boarding party removed the three men, clearly American citizens, but also one British subject who was later hanged.

The American reaction was instantaneous and outraged. Threats of war filled the air, and undoubtedly a near-united country could have embarked on war in 1807. Americans were offended by the effrontery and the injustice of the act; they were also humiliated by the failure of the *Chesapeake* to defend herself.

By proclamation, President Thomas Jefferson ordered all British armed vessels out of American waters. He referred to the attack as "this enormity" which had neither provocation nor justification.[2] Yet his voice of moderation was a leading factor in the prevention of a war that he opposed. He sought reparations and an apology from Britain, although ultimately getting neither; he counselled patience; and he refused to call Congress into session until October, by which time the war fever had abated. Nevertheless, Jefferson acknowledged that although Napoleon had established a tyranny on land, the United States was more immediately threatened by Britain's tyranny on the seas.

His solution to the crisis was economic coercion in preference to war. He proposed, and Congress quickly approved, a total embargo upon all American foreign trade. He was convinced that American commerce was so vital to

Europe that its cessation would bring the belligerents to their senses and cause them once again to respect a neutral flag. He was well aware that as much as 80 percent of all American exports went to Great Britain and its dependencies; that one-third of all imports came from the British, and that the latter benefited by many millions of dollars from a favorable balance of trade.[3]

Under normal conditions the embargo might have been effective, but France and Great Britain were too committed to defeating each other by maritime regulations to soften their policies. The British manufacturers, who were severely hurt, protested and submitted petitions, but the Whigs were a minority in Parliament, and their arguments were lost in the louder clamor over the necessities of the war with France. Furthermore, although British exports to the United States dropped from £11,850,000 in 1807, to £5,240,000 in 1808, they at first showed a 50 percent increase to the rest of the Western Hemisphere, chiefly to the newly opened markets of independent South America.[4] Consequently, some of the dismay of the merchants over the embargo was compensated for by new outlets for their goods. The Tory government came to look upon the embargo as a positive blessing: the Americans had voluntarily removed both aid to Napoleon and competition with British commercial interests. Viewing the embargo with intense satisfaction, the Tories were content to leave matters alone.

While failing to have the desired effect upon Great Britain, the embargo was a disaster in the United States. The South, which loyally supported Jefferson, suffered an agricultural decline from which some areas, especially Virginia, never recovered. The West entered upon a period of hard times with the loss of its foreign markets. Westerners considered the British restrictions chiefly responsible and loudly denounced that nation's maritime policies.

On the other hand, the shippers of the Northeast were able to make considerable profit in their carrying trade, despite British regulations. They preferred to take the risks that went with wartime commerce rather than have it stopped. A revival of the Federalist party took place in New York and New England in vigorous opposition to Jefferson's policy. As early as 1807, Massachusetts elected a Federalist governor, but the wider revival of the party came more gradually as a result of the failures of Madison's policies and the drift toward war. Although northeastern shipping declined disastrously, illegal trading was carried on all along the seacoast. The only incidental benefit to accrue from the embargo was the stimulation of the domestic manufacture of textiles and iron products in the middle states and New England, but at the time this was not seen as the blessing it later turned out to be.

Opinions in the Champlain Valley were formed in reaction to the distressing *Chesapeake* crisis and the war scare it engendered, followed by the locally abhorrent laws forbidding trade with Canada. In this situation, the people of the exposed New York border reacted strenuously to the fear of war. The inhabitants of Chateaugay begged Militia General Benjamin Mooers in Plattsburgh for help in obtaining arms in 1807: "Our people are courageous and patriotic, and are determined not to leave their Habitations provided they can be placed in a situation to defend themselves."[5]

At the same time the citizens of Champlain formed a Committee of Safety, which sent Pliny Moore to Albany to ask Governor Daniel Tompkins for arms. He obtained them but only on condition that they would be used only in a real emergency and that they would be returned on demand. Moore personally brought back the 130 stands of arms and ammunition, by wagon from Albany to Whitehall and then by boat, in October 1807. His expenses were covered by subscriptions of a dollar or two from a large number of individuals. The arms were turned in to the Plattsburgh arsenal a year later, when the war scare had abated.[6]

On the other hand, the reaction to the prohibition against trade with Canada was stronger, but only in degree, on the Vermont side of the lake, which had an older and more extensive export business. Trade with Canada did not become illegal until Congress passed the Second Supplementary Act on March 12, 1808, which closed a large loophole in the Embargo Act of the previous December. Soon the citizens of Burlington called a town meeting "to deliberate the question whether any, or what measures can be adopted to avert the evils of the late embargo act," and demanded that the act be repealed. Towns from north to south on the Vermont side held similar meetings which produced similar results.[7]

By 1808, the trade both ways with Canada had become crucial to the economy of the Champlain Valley. In addition to exporters and importers within the valley itself, Troy, Albany, and Boston merchants were also involved. John Jacob Astor, who was in Canada periodically on his fur business, estimated that 75 percent of all potash, 20 percent of the flour, much timber, and nearly all the beef and lard exported from Canada in 1808 originated in the United States.[8]

According to a recent study by Richard P. Casey, the two most valuable exports were potash and pearlash, which leads him to dub the subsequent disturbances as the "Potash Rebellion." These products were used in bleaches, fertilizers, soaps, oxidizing agents in British manufactures, and scourers of newly clipped wool. Its price remained consistently high in Montreal, pearlash commanding from $200 to $350 a ton in 1808. By one estimate for that year, and in spite of the embargo, thirty thousand barrels of American potash reached Montreal.[9]

Muller's careful study of the Canadian trade of this period throws much light on the huge quantity and variety of goods that moved north and south. By 1807, there were 110 different commodities involved in this traffic. At the opening of the rafting season in 1808, Burlington merchants claimed lumber intended for the Canadian market and stacked on the shores of lake and rivers to the value of $400,000. Despite the embargo, it was sent on rafts whose cargo ranged from $5,000 to $30,000 apiece in value.

According to Muller, the goods smuggled out of the Champlain Valley in that year included potash and pearlash (more than half of the value), lumber, pork, cheese, butter, grain, and much else to the value of about $260,000. In 1809 this figure was more than doubled, with an additional $200,000 in goods moving southward. The value in 1810 was 41 percent higher than the year before; the exports and many of the imports were illegal for most of this period under the administration's measures.[10]

The customs services on the two sides of the lake were ill-equipped, either temperamentally or physically, to cope with the unlawful traffic that sprang up. On the New York shore Collector Melancthon L. Woolsey maintained one station near his home on Cumberland Head. Several attempts to kidnap him perhaps discouraged him from making very vigorous efforts at enforcement. President Jefferson received reports which accused Woolsey of everything from corruption to irresponsibility. At the president's urging, Governor Tompkins reluctantly ordered a detachment of militia to Cumberland Head in June 1808, and he placed General Mooers in charge of them to help enforce the embargo. The governor's instructions emphasized the delicacy of the militia assignment: to sustain the collector enforcing the laws while avoiding giving "any uneasiness or offence to the peaceable Citizens of the State," as well as exciting "irritation, offence or alarm in our Canadian neighbors."[11]

Woolsey was relieved from his duties in 1809 and was replaced by Peter Sailly of Plattsburgh, who held the position until his death in 1826. Sailly expanded his operation by establishing his main station at Rouses Point and by maintaining twenty-two special inspectors in the field. He learned to keep loaded pistols at hand at all times; in spite of that his home on Bellevue (now Cumberland) Avenue in Plattsburgh was attacked at least once.

On the Vermont side, Jabez Penniman was the collector in 1808, followed later by Cornelius P. Van Ness. Penniman, who received threats on his life, reported to Secretary of the Treasury Albert Gallatin that the embargo was unenforceable without military help. He was directed to arm some vessels, which he did. If more help was needed, the U.S. marshall could raise a posse; if that was insufficient, the militia would be used. The militia from Franklin County, Vermont, were ordered to duty at Windmill Point in Alburg, but perhaps because they knew many of the smugglers, rafts continued to get by at night. The men were replaced by militia from Rutland County, who marched 120 miles to reach their post. In July, fourteen of them departed without leave. This unit too was suspected of winking at evasions of the law and was replaced by a detachment of federal artillery, which constructed an extensive cantonment in Swanton village.

Jefferson was sharply criticized locally for using troops against so-called "peaceable citizens," but for him the issue was war or peace, and he was determined not to let the embargo fail for lack of enforcement. On April 19, 1808, he issued a Proclamation of Insurrection on Lake Champlain, which urged illegal operators to retire peacefully, and expanded the powers of customs officers to seize property merely on a suspicion that it was headed for Canada. A St. Albans town meeting in June rejected the insurrectionary label, believing it was not justified by individual evasions of the law. Protests to the president were forwarded such as the one from North Hero: "Can the danger, which awaits our vessels and our merchandize on the high seas, be a good reason for stopping our boats, our carts and waggons, where no such danger exists?"[12] Smuggling continued after 1808, but not quite as blatantly whenever troops were stationed in the area.

The techniques evolved by the smugglers were always bold, often ingenious, and sometimes violent, and they form a large volume of the folklore of the Champlain Valley. On the water the favorite device was the large raft carrying huge cargoes and operated by sail and a crew of dozens of men. Since they were clumsy and slow moving, the rafts usually were operated only at night. On land a variety of expedients was used. Cattle were driven through the woods. Goods were stacked near the border and carted across on human or animal backs. One of the cleverest schemes for avoiding prosecution was the construction of rude huts on slopes leading down to the border. A hut was then filled with produce and caused to collapse, whereupon the barrels of flour or pork rolled obligingly into Canada.

Tea was one of the profitable shipments into Canada. A New York barrel would just hold two chests of the leaves. Tea was obtainable at a dollar a pound in Plattsburgh. Smuggled to St. Jean, it sold for two dollars. The return trip was made with sugar which also doubled in price. Another profitable export was always potash, of which there were frequent seizures. A supply of sixty or seventy barrels was once captured and stored in a barn on Windmill Point, whereupon a group decided to rescue it. One man reconnoitered the location, found that the officer was absent, and the property guarded by only one man and a housekeeper. That night two men visited and preoccupied the single guardian indoors while the rest raided the barn. Because it was locked, they removed the siding and sped the potash across the ice of the Richelieu. One of the teams made three trips before the job was completed.

In his confrontations, Deputy Collector Samuel Buell of Vermont, son-in-law of Peter Sailly, was plagued with bad luck. He and two boatmen pursued Harrington Brooks and Miner Hilliard in their boatload of salt and dry goods. Overtaking them, the officer gave one of his boatmen the order to fire a warning shot. Unintentionally, the shot killed Brooks. A sensational trial ensued, and the jury found the boatman guilty of murder, but further proceedings led to his acquittal. On another occasion Buell managed to board a smuggler's boat, but he was marooned there when his revenue cutter pushed away. His own men refusing to use their guns to rescue him, the smugglers took Buell across the line and deposited him in water up to his chin, then made good their escape.

The most notorious escapade involved a shoot-out in the Winooski River in August 1808. The customs service had acquired an efficient, twelve-oared cutter, the *Fly*. It was defied by a smugglers' vessel, the *Black Snake*, which had a load of about 100 barrels of ashes, much of it from St. Albans Bay. During the melee, two soldiers and the captain of the *Fly* were killed and another officer seriously wounded. All of the smugglers were captured on the spot or shortly afterwards. After their trials, one was executed, two were sentenced to fifty lashes and ten years in prison, and one received only a ten-year sentence. Their leader, Captain Truman Mudgett of Highgate, was tried but the jury deadlocked and his case was finally dropped.

The violations of the Embargo and Nonintercourse acts were, however, much more than amusing but passing episodes. For one thing, they demonstrate the degree of lawlessness that can prevail when economic self-interest is pitted against national policy. More importantly, they taught the smugglers of Vermont and New York that the profits were enormous and the risks minimal. Since the men knew all the routes and subterfuges, they had no reason to stop their illicit trade just because the United States declared war, and their supplying of the British army in Lower Canada was a major blot on the American war effort.

The embargo succeeded chiefly in dividing and impoverishing the United States. A discouraged Jefferson, eager to prevent it from becoming a millstone around the neck of his successor, James Madison, persuaded Congress to repeal it as one of the last acts of his administration. The Congress was far less willing, however, to prepare the country for possible military involvement. From a wide range of urgently proposed measures during 1808, it rejected the project for raising a large corps of volunteers, but on paper it added eight new regiments to the existing three in the regular army.

This modest acknowledgement of the need for a regular army ran counter to the traditional Republican mistrust of standing armies, a carry-over from the Revolutionary experience. The young republic consequently put its defense into the hands of the militia, its "citizen soldiers." Yet prior to the War of 1812 few clarifications had been made of the relative responsibilities of state and federal governments. Although the Constitution empowered Congress to organize, arm, and discipline the militia, these functions had been left almost entirely to the states. The War Department did very little, for it seemed to lack both power and money. No answers were formulated to these vital questions: Who decides that an emergency warrants calling out the militia? Do they serve under state or federal authority? Can they be required to serve outside their own state? Since the Constitution authorized their calling forth only to execute the laws, suppress insurrections, and repel invasions, some states legalistically confined its meaning to defensive action within the state. The war effort was to be critically hampered by this failure to agree on basic principles.

Nevertheless, in 1808 Congress committed the country to a new practice — the loaning or selling of arms to the states. Since the annual appropriations were small, the law only gradually began to be effective. For three and a half years after this act, during a period of crises and mounting tension, the federal government failed to take any further steps to organize the militia or substantially expand the navy.

At the time of the *Chesapeake* crisis, Jefferson revealed the extent of his aspirations. In a confidential talk with the French minister, Louis Marie Turreau, he threatened that if the British did not give satisfaction, "we will take Canada, which wants to enter the Union; and when, together with Canada, we shall have the Floridas, we shall no longer have any difficulties with our neighbors; and it is the only way of preventing them."[13]

During the period of international tension, the governor general of Canada, Sir James Craig, employed a secret agent, John Henry, to investigate and foster the antiwar sentiment in New England. Henry, a native of Ireland, was a naturalized American who had lived in Vermont, studied law, and edited a newspaper, during which time he developed a violent antipathy to Jefferson and went to Canada late in 1808. There he was provided with a cipher and directed to travel across New England from Burlington to Boston. He spent two days in Burlington and reported that the embargo was considered "unnecessary, oppressive and unconstitutional." He singled out Governor Isaac Tichenor for particular mention:

> I learn that the governor of this state is now visiting the towns in the northern section of it; and makes no secret of his determination, as commander in chief of the militia, to refuse obedience to any command from the general

government, which can tend to interrupt the good understanding that prevails between the citizens of Vermont and his majesty's subjects in Canada. It is farther intimated, that in case of war, he will use his influence to preserve the state *neutral,* and resist, with all the force he can command, any attempt to make it a party. I need not add, that if these resolutions are carried into effect, *the state of Vermont may be considered as an ally of Great Britain.*

Henry believed he had found sufficient evidence to assure Craig that the prospect of war was anathema in all of Federalist New England, whose people "will be ready to withdraw from the confederacy, establish a separate government and adopt a policy congenial with their interest and happiness.[14]

It is possible that Henry reported what he thought his employer wanted to hear. Dissatisfaction was easy to find, but in the case of Governor Tichenor, for example, although he was a strong Federalist, there is no evidence of disloyalty in his thinking. Nevertheless, Henry's reports sufficiently impressed Craig that he sent them to London as "useful information." There they would undoubtedly have been forgotten if Henry had not changed sides. After applying for a large reward, and being turned down in both Canada and England, he sold copies of the correspondence to President Madison in 1812.

Madison, no less than Jefferson, wanted peace, but he had witnessed the failure of economic coercion to assure it. Consequently, he set out to obtain the repeal of the British Orders and the French Decrees by inducement and persuasion. Jefferson had bequeathed to him not only the repeal of the embargo, but also, by his signature on March 1, 1809, the Nonintercourse Act. This legislation reopened American commerce with all the world except France and Great Britain, but allowed the president to suspend its operation against either upon repeal of their restrictive regulations. The measure was as satisfactory to Napoleon as the embargo had been, and while the Tory government in London preferred the complete abandonment of trade that the embargo had provided, it viewed with satisfaction the continued denial of American trade to France. Consequently, neither power was moved to seek any accommodation. On the contrary, the heavy costs of nonintercourse still rested upon Americans. Their exports before 1807 had gone mainly to British markets; unlike British merchants, Americans were unable to find compensatory new markets for their products. Thus nonintercourse was only slightly less distasteful to the commercial sections of the nation than the embargo had been. Moreover, unlawful trade was far more difficult to control than previously because of the impossibility of knowing the real destination of ships once they had cleared American ports.

The frustrations of 1809 aroused a new outburst of anti-British feeling in the United States and renewed threats of war. Henry Clay early in 1810 openly advocated it as the only way to force England to recognize American rights, and the invasion of Canada as the place where the British were most vulnerable. Anti-American sentiments also continued in the British Isles, where all issues were subordinated to the war with France. Resentment over America's commercial rivalry and scorn for its weak defense efforts pervaded the ruling circles. The government displayed no concern for making even the slightest gesture toward recognizing the American position.

The Madison administration was determined to keep trying. In May 1810, Congress passed Macon's Bill No. 2, which removed all restrictions on trade with Europe; but if either Britain or France repealed its regulations, the United States would reinstitute nonintercourse against the other within three months. The bill was prompted by the hope that one or the other of the belligerents would welcome the opportunity to regain American trade and embarrass its opponent at the same time. Since neither previous measure had succeeded in this object, and since both had apparently overemphasized the importance of American trade to the belligerents, Americans no longer expected miracles. Madison himself thought that the act was futile. American humiliation and frustration influenced the outcome of the fall elections of 1810, when many Republican congressmen were replaced by new and younger men determined to stand up for American rights, by war if necessary. This was the first appearance of Henry Clay and John C. Calhoun in a Congress that was still three-fourths Republican.

Events now moved ponderously toward a showdown. The wily Napoleon seized the opportunity offered him in Macon's Bill by promising to revoke his Decrees as of November 1, 1810; in return he expected the United States to revive nonintercourse against Britain. Dutifully the American government gave London the required three-month warning, after which all trade with Britain was forbidden beginning in March 1811. Although the Americans had no proof that the French Decrees were in fact revoked or that Napoleon would keep his word, which he did not, they eagerly accepted his offer. At best, it might coerce Britain into following suit; at the least, it might pinpoint the real enemy if Britain failed to do so.

American resumption of nonintercourse with Great Britain exacerbated the stresses within British society. In the latter half of 1810, Britain entered upon a period of sharp commercial depression. The causes were only partly related to American actions, for they also stemmed from the loss of continental markets, industrial changes at home, and overspeculation and losses in the new Latin American markets.

Throughout 1811 petitions to Parliament increased in number and the vigor with which they denounced the Orders in Council. Great pressures were applied upon the government by the Whig opposition, but the Tory leadership remained convinced that its commercial policy was necessary for winning the war and keeping the carrying trade out of the hands of American rivals. Not even the final insanity of George III and the accession to authority of the Whiggish prince regent produced any change of policy. Nor did the recall of Francis James Jackson and his replacement in Washington by Augustus J. Foster in 1811. Although he was an improvement upon the arbitrary Jackson, Foster was no friend of America, and his instructions left no room for maneuver, since they included all the old stipulations of an agreement solely on British terms. Yet Foster was the only negotiator during these final months, because the United States had no minister in London after February 1811.

The Tories held fast throughout 1811. They viewed Macon's Bill as a surrender by the United States and considered it a vindication of their policies. They correctly regarded Napoleon's announced repeal of his Decrees as a fraud, repeatedly demanded clear proof of his actions, and were persuaded by the Federalist clamor in the United States that the nation was far more divided than it was. Ever since 1808, reports such as those of John Henry had tended to exaggerate the disunity and the disloyalty of New Englanders. Federalist views were given disproportionate publicity in England, where they helped to confirm British opinion that there was nothing to fear from such a divided country.

New fuel was added to anti-British feeling in the United States with the outbreak of an Indian war late in 1811. Americans in the West had worried for some time about a new confederation of tribes in the old Northwest, astride the international boundary. A new leader, Tecumseh, of great vision and force of character, sought to unite the Indians in opposition to American encroachments upon their tribal lands. There was nothing new in Indian resistance, for land-hungry Americans of every generation had had to deal with it. What was new this time was the growing American conviction that the British were arming and inciting the Indians to war. There is sufficient evidence to prove that British policy toward the Indians was quite the opposite — that although arms and other goods were dispensed freely in order to ensure Indian friendship, British officials sought to restrain the warlike enthusiasm of some of Tecumseh's followers. An Indian war which might involve them was the last thing the British wanted.

After William Henry Harrison's campaign in November, and the dispersal of the Indians at the battle of Tippecanoe, the western conviction deepened that the British were subsidizing the Indian confederacy. This suspicion was added to the other grievances against Great Britain. Also promoting the war fever was the belief that the Spanish in Florida, and the British fur interests based there, were fomenting the militant behavior of the Creek and other Indian tribes in the Southwest. In a war for national honor and neutral rights, many Americans came to view the conquest of Canada and of Florida as the means of bringing the British to terms, abolishing the Indian menace, and greatly expanding the national boundaries at the same time. However, the administration and most of the "War Hawks" looked upon foreign conquests as only a weapon with which to achieve the primary goal of justice on the seàs.

The Congress which had been elected in 1810 did not meet until November 1811, upon special call of the president. The nationalists, often dubbed the "War Hawks," quickly captured the machinery of the House of Representatives. Henry Clay was elected speaker, and he staffed the key committees, such as foreign relations, with War Hawks like himself. Although Madison's message to Congress revealed some of his anxiety over the failure of Napoleon to implement his promises and to make restitution for past wrongs, its main target was Great Britain. He reviewed the history of British arrogance and abuse of American rights, which he described as having "the character as well as the effect of war on our lawful commerce." He suggested "putting the United States into an armor" and recommended a series of warlike preparations.[15]

Although Sir George Prevost saw "dynamite" in Madison's message, English newspapers in Canada tended to ridicule it. From Quebec came a particularly biting comment:

> With syllogisms 'twill make a clatter,
> With abstract rights, three-deckers batter;
> An empty purse at millions shake,
> And no trade 'gainst a free trade stake;
> Of rotting produce count the gain,
> A seaboard coast shut from the main;
> To seamen recommend the loom,
> And on each mast to fix the broom;
> Merchants for each of foreign wares,
> To retail apples, plumbs and pears.[16]

An extended debate ensued in Congress and the country. Former President Jefferson in January expressed the confusion of the times when he wrote, "As for France and England, with all their preeminence in science, the one is a den of robbers, and the other of pirates." By April he was putting it somewhat differently: "When the wrongs of France shall reach us with equal effect, we shall resist them also. But one at a time is enough; and having offered a choice to the champions, England first takes up the gauntlet." Clay and the other War Hawks loudly advocated war; Clay had felt it was inevitable since at least August 1811. In December, he urged Congress to approve a large military expansion for use in conquering Canada, for "do not wisdom and true economy equally decide in favor of the larger force and thus prevent failure in consequence of inadequate means?" He denied the charge that France was as great a threat as Great Britain: "Shall we bear the cuffs and scoffs of British arrogance, because we may entertain chimerical fears of French subjugation?. . . . Whoever learned in the school of base submission, the lessons of noble freedom, and courage, and independence?"[17]

Calhoun, chairman of the House Foreign Affairs Committee, added to the bellicose arguments. He too deduced that war was the only solution to American grievances despite evidence that the army contained only a skeleton of its authorized strength of ten thousand, that the navy consisted of only fifteen ships of war, and that the British peacetime strength in American waters alone was six times the strength of the entire American fleet. Such facts were brushed aside by Jefferson, who believed that the conquest of Canada was merely a matter of marching, and by Calhoun, who declared in May, "So far from being unprepared, sir, I believe that, in four weeks from the time that a declaration of war is heard on our frontier, the whole of Upper and part of Lower Canada will be in our possession."[18]

Madison, by this time also convinced of the inevitability of war, tried to fan the flames by sending the correspondence of John Henry to Congress. For $50,000 he had bought the fourteen documents from Henry, who felt the British had not sufficiently rewarded him. Since the letters were only paraphrases of the three-year-old originals, with comprising names omitted, they were received somewhat skeptically by Congress and the public despite some vehement Republican accusations against the British for their treachery.

There was no unanimity about the drift toward war. Some Republicans, paced by John Randolph of Roanoke, sought by ridicule or reason to stem the trend. The Federalists were solidly opposed to war, as were the Clintonian Republicans. Balancing the enthusiastic preparations of Kentucky and Ohio were a series of petitions from the Northeast. The merchants of New York asked Congress to postpone war in the confident expectation that British repeal of the Orders in Council was in the offing. The Massachusetts House of Representatives told Congress that "our constituents cannot be reconciled to the belief that an offensive war with Great Britain is demanded by the interest or honor of our country. . . . The conquest of Canada, the only point in which she is assailable, would afford no indemnification if achieved, for the losses to which we should be exposed upon our unprotected seaboard and upon the ocean."[19]

The Twelfth Congress was hampered in its war preparations by the feeling of many that negotiations had not been exhausted, by opposition to a large regular army, and by factors of economy. Receipt of word in March that the French had seized and burned American ships undermined the administration's position and revived the Federalist campaign against any war. Madison for a short time considered a declaration against both France and Great Britain. Factions in Congress developed around alternatives to immediate hostilities: postpone the inevitable until the country was more nearly ready, or wage a limited naval war against one or both countries. Administration leaders opposed both ideas.

Congress also steered an ambiguous course in its military preparations. On the one hand it voted to prepare three old vessels for action, but then it refused to order the construction of new frigates. It also defeated efforts to organize the militia on a uniform plan or raise sufficient revenue for its new commitments. Yet in December, in order to speed the build-up of the regular army to its full ten thousand men, Congress provided a sixteen-dollar enlistment bounty, plus 160 acres of land and three months' pay on honorable discharge. This measure failed to achieve its purpose, because potential recruits could find high wages and abundant employment elsewhere. Nevertheless, Congress in January increased the regular army to thirty-six thousand men and voted the first appropriations for coastal fortifications, ordnance, military supplies, and quartermaster's stores.

In February, Congress authorized fifty thousand volunteers who would be officered by the states, report directly to the president, and be subject to one year of service. In April, it created a Quartermaster's Department. It also passed an act providing for one hundred thousand militia detached into special units from the mass of the enrolled militia. Each state had a quota to fill. And the men, if called, were subject to six months' service. During the debate on this measure, Henry Clay and others pressed for a clear recognition of the legality of sending militia outside the country. If war came, Clay maintained, it would be defensive but "in making the war effective, conquest may become necessary; but this does not change the character of the war—there may be no other way of operating upon our enemy, but by taking possession of her provinces which adjoin us."[20] But the problem was too controversial for a quick solution, and the act failed to clarify the geographical extent of the militia's services.

By the end of April, the American armed forces *on paper* consisted of thirty-six thousand men to serve five years; fifty thousand volunteers for one year, and one hundred thousand militia for no more than six months. Recruiting of regulars was slow, and when war was declared only ten thousand were enrolled, of whom four thousand were inexperienced recruits, as were many of their officers. Volunteer units were never popular in spite of the special inducements that were offered, and their numbers remained negligible. The militia were enrolled by the thousands but were not with certainty considered available for use in Canada.

All these undertakings proved almost too much for the dentist-cum-secretary of war, William Eustis, and his little staff of seven or eight clerks. He notified each state of its quota of militia under the one hundred thousand-man law. Quotas ranged from one thousand for Delaware to thirteen thousand five hundred for New York; men were to be alerted by the governors for call if needed. He asked Governor Daniel Tompkins of New York to send fifteen hundred men to the Canadian frontier. The act of 1808 for arming the militia was becoming effective, although supplies were never available in sufficient quantities to meet all the demands. Quartermaster issue of clothing was also stepped up in the spring; all the states and territories received allotments except four New England states, which did not desire them.

As the war clouds gathered, military and political leaders volunteered patriotically or were sought out by the administration. Morgan Lewis, former governor of New York, was made quartermaster general. The senior major general, Henry Dearborn, was appointed in January. He spent weeks in Washington contributing his ideas on strategy. The other major general was Thomas Pinckney, who at sixty-two years, and lacking military experience since the Revolution, received the command of the Southern Department.

Five brigadier generals were named from among civilians or promoted from within the service. All had served in the Revolution, all were between fifty-five and sixty years of age. The senior officer was James Wilkinson, who was dispatched to New Orleans for the defense of the Southwest. The administration's confidence in him can be explained mainly by its desperate lack of men with command experience. The second brigadier was the unproven South Carolinian, Wade Hampton, who had entered the service in 1808. The third was Joseph Bloomfield, who was completing ten years as a Federalist governor of New Jersey. The fourth was James Winchester, called out of retirement in Tennessee.

The fifth brigadier was William Hull. As civil governor of Michigan since 1805, he hurried to Washington during the winter to urge the defense of the Northwest. For weeks he resisted the administration's urging that he accept the command; reluctantly he agreed during the spring. He was assigned to organize the few hundred regulars in the Northwest and the forthcoming Ohio militia for a probable invasion of Canada. The war preparations of Madison, Eustis, Monroe and Dearborn were extremely hazy; they were based upon a regular army that did not exist and upon untrained militia, to be led by elderly officers mostly called out of civilian life for the emergency.

The warlike actions and words of the Americans did not go unnoticed by the British. Foster in Washington kept his government fully if not always accurately informed of the trend of events. He misjudged the divisions within the Republican party, and he also misinterpreted Madison's vague utterances. He was encouraged by certain Federalists to hold fast and to push the administration to the brink and, if necessary, into a war it could never win. Some of his reports, always belatedly received in London, served to reassure an unimaginative government that by all the laws of logic and self-interest, the United States would never carry out its war threats. As late as May, the colonial secretary wrote Governor General Prevost in Canada not to expect a rupture with the United States, but also to avoid the slightest act that could give offense or be viewed as "proof of want of good faith."[21]

One reason for British complacency was their slow drift toward accommodation late in the spring. Ever since Parliament convened at the beginning of the year, the Whigs had stepped up their attacks on the Orders in Council. Repeal became the rallying cry of the manufacturing interests in the Midlands and the north of England. Endless petitions to Parliament revealed unemployment and a business stagnation, as well as the manufacturers' anxiety that they would permanently lose the American market if Americans were compelled to manufacture for themselves.

At a time when the American Congress was floundering in a sea of indecision, almost any conciliatory act in London would at least have postponed war by invalidating some of the arguments of the War Hawks. But no such evidence was discernible to Washington policymakers. Yet the British government was in fact yielding bit by bit to the pressures. Meanwhile, the foreign secretary ordered Foster to do everything he could to maintain the peace.

The slow yielding of the Tory government was halted by the assassination on May 11 of Prime Minister Spencer Perceval. The death of the author of the Orders in Council was not greatly mourned in the manufacturing areas. Unfortunately, the country was without effective leadership until June 8, when Lord Liverpool was able to form another Tory government. On June 16 his ministry promised to withdraw the Orders. This was done officially one week later.

As the British drifted toward accommodation, the Americans drifted toward war. Congress passed a ninety-day embargo early in April to allow American ships to reach home port, after which war could be expected. Yet some congressmen were still advocating a war against both Britain and France. When the *Hornet* arrived from England late in May without any conciliatory news, Madison submitted his war message to Congress on June 1. Reviewing the British record of misdeeds on the seas and in Indian affairs and terming them "this crying enormity," he declared: "Whether the United States shall continue passive under these progressive usurpations and these

accumulating wrongs, or, opposing force to force in defense of their national
rights . . . is a solemn question which the Constitution wisely confides to
the legislative department of the Government." While refraining from asking for a declaration of war, he plainly indicated that there was no other
choice. He just as clearly suggested taking no action against France until the
result of current talks in Paris could be known.[22]

A bill for the declaration of war was reported on June 3, and Congress
went into secret sessions to debate it. The House carried the measure the day
after it reached the floor by a vote of 79 to 49, the Senate on June 17 by the
close count of 19 to 13. The Senate spent thirteen days to come to its decision.
All of the alternatives to war were explored once more. Most Republicans had
thought for some time that war was inevitable; that they were finally induced
to agree on its timing and nature is attributable to the skill and determination of administration leaders in the Senate. But it was to be a war of sectional orientation. Only Pennsylvania and Vermont in the North strongly
favored it; no southern or western state showed much opposition.

Throughout the months of debate, the necessity of upholding the national honor undergirded much of what was said, but the final decision
rested upon the more tangible issues of Orders in Council, illegal blockades,
impressment, and British Indian policy. Recent scholarship has offered new
insights into the American war-making mentality. One of them emphasizes
the "nations's honor" as a leading factor. The south Atlantic states, which
provided nearly half of the war votes in the House, blamed British interference with American trade for the decline in the price of agricultural products
like cotton. Afters years of Republican efforts to reconcile their antiwar
dogma with the need for a vigorous defense of American rights, they had
concluded that the only alternative to submission to the British commercial
system was war.[23]

Another recent writer analyzes the disarray in the Republican party during Madison's first term. The middle states, especially New York, resented
the continual domination of the presidency by the "Virginia dynasty," and
they coalesced around the Clintonian wing of the party. The current leadership of the movement was to be found in DeWitt Clinton of New York.
Other dissidents were the old "Quids," or Republicans of "pure" extraction;
champions of John Armstrong in his ambition for high office, and sympa-
thizers with the demoted secretary of state, Robert Smith, who was succeeded
by another Virginian, James Monroe. The declaration of war restored "a degree of order and stability to the highly factionalized politics of Madison's administration," although precarious at best.[24]

A third view suggests that party Republicanism, and especially republicanism, was in extreme peril. Robert H. Brown concludes that "To a great

majority of Republicans war seemed necessary in 1812 because the alternative to war, submission, presented unacceptable consequences." One of the consequences would be a political disaster for the Republican party and for republicanism everywhere from the return to power of the aristocratic Federalists. Republicanism seemed to be in great danger which could be met only by defying British *and* Federalist pretensions.[25]

American policy before the war was based upon a number of misapprehensions. One was an overestimation of the importance of commerce as a bargaining tool. The more complete the American embargo, the more satisfied were the British; the American government came reluctantly to realize that it was hurting its own people more than its opponents. Americans also failed to recognize the threat of Bonapartism, and the depth of feeling about it in Britain. So wrapped up were they in their own grievances that they refused to acknowledge the British contention that their war against Napoleon was a struggle for free men everywhere. Not only did Americans not see any danger, but in spite of repeated injuries from the French, they found a pretext for considering them more innocuous than the British. Yet no wartime collaboration developed between the United States and France; no American official ventured to remind his countrymen that they were fighting on the same side as Napoleon. Silence suggests an American embarrassment on the subject.

The British also miscalculated. Their preoccupation with affairs in Europe led them to gamble recklessly on the possibility of a war in North America. Yet they did not consider it a serious risk, for they were not impressed by the weak American protests or unity, which they underestimated. They were arrogant in enforcing their Orders on the high seas, and in refusing to meet the Americans half way at the diplomatic table. They failed to anticipate the inevitable results upon a proud, independent state of a long-continued policy of harrassment and humiliation. Finally, the British government refused to recognize the ruin that its policy was bringing to its own manufacturing interests. After the declaration of war, the British were bewildered and furious at American perfidy. In speaking plaintively on the subject, the colonial secretary, Lord Bathurst, asked Parliament:

Was there any country in Europe that had in the same time made the same advances in population, commerce, products of industry? And to what did she owe this very commerce of which she was so jealous, but to the superiority and protection of the British navy? And was it not reasonable to have expected this might be felt by her and that if there were any casual irritation it would be passed over—any little object of dispute, it would be left to the decision of sober and friendly arguments?[26]

The government thus blamed an unwanted war upon the Americans who, after seven years of "sober and friendly argument" and "little objects of dispute," had decided unreasonably to make a mountain out of a molehill.

3

THE EVE OF THE WAR—THE NORTHEAST

Canada

When war broke out on the North American continent, the British government sought for the first two years to continue its cautious prewar defensive strategy in Canada. They had little choice in view of the tremendous demands of the British war in Europe, which were straining the resources of the empire. They also had to adapt to the geography of Canada. Their defensive warfare, as executed by their leaders in Canada, was a brilliant delaying action which literally saved the colony for the empire.

The potential war zone in Canada stretched for thirteen hundred miles from the Atlantic Ocean to Lake Michigan. The British had no comparable front in their European war, nor did they have the manpower, British or Canadian, to man such a line. A country of half a million people faced an arming nation of nearly eight million. The centers of American population—New England, New York, and Pennsylvania—were in the northern part of the country so that, insofar as numbers could be expected to prevail, the Americans might invade and conquer Canada with ease if they chose to try.

The people of Canada, on the other hand, were thinly stretched over many hundreds of miles. These inhabitants must somehow be persuaded to provide most of the fighting force for Britain's war if it came. Administratively, Canada was divided into several provinces, only two of which are pertinent to this study. Upper Canada, the modern province of Ontario, had perhaps eighty thousand residents, sparsely settled from the upper St. Lawrence along Lakes Ontario and Erie to Amherstburg, nearly opposite Detroit. Its administrative center was York (Toronto), the seat of its own legislative body and a governor who was subject only to the governor general of Canada.

The inhabitants of this area were largely British or American in origin. The older American stock consisted of Loyalist refugees from the American Revolution who had no love for the United States, but the later and larger group included westward-moving Americans who either had little interest in the war or were actively pro-American. By American choice, this province developed into a major theatre of war. It had to deflect repeated campaigns on three widely separated fronts: at Detroit, on the Niagara peninsula, and along Lake Ontario. A cautious, nimble and skilful war of defense was called for. With some notable exceptions, this was the type of war waged in Upper Canada.

Lower Canada, with which this study is primarily concerned, contained the larger centers of population, Montreal being the largest with twenty-two thousand people. Administratively, Lower Canada was centered in Quebec City. Here another legislature sat, and the governor general made his headquarters. The people of Lower Canada were overwhelmingly French, and their loyalty at the approach of war was an uncertain factor in all war plans.

Beginning in 1811, the governor general, as well as commander in chief of the armed forces, was Sir George Prevost. He served in this dual capacity throughout the war, and consequently any judgment concerning British success or failure in its political and military objectives must rest firmly on the character and leadership of this man.

For a century and a half Sir George has borne the brunt of British and Canadian censure for all the misadventures of his years in Canada. A few recent studies have reassessed his political record and found it impressive.[1] But most of the older studies severely denigrated Prevost. The sharpest attacks date from 1815 and a series of articles in the *Montreal Herald*. Since then, Prevost has been found "not the man to save an empire. A politician rather than a soldier, irresolute and down-hearted, with no confidence in himself and no military skill;" or again, that he was overcautious and vacillating; or that he "hung like a dead weight on more enterprising officers who commanded armies in Canada;" or that he and his adjutant general, Edward Baynes, were "the two weakest spots in the defense of Canada;" or more recently, that he was a "fussy incompetent, timid and lacking foresight."[2] This wholesale condemnation of Prevost stems from an unwarranted disregard of the importance of politics in this war and an undue emphasis upon certain aspects of his military record.

At forty-four years of age Lieutenant General Sir George Prevost assumed his position of civil and military chief in September 1811. He found a sullen and discontented French population and an Indian movement about to burst out of control. But he came admirably prepared to deal with the problems of British Canada. His government picked him for his proven capacities for tact

Lt. Gen. Sir George Prevost (1767–1816), mezzotint by S. W. Reynolds. *Courtesy of The Public Archives of Canada.*

and conciliation. If anyone deserves the title "Savior of Canada," Prevost is a prime candidate. Son of a Swiss officer, he spoke French fluently. He possessed considerable bodily energy and strength of will, combined with graciousness and personal charm. He was also suave and diplomatic; he later showed a tendency to temporize, probably enhanced by declining health. He had gained a high reputation in the West Indies, where his tact, diplomacy, and knowledge of the French language gave him success in the delicate role of conciliator in the conquered French islands of St. Lucia and Dominica. From there he went as governor to Nova Scotia, where his reputation was further enhanced.

When he arrived in Quebec, Prevost had again to deal with a native French population. His British advisers, including his deputy in Upper Canada, Major General Isaac Brock, felt that the French were disloyal; Brock was sure that Napoleon with five thousand troops could conquer Canada, and that the French would eagerly join him. The Americans too misjudged the temper of the French and counted on being welcomed in case of war. Actually, the Canadian French had a basic loyalty to the empire and quarreled only with its administration. They desired nothing more than "to live their French-Canadian lives in a French-Canadian way." They realized that their constitution under the British protected their language, religion, laws, and customs far better than any conceivable treatment under Napoleon, nor were they prepared to exchange British rule for the more uncertain American. Prevost's statesmanship fostered this basic feeling and, miraculously, he succeeded in attaching the French firmly to the British cause in the few months between his arrival and the outbreak of the war.

During that brief nine months, he had to repair the damage to French-British relations that had occurred in the regime of his predecessor. Sir James Craig, sometimes known as the "Anglophile Governor," had served as governor general from 1807 to 1811. He blatantly aligned his administration with the English minority in its struggles with the huge French majority.

The religious aspect of this struggle involved Anglican Bishop Mountain's efforts to obtain a reversal of the appointment of Joseph-Octave Plessis as Catholic bishop. On the political level, the English intended not only to continue their domination of the Legislative and Executive councils, but also to obtain changes in the Constitution of 1791, which made a French majority in the Assembly inevitable.

Craig used repression to deal with all signs of French nationalism. He dissolved the Assembly whenever it tried to assert itself, arrested the proprietors of *Le Canadien* for its alleged treasonable tone, and cancelled many French commissions in the militia. His measures were so effective that active opposition came to an end, even if a burning resentment remained.

Sometimes known as the "Francophile Governor," Prevost's chief error was his failure to recognize the depth of the national divisions in Canada. He ran the risk of alienating the official class and being seen as too friendly with the French. Referring to the "system of coercion practiced by my predecessor," he set about reversing the anti-French bias of the previous administration. He started with the Catholic clergy, and especially with its head, Bishop Plessis. Prevost sought his friendship, obtained a large increase in salary for him, and also official confirmation of his bishopric, in effect establishing the Catholic Church in Quebec. In consequence, the Catholic clergy became his firmest supporters, and Prevost credited them with the general acceptance of the militia and currency laws and a broad support of the war.

Prevost's next efforts were directed toward his Assembly, which convened in the early months of 1812. He found its members less cordial than he had hoped, which he attributed to the "reign of terror" under Craig. But his tact enabled him to obtain a strengthening and financing of the militia. He was even granted the power to suspend the writ of habeas corpus. After the beginning of the war, he won the most important financial measure of the war in the Army Bill Act. An issue of paper money was provided which was to be legal tender and on which the province, backed by the British government, paid interest. It was the first paper money ever redeemed at par, a forerunner of the selling of bonds by later governments. Received suspiciously at first, the notes were accepted with increasing confidence and by September 1812, the sum of £150,000 had been issued. At the end of the war there were £1,300,000 of army bills in circulation.

Quite early in his administration the British elite, the "Château Clique," began to suspect that Prevost was weakly submitting to French control. He restored the French to their cancelled militia posts. He elevated Pierre Bedard, in jail under Craig, to the bench. He added seven new members to the Executive Council, of whom four were French Canadians, and several more French to the Legislative Council. By the time war came, Prevost was able to count on the support of the Assembly for his war measures, although its members never abandoned their sometimes strident demands for more authority. In their wartime cooperation they apparently welcomed the opportunity to prove Craig wrong in charging them with disloyalty; they also reacted strongly against American boasts about the ease of conquering Canada. Optimistically, Prevost wrote to London in March: "My endeavours to rouse the Canadians from their lethargy and to inspire them with loyalty towards the Crown protecting them received considerable assistance from the arrogant declarations made in Congress respecting the easy conquest of their country."[3]

Nevertheless, when 1,577 troops were sent to Canada in April, Prevost was required to send two British regiments back to England unless war was imminent: "The exigencies of the public service in Europe render it desirable that every reduction of the British force should be made in our distant possessions."[4] In other words, France was *the* enemy and war with the United States was not likely.

The British minister in Washington and the American newspapers kept Prevost informed of the drift toward war and of the deep divisions in American opinion. Prevost saw the text of Madison's message to Congress in November 1811 and thought it was "full of gunpowder." The British government sent him continuous exhortations to avoid any action that would create a breach with the United States; but no instructions for the disposition of troops or the preparation for possible war arrived. Denied reinforcements and instructions, he referred to "the infatuation of His Majesty's ministers upon the subject of American affairs, and show how entirely I have been left to my own resources in the event which has taken place."[5]

Closer to the scene of action, perhaps more aware of the trends than the secretaries in London, undistracted by the European war, and deeply conscious of his own responsibility to Canada and the empire, Prevost was unable to accept the hopeful assurances of peace from London. Left to his own devices he prepared for the worst. His chief advantage in the approaching conflict was a small but well-trained body of imperial troops in Canada. For emergencies, universal service was to be expected from the militia, who were loosely organized, untrained, but subject to six months' service. Because of their lack of training and short-term liability, the British encouraged the formation of volunteer groups of Canadian regulars, who received good training although subject to duty only in British North America. These fencible regiments, as some were called, had originated in the Maritime Provinces and their success led to the creation of other units in Lower and Upper Canada. A dozen Canadian battalions of infantry—Voltigeurs, Chasseurs, Fencibles, Select Embodied Militia, Incorporated Militia—contributed about half the strength of regular units in Canada. Together with the imperial regulars, they were by conscious British decision kept approximately equal to the number of American regulars.

Disturbed by the rising tensions during the winter before the war, Prevost in December 1811 sought permission from London to create a Glengarry Light Infantry Fencible Regiment from among the Scotsmen of Upper Canada. Without even waiting for an answer, he formed a unit of men taken from the seventeen-to-forty-year age group to serve in North America until peace or for three years.

One of the corps of volunteers in Lower Canada was the Canadian Voltigeurs, which Prevost created in the spring of 1812. This unit was to be recruited primarily from the French population and be under the command of Major Charles de Salaberry. Initially planned for 670, owing to the difficulties of recruitment it was finally stabilized at 350, with a company of Indians attached to it. A commission as captain went to anyone who enlisted thirty-six men, a lieutenant for sixteen, and adjutant, quartermaster, and surgeon for smaller numbers. Enlistment bounties were originally £4 but were later increased to £5. Prevost obtained permission to make land grants to its members upon termination of service.

The Voltigeurs opened their career unpromisingly early in June. A short-lived mutiny occurred among members recruited around Montreal when they refused to follow orders. Force had to be used to arrest the ringleaders and form the companies. De Salaberry reported, however, that during his absence short rations had been issued, and that a rumor gained circulation that an officer had come from Montreal to enlist them as regulars.[6] With firmness combined with tact, the crisis was surmounted and the Voltigeurs, centered at Chambly, became one of the most effective adjuncts to the forces along the border with the United States.

Thus the British fought the war with a dozen battalions of Canadian regulars, totalling fewer than four thousand men. There were also 4,450 imperial regulars in Canada at the outbreak of war. Prevost's problem was the disposition of the two forces. For the most part, provincial regiments saw service in their own province. He did not dare denude the Maritime Provinces in case they were attacked. Expecting that Montreal would be the prime American target, he maintained substantial units in Lower Canada. At the outbreak of war only fifteen hundred regulars were stationed in Upper Canada to protect a frontier of one thousand miles. All across Canada too few regulars were available to resist conquest, which appeared likely if not inevitable, and they were expected to do most of the fighting, because no one in authority dared to count on effective help from the militia.

Owing to the deep divisions of opinion in both Lower and Upper Canada, neither Prevost nor Brock had much confidence in the willingness of the people to defend themselves, but both knew they must make the effort. Each of the provinces had militia organizations, the underlying principle of which was universal liability. In Lower Canada, when war was expected during the crisis of 1807, one-fifth of the total militia was called out. Both French and English reported quickly and willingly. But the Craig regime subsequently raised questions about the future reliability of the French.

In 1808 the militia were reorganized under a comprehensive act. There was to be an annual muster day, with a fine of five shillings for absence. Most of the men were considered Sedentary Militia. In Lower Canada they numbered sixty thousand from whom Prevost incorporated into an Embodied Militia about two thousand for further training. They were chosen by ballot from among the unmarried men to serve for two, later three years. One of the flimsiest charges made against Prevost by his British critics was his prohibition of substitutions and the use of Embodied Militia as servants to officers. It was called unreasonably prejudicial to the traditional British use of the French as substitutes and for menial work. In Lower Canada a form of special corps called the "Select Embodied" battalion was used successfully. It was left permanently in service, but consisted of successive drafts of six-month men. They were used principally on garrison duty. Few sedentary militia saw action, but some were used to relieve the better-trained men at the bases. In spite of the six-month limitation, the enrolled militia of Canada remained constant throughout the war at about four thousand men. The regular and militia forces that carried on the first two years of the fighting thus totalled about twelve thousand men at one time.

As a consequence of Prevost's activities, when war came the French embraced the British cause and gave their governor solid if not enthusiastic support. A people traditionally suspicious of paper money was persuaded to issue and use the army bills, which helped greatly to finance the war. And a people who opposed militia service because it had been so long unused and because its organization had been dominated by the British, embodied and financed a wartime militia to fight alongside the British regulars. Prevost was able as early as June, in the face of almost certain war, to praise "the loyalty, zeal and public spirit" of the people of his province.

During the long spring before the war, the colonial secretary, Lord Bathurst, repeatedly warned Prevost to avoid any action that could give the United States offense, or be used as "proof of want of good faith," or "accelerate the resort to actual hostility," or interfere with British commitments in their war against Napoleon. Prevost consequently warned his commanders to adopt a system "strictly defensive," and to avoid being led into any act of aggression that might unite the United States and strengthen their government, "without which their ability to raise one additional Regiment is now questioned."[7]

Prevost hoped to establish a firm control over Indian affairs. He tried to repair the damage to imperial policy created by the battle of Tippecanoe. He urged his commanders to use the "utmost caution and forbearance" in their Indian relations to avoid irritating the Americans; on the other hand he instructed Brock to "find a clear but delicate way of letting the Indians know that in case of war, we expect aid of 'our brothers.'"[8] The British subsequently obtained the services of several hundred Indians, and the invaluable support of their great leader, Tecumseh.

As a military officer, Prevost did not display a deep understanding of naval strategy, but he early grasped the supreme importance of control of the lakes. He also knew that much of the campaigning would have to be combined military-naval operations. Ever since the British conquest of Canada, the naval force on the lakes was known as the Provincial Marine. It was primarily a transport service, especially on Lakes Ontario and Erie, and was administered by the quartermaster general's department of the army. Both before and after the start of war, Prevost begged for men and supplies from the Royal Navy, but not until the second year of the war were his petitions heeded.

Prudence demanded a defense in depth of Montreal, which Prevost assumed would be central to American war plans. Since the town was essentially indefensible except for any advantage that could be taken of its island position, its protection would depend upon a series of outposts from Laprairie southward to Chambly and St. Jean. A month after his arrival in Canada he visited the Richelieu Valley and decided that the old works at both these places were not worth repairing, although needing garrisons.[9]

If history had any message for him, Prevost could expect the Lake Champlain-Richelieu waterway to be the major American invasion route. It pointed like a dagger into the heart of populated Quebec, entering the St. Lawrence at Sorel. This town was 100 miles southwest of Quebec City and about 25 miles northeast of Montreal. The British were aware of both advantages and disadvantages from the interrupted flow of the Richelieu at St. Jean. They could take comfort in the fact that no American warships could sail from Lake Champlain into the St. Lawrence. On the other hand, their own efforts on the lake could be successful only with immense efforts on their part. Cartage by land to St. Jean would be required; no vessel larger than a gunboat could be winched around the rapids between Chambly and St. Jean, and all others would have to be built south of the rapids. At the start of the war the British naval power consisted of only the rotting hulk of a schooner and a couple of old gunboats at Isle-aux-Noix.

In any case, Prevost prepared for invasion along the Richelieu. Consequently, he denied many of Brock's requests for troops in Upper Canada, leading Brock to tell his officers about "the old parrot cry from headquarters, 'Not a man to spare.'"[10] Prevost was proven wrong about where the early battles would be fought, but he was flexible enough to move troops around with great agility. In theory, however, he was correct. One large-scale American offensive against Montreal early in the war, if successful, would have removed the need for campaigns farther west. American control of Montreal would have effectively denied help to Upper Canada along its only usable highway, the St. Lawrence River, or the only alternative, the Ottawa River, a route that was not developed until years after the war. Thus Upper Canada would almost certainly have succumbed to American occupation without its lifeline to Montreal.

The United States

If Lower Canada approached war with divisions in its political and social structure, so did the states bordering on Lake Champlain. This was even more true of southern New England. The polarization of these areas began with the enactment of the Embargo Act in 1807. Opposition to any federal interference with foreign commerce, coupled with frantic disapproval of the drift toward war, brought about a revival of the nearly defunct Federalist party in the northeastern states. Historically, the Federalists had spoken for the commercial interests, wanted close relationships with Great Britain, and mistrusted France. The Jefferson-Madison leadership was clearly violating these cherished principles.

As early as 1807, Massachusetts elected Federalist Caleb Strong to the governorship and maintained him in office for years. The Federalists had always controlled Connecticut, and they now captured Rhode Island as well. In Vermont, after the *Chesapeake* affair, the assembly by a vote of 169 to 1 supported Jefferson with "the most perfect confidence in his wisdom, integrity, and ability" to handle the crisis with honor. However, in December of that year, two Vermont congressmen voted for the Embargo Act and two against it.[11]

In the following year the Federalist, Isaac Tichenor, was elected governor. Since he had served in the office for ten successive years until he lost the election of 1807, his return to office is not surprising, although it probably reflected the state's reaction to the embargo on Lake Champlain. It was the opinions of Tichenor which John Henry exaggerated in his reports of 1809. The Federalists also controlled ten of the twelve council seats, but the Republicans maintained a seventeen-vote margin in the assembly. The Federalist Martin Chittenden was re-elected to Congress. However, in 1809 and in the next three annual elections, Vermonters elevated the Republican, Jonas Galusha, to the governorship, together with Republican majorities in both the council and the assembly. Thus the state approached the war with the Republican party dominant and happily prepared to support the administration in Washington. It was one of only two states in the Northeast whose congressional delegation gave majority support to the declaration of war — three to one in the House and one in favor and one unrecorded in the Senate. Ultimately, Vermont contributed more men to the regular army than any but the four most populous states; it promptly raised its quota of three thousand militia, and at first allowed them to serve outside the state.

However, the Federalists were by no means submerged in Vermont, and they would capture the state during the war. A typical expression of the bitterness of the prewar period is to be found in the letters of Royal Corbin, a federalist businessman of Craftsbury, member of the assembly and brother-in-law of Pliny Moore of Champlain:

I have once more happily returned from our Hon'l Legislature, so call'd. I say happily for sure I am, I had rat[h]er be at home with my own family &

concerns, than at our hott bead of democracy, where intreague (& I say tirany) reigns, in its almost full extent, in leu of blood bought & boasted American liberty, but such are the times, & I see no way but we must groan under them at present, but I pray not much longer.

Lamentable it is to relate the strongly appearant depravity of the ruling party & to me it is astonishing, to hear men standing on the highest ground as it were in our State, utter & deliver such corrupt sentiments as was at some of those democrattick caukasis . . . to see Mr. Shaw git up, harrangue & strongly impress, & declair it to [be] absolutely necessary to vue a certain part of [the] community, say the Federalists, as British hirelings & that much British gould had been distributed all ready to news paper presses & among the leading charrictors of the Federalists.[12]

In New York State the Republican, Daniel Tompkins, was elected governor in 1807 for a three-year term and was re-elected in 1810 and 1813. He eventually became vice president of the United States under President Monroe. A popular and effective, even great, wartime governor, he was a loyal Jeffersonian and a supporter of the war when it came, but his frustrations were momentous. New York was almost equally divided between the shipping and commercial interests, which opposed administration measures and the drift toward war, and farmers and frontiersmen of the north and west, who generally favored them. As in the Revolution, the state's geography again threatened to make it a main theatre of military operations. The uncertainties of the prewar years gave the Federalists growing leverage, until in the spring of 1812 they captured control of the assembly. Thus unlike Governor Galusha in Vermont, Governor Tompkins entered the war with one chamber controlled by the opposition, and he had a great deal of trouble in obtaining the money, supplies, and even the militia officers, that he deemed necessary. The political complexion of both states would have an important impact on the conduct of the war in the Champlain Valley.

Even in northern New York, outposts of Federalism began to emerge in normally Republican territory. Although Clinton County, for example, continued to support Republican legislators in Albany and Washington until the year the war began, the Federalists repeatedly carried the elections in some towns like Champlain as early as 1809, even voting against Governor Tompkins in 1810. This town seems to have taken some of its political coloration from the town's founder and leading citizen, Judge Pliny Moore, a firm Federalist who disliked Presidents Jefferson and Madison and most of what he thought they stood for, although tolerating the war when it came. Champlain is typical of other towns along the border of Canada in Vermont and

New York. These communities enjoyed important trade connections with Canada which they did not want to see disrupted, but more urgently they realized that if war came it would strike them first.

Representative of the deep-seated convictions of the Federalist party in northeastern New York are the opinions of John Freligh, a Plattsburgh businessman who rafted his own goods to Canada. Writing of the embargo in 1808, he said: "We are obliged to submit to the orders of the petty officers of Government, without a murmur, however unjust and violent. And what is still more allarming, the people are duped into a belief that these measures are necessary, and perfectly consistant with the principles of liberty and genuine republicanism."[13]

Rejoicing over the fact that the Federalists of Clinton County had finally elected an assemblyman in the spring of 1812, he exulted: "Federalism is again triumphant after so long a struggle against 'principalities and powers,' and the workers of political iniquity in our country. . . . The fact is, republicans begin to open their eyes to the truth, and many of them have already been convinced of the deceptions practiced upon them, and have consequently left the ranks of their party to return to it no more."[14]

Meanwhile, the war scare of 1807 jolted New York officials into bolstering the defensive capabilities of the northern regions. In the summer of 1809, a brick arsenal was built at Plattsburgh large enough to hold ten field pieces and two thousand stands of arms, plus equipment and ammunition. At its completion it already contained 500 stands of arms, some brass field pieces, and other supplies. By the summer of 1810, another arsenal was completed, at Elizabethtown, to serve Essex County.

The militia was improved by a series of promotions and reorganizations. Under the provisions of the federal act of 1808, New York's quota of detached (specifically designated and trained) militia was 14,389. At that time New York's Third Division consisted of the militia of Clinton, Essex, and Franklin Counties. Within that division the Fortieth Brigade was commanded by Brigadier General Benjamin Mooers of Plattsburgh. His quota of detached militia was 262 men. Mooers had been a lieutenant and adjutant in Moses Hazen's Canadian Regiment during the Revolution, seeing his first service at the age of eighteen. After settling in northern New York, he joined the militia and rose rapidly to positions of command. Born in 1758, he was in the prime of life physically. A large landowner and prominent citizen of the young village, he was the first sheriff of Clinton County, had represented it in the Assembly, and was the county treasurer.

In 1811 Mooers was promoted to major general and put in command of the entire Third Division. But the state's brigade commanders in peacetime were not very conscientious in their paper work, and the governor took

Maj. Gen. Benjamin Mooers (1758–1838) by an unknown artist c. 1812. The painting was damaged in the Chicago fire of 1871. *Courtesy of the Clinton County Historical Museum.*

Mooers to task for the shortcomings of his brigadiers. In the spring of 1812, Tompkins complained that since the middle of 1811 no brigade in the state had made full returns, and he threatened courts-martial if the practice were allowed to continue.

Early in 1812 Congress revamped its militia requirements. New York's new quota of 13,500 detached militia was broken down by the governor so that, for example, the quota of the Fortieth Brigade was 300 men. Mooers' division was extended in May to include Washington, Rensselaer, and Columbia counties, and in June to other counties on the west bank of the Hudson River. In the same month the governor created an organizational structure paralleling the existing one for the whole militia, in order to give a framework for the units of detached militia. Mooers continued to command the Third Division of the total militia, but now he also headed the Second Division of Detached Militia, consisting of three brigades. The Third Brigade, nearest to the scene of future action, was commanded by Brigadier General Micajah Pettit of Washington County. Within that brigade the Seventh Regiment was headed by James Green of Washington County, the Eighth by Thomas Miller of Clinton County, and the Ninth by Peter Vosburgh of Columbia County.[15] As the commander of the militia nearest the border, Colonel Miller will be heard from throughout the war. His memorials in the North Country are his lovely stone house and the street on which it is located, the Tom Miller Road in the town of Plattsburgh.

The old militia structure maintained the activities of the great majority of the militia who were in the exempt classes, provided replacement for the detached units, and organized and sometimes provided leadership for the many exempts who rushed to volunteer with the declaration of war. Ultimately New York fielded 77,896 militia in the war of 1812, a figure that does not show the number that served more than once or the men who enlisted in the regular army. This is from a population of about one million in 1813.

As war came nearer, Mooers was ordered to "keep up a communication and understanding with the officers on the Vermont side of the lake." He was authorized to call out the entire 13,500 militia from Clinton, Essex, and Franklin counties "whenever you may think proper to call on them." Pettit was ordered to Plattsburgh to serve under Mooers in command of these men.[16]

The militia structure was similar in Vermont, which also had a quota under the presidential directive of April 1812. They were no better prepared than the New York militia, for both put their trust in one day's training a year. But whereas General Mooers was the sole military commander in the Plattsburgh area during the first months of the war, Burlington had a small detachment of regulars. Just before the declaration of war, Colonel Isaac Clark of the Eleventh U.S. Infantry, a veteran of the Revolution, arrived to prepare for almost certain conflict. His most important achievement was the purchase for government use of two five-acre lots on the bluff overlooking the lake, land now included in Battery Park. The site was eventually used as intended — the erection of a battery of guns along the bluff and the construction of a cantonment behind it.

However, at the outbreak of war there were no usable fortifications in the entire Champlain Valley. Even the cantonment at Swanton was only occasionally garrisoned. The old forts at Ticonderoga and Crown Point had long since fallen into decay and private hands. There was no fort guarding the entrance to the lake from the Richelieu River. The wooden blockhouses erected in Plattsburgh, Peru, Essex, North Hero, and elsewhere during the Revolution and the Indian scares of the 1790s had likewise been abandoned except the one on the lake shore in Plattsburgh, which had been enlarged and used as a courthouse, schoolhouse, and church. Physically, the whole valley had a most unmilitary character early in 1812.

On the lake there was nothing that could be called a navy. The Americans could not even match the British gunboats at Isle-aux-Noix until 1809. In that year Naval Lieutenant Melancthon T. Woolsey, son of the collector, was assigned to Lake Champlain with orders to construct two gunboats at Whitehall, primarily to help in enforcing the embargo. Young Woolsey had entered the navy in 1800 and had fought well in the Tripolitanian War. The chasing of smugglers seemed tame to him and so, delegating his work on Lake Champlain, he obtained a transfer to Oswego, later to Sackets Harbor, where he earned a considerable reputation and rose to second in command under Captain Isaac Chauncey.

The Champlain Valley was still, in 1812, overwhelmingly rural. The population was relatively sparse on both sides of the lake but especially in northern New York. New York's lake counties (Clinton, Essex, Washington) numbered 61,750 inhabitants in the census of 1810, but three-fourths of them lived in Washington County, at the south end of the lake and extending southward to the Hudson. The residents of Clinton County, which was to become a main theatre of operations, numbered only eight thousand people. The border town of Champlain had twelve hundred, but they were divided among the hamlets of Champlain, Rouses Point, and Cooperville. The town of Plattsburgh numbered 3,112 souls, including 28 slaves. But Plattsburgh then included the later towns of Beekmantown, Dannemora, Schuyler Falls, and Saranac. Indeed, there were only five towns in the entire county, all but one bordering on the lake.

Nevertheless, the central settlement in Plattsburgh was a bustling lake port, whose industries were powered by the Saranac River along its southern edge. The town had a bloomery, a carding and a nailing machine, a fulling mill, a furnace, and two tanneries. It produced hollow ware and pottery. The extended town was governed as one unit until 1815, when the center on the lake obtained a charter to run its own affairs as the Village of Plattsburgh.

The five lake counties in Vermont (Grand Isle, Franklin, Chittenden, Addison, and Rutland) numbered eighty-seven thousand people, more than a third again as many as the residents on the New York shore. Vermont towns in the valley were also all small, the largest being Rutland (2,370), followed by Middlebury (2,130), and Burlington (1,690). But Burlington was the fastest growing and in another thirty years would be the largest town in the state.[17] In 1812 it was probably at least as large as the village of Plattsburgh. Like that town, it was also a lake port and a place of small, diversified industries. It had gone farther in developing the commercial potential on the lake, and its Gideon King was already dubbed "The Admiral of Lake Champlain." Plattsburgh's leading citizens, on the other hand, were more likely to be big landowners and speculators, such as the Platts and Benjamin Mooers.

Few as they were, the inhabitants of the lower Champlain Valley alternated between fear of war and irritation with restrictions on their trade with Canada, which was their commercial lifeline. When war came, the fears of invasion, always present, rose with the summer months and waned somewhat in winter. Before the war was over, they would be subjected to the harrowing experiences of raids, invasions, and the profound dislocations of their social and economic life.

4

WAR COMES

Although Congress declared war on June 18, it was the 23rd before Governor Tompkins knew it and the 27th before General Mooers in Plattsburgh received word. With his immediate issuance of division orders, the wheels of mobilization started to turn. He continued to receive directions from the governor concerning the militia, but technically, as the governor explained, Mooers was under General Dearborn. This was a sensible recognition of facts by the governor because for the entire first summer of the war Mooers commanded the northern front, which was defended almost entirely by militia. Early in July, for example, the regular army strength in Plattsburgh numbered five men, the highest rank being a lieutenant. "Happy however for us," grumbled a Plattsburgh businessman, "the pacific disposition of our enemy affords us a better security than the troops stationed among us."[1]

Early in 1812, Henry Dearborn, a colonel in the Revolution, had been called to Washington from the customs house in Boston. He had served as secretary of war in both Jefferson administrations, and his experience prompted President Madison to make him one of two major generals, although he had passed his sixty-first birthday. Augustus Foster, the British minister in Washington, described him as "a heavy unwieldly looking man" of no great military reputation who had accepted his appointment with great reluctance.[2] During his two months in Washington, he performed the functions of a chief of staff, and by April had developed the outline of a plan for the conquest of Canada. Its main thrust was to the north along Lake Champlain to Montreal although supporting campaigns were to be launched from Sackets Harbor, Niagara, and Detroit.

It was a good plan, and its prompt and vigorous execution might have knocked Canada out of the war in the first season. This is what the British feared. There was, however, a vast difference between secret plans drawn up in peacetime, and their translation into an army trained and equipped to carry them out in wartime. Assigned the command of a northeastern army not yet in existence, he went first, in May, to supervise the defense of New York City preparatory to turning it over to Brigadier General Joseph Bloomfield. Then he chose Greenbush, across the river from Albany, as his headquarters. The task confronting him was impossible for one man to execute. He was expected to raise troops in New England and New York, then train and equip them for the invasions of Canada. For the sake of the war effort and his own reputation, it is unfortunate that he was not kept in Washington as a coordinator, a job he probably would have done well, but he left the capital without his duties having been made clear. He did not know until August that he was expected to aid General Hull at Detroit, and he did not understand that his direct responsibility included the western borders of New York state.

Many of Dearborn's troubles were not of his own making. Fumbling in Washington threw many plans out of joint. President Madison's wartime administration came under constant attack from his enemies, whose bitterness increased after each new military failure. An occasional victory might have taken the sting out of the attacks and perhaps even have made Madison a notable war president, but there were to be no victories in 1812 and few thereafter. Furthermore, Madison's poor judgment of men and the desperate lack of qualified personnel led him to make weak appointments in the War and Navy departments and the military commands. He involved himself, moreover, in military tactics and strategy more than his background warranted. On the other hand, his modesty, steadiness of purpose, and self-control made him the only symbol of unity that a divided nation possessed.

As an agent of a peace-loving president with no military experience, the head of the War Department took on added significance, and Madison was unfortunate in his choices. At the start of the war the secretary was Dr. William Eustis of Massachusetts. Born in 1753, Eustis had served as a surgeon in the Revolution, after which he practiced medicine in Boston. He had been a member of Congress prior to his appointment to the War Department in 1809. If the army had remained small and the country at peace, Eustis would probably have filled the position adequately, but the mere approach of war was too much for him and his small staff. Without the background to do so, he participated with Madison, Dearborn, and Hull in laying out the strategy for the coming war. He dispatched Dearborn to New York without clearly defining his military jurisdiction. During the final Congressional debate on war, he answered an urgent request for information by admitting that he did not know whether the authorized ranks were filled, or how many militia were enrolled under the new act. This lack of information reflects slow communications with distant posts, a hold over from a leisurely peacetime army, but also the secretary's failure to cope with the rapid pace of events. A penny pincher, he wasted time on unimportant matters instead of the major ones. Secretary of the Treasury Gallatin said of him, "His incapacity and total want of confidence in him were felt through every ramification of the service."[3] He finally resigned under pressure in December 1812.

Madison was no more fortunate in his choice for the Navy Department. Paul Hamilton, the secretary, was a veteran of the Revolution and subsequently a politician in South Carolina, where he rose to be governor. But nothing in his background qualified him in naval matters, and he seems to have learned little in the office. According to the gossip of the day, he was frequently intoxicated by the middle of the day. Overcautious in all his decisions, he soon lost the confidence of Congress and the president, and he also resigned in December.

Thus the national command structure was not capable of evoking respect. Yet Dearborn did the best he could in his difficult assignment. From Greenbush he went to Massachusetts in May to raise troops. He wrote Governor Strong three times before getting an answer and then received a flat rejection. Strong, an extreme Federalist, took the position that only he had the power to determine when an emergency warranted putting the state's militia under national authority. Since the federal Constitution limited such an emergency to foreign invasion or domestic insurrection, the militia of Massachusetts would be used only in the state and under his direction. When war was declared, the lower house of the state legislature had condemned it by a vote of two to one. "Mr. Madison's war" was greeted by a day of public fasting, humiliation, and prayer as well as flags at halfmast and peace memorials from numerous towns around the state.

The Federalist governors of Connecticut and Rhode Island arrived at conclusions similar to Strong's regarding their militia. Governor Roger Griswold of Connecticut temporized even longer than Strong but eventually fell back upon the Constitution's definition. "No such case existing," he proclaimed, "the officers and soldiers have not been ordered from their farms and other occupations, and from their homes into the service required."[4] So Dearborn returned from southern New England with empty hands, and the militia of those states never served outside their own states. He arrived at Greenbush on July 26, to find no troops assembled and a shortage of every kind of equipment for the New York militia already at the front, in spite of heroic efforts by Governor Tompkins. At least the militia *were* at the front, in both northern New York and Vermont, and by the time of the fall campaign Vermont militia were serving on the New York side of the lake as well.

Opponents of administration policy before the war were not reconciled to it after it arrived. Concerning the Republicans, Federalist John Freligh said: "This war, like all the rest of their measures, has been commenced in folly, directed in weakness, and will end in ruin."[5] Waxing even stronger about the war a month later he wrote:

> I regard it as ominous, pointing to the final downfall of our liberty and independence. . . . It was a maxim among the heathens, that those whom the Gods intend to destroy were first struck with madness. Is not this maxim verified in our case? It is acknowledged by every man of common sense, that our country has for several years back, been travelling the down hill road with the most rapid and portentous pace; and it is equally obvious that we have been driven into this path by the folly or wickedness of the present administration.[6]

His frenzied denunciations can be countered by any number of patriotic utterances such as those of Abraham Per Lee at Champlain:

> War is the constant theme of the people on the frontier, and well they may be alarmed. The British are making every exertion for defense, they are giving great bounties for enlisting and fortifying every place that admits of it.
> They intend we shall purchase Canada, if we have it, at a very dear price, even the blood of thousands of our best Americans. But it is better we should bleed on the tomb of Montgomery than have our country dishonorably submit to the dictates of a British Cabinate, the insults of a British ministry or the oppression of a British navy.[7]

The border towns were indeed frightened. At the start of the war not a single uniformed man was stationed at the frontier, and during the summer only small militia units were sent there. Large numbers of the inhabitants prepared to abandon their homes and flee southward. General Mooers bombarded the governor with requests for more troops and supplies, reporting "the greatest consternation and dismay" on the frontier. In June: "Our inhabitants are much alarmed & if prompt & immediate protection is not given them, all that can will move to some place for safety." In July, he reported that many families were leaving, which meant a great loss of crops. He believed that a campaign into Canada would reassure the border residents. In September, he was again urging an invasion because it would "give spirit to the residents;" but, he warned, "if the force is too small or it falls back, the people will leave and ruin & distress the consequence."[8]

Mooers was besieged by requests for arms from Jay, Malone, and Chateaugay, all of which he tried to satisfy. The Franklin County Committee of Safety told him that people were already moving inland. With a sparse population and no large centers nearby, they felt exposed to both the British and the Indians, whose loyalties were suspect. The people wanted enough protection so they could stay neutral, perhaps partly because of their antiwar Federalism. Mooers sent them shipments of arms in June and July. The latter load was carted in a rain that ruined the powder and rusted the guns; those could be cleaned, but many of them still needed repairs. One shipment contained ammunition that did not fit the guns already there and had to be exchanged.

The same refrain was heard from the Committee of Safety in Champlain, which wrote to learn if they would have government protection. Local citizens were keeping guard duty until they could be relieved by troops, but they also feared that the military might invite attack. Reacting to a report that soldiers were going to be stationed in Chazy, they wrote: "The people in this place (if the report is true) will one and all quit their property and move to the south. They would rather that the troops were stationed at Albany than at Chazy for then we could stay neutral." Their tone changed somewhat during the summer when militia were sent to Champlain, but in September they were still stating their case: "We confidently believed the Government intends ample protection to the inhabitants of the frontier & are persuaded you are disposed to second the views of government in this respect."[9]

One of the most curious requests received by Mooers came from Daniel Robinson at Little Pond on the Military Turnpike. He wrote to say that a group had formed the "True-Harted Amaracan Volentears" which wanted him to visit them because "Your coming to se us will rais our ambition and prhaps eas the mind of sum of our wiming that now air vary much alarmd." Two days later he wrote again: "We have nither arms nor anention and we mus be emedely furnished with them or we shall lose all our wimen. Pray help us if posebel for we air determed to se sum blud run before we give up our propety if asisted." He offered to march his company to the "asnel" if Mooers would give them arms; he also wanted to borrow a fife and drum until cold weather.[10] Robinson received his arms about four days later.

When London learned of the outbreak of war, the British government expected that the repeal of the Orders in Council would bring an early termination; consequently, the governor general was exhorted to wage war defensively. Prevost bombarded his commanders with instructions to use caution:

> Our numbers would not justify offensive operations being undertaken unless they were solely calculated to strengthen a defensive attitude. I consider it prudent and politic to avoid any measure which can, in its effect, have a

tendency to unite the people in the American states. Whilst division prevails among them, their attempts on these Provinces will be feeble; it is therefore our duty carefully to avoid committing any act which may, even by construction, tend to unite the eastern and southern states, unless by its perpetration we are to derive a considerable and important advantage.[11]

For two years the British policy remained a defense of Canada. Some measure of the success of this strategy can be found in the repulse of eleven distinct invasions of Canadian soil.

Prevost soon found another good reason to fight a defensive war. Every time British regulars were stationed near the border or operated on the American side, large numbers deserted into the United States. When caught, they were often punished by death but without noticeable deterrence on the others; thus Prevost learned to avoid campaigns on American soil. If his militia deserted, they were more likely to head for home than abroad, but their punishment had to be lighter because of the numbers involved in single movements.

Awareness of this tendency by British regulars stimulated a unique American proposal to capitalize on it. Caleb Nichols, a Plattsburgh lawyer and occasional intelligence agent for the War Department, suggested to the secretary that American troops should be stationed just over the line in Canada. They should bring on as many skirmishes as possible so as to give British soldiers the opportunity of deserting while fighting in the woods. "No place on the whole frontier," he argued, "is so favorable to ensure successful desertion as from the Stone Mill [Lacolle] to Champlain, there being neither river nor lake to cross." Such a policy from the beginning of the war, he believed, would have drawn off a quarter of the troops in the area.[12]

Prevost bolstered his reasons for a defensive war as he learned about the weaknesses of the American militia system. Even before the war Foster in Washington informed his government that the president lacked the clear power to send the militia outside the country. If the bulk of the American forces could not be used except in case of invasion of their own country, Prevost surmised, Canada would be saved. His adjutant general, Edward Baynes, after his public mission to Dearborn at Greenbush, described the militia in these terms:

The men are independent in their habits and principles, their officers ignorant and totally uninformed in everything relating to the profession of arms and possess no influence over the militia but in proportion as they court it by popular and familiar intercourse. . . . There appears to exist in the United States the greatest contempt and repugnance to the restraint and

discipline of a military life, and few gentlemen of respectability are willing
to become officers but prefer the militia where they obtain high rank without serving.[13]

Some elements of truth can be recognized in this assessment, and even
American officers of the regular army voiced similar opinions about their
own militia. However, it dangerously underestimated the willingness of the
average militiaman, when fully aroused and properly led, to fight heroically.
To the extent that Prevost was swayed by this disparaging outlook, which was
probably very little, his war plans could have gone awry. He needed every
shred of comfort he could find in his situation, which was desperate beyond
belief. His military strength was weak and his border population terrified.
The Canadian economy was to be severely damaged by frequent militia calls
which disrupted the farmer's year as well as preventing the development of
any large enterprises such as making potash or the cutting and preparing of
masts and timber, most of which continued to be imported at great expense.
Recognizing the hardship upon the militia and their families, a meeting of
London merchants, presided over by the duke of Kent, started a subscription
for war sufferers in British North America.

Nevertheless, Prevost maneuvered his small forces brilliantly. The initial
rebelliousness among some of the militia units around Montreal was met
with a firm but tactful hand, and throughout the war they rendered steadier
service than their counterparts in the United States. Viewing Montreal as the
Americans' prime target, he strongly fortified the area between Laprairie and
Champlain with militia and a few regulars. By the end of July, he had about
4,000 troops in place, including 1,600 at Half Way House (the mid-point between St. Jean and Laprairie and 27 miles from Champlain), 600 at Lacadie,
300 at Isle-aux-Noix, and others at St. Jean and Chambly. Isle-aux-Noix was
fortified as an advance post and gunboats brought overland as the basis for a
fleet. When Prevost became certain that the summer efforts for an armistice
had failed, he ordered the blocking of all the roads leading to the United
States border. De Salaberry and the Voltigeurs accomplished this work
swiftly; Prevost let the border residents know that if they did not like to have
their roads blocked, they were free to move away.

The mobilization for war was slow on both sides of Lake Champlain. Vermont had the advantage of a small force of regulars under Colonel Clark at
Burlington, and his numbers were increased to about 300 men by the first of
August. On orders from Dearborn, Governor Galusha ordered out one regiment of detached militia, who put them under Clark. During the summer,
other units were mustered and sent to the border. By August, there were
about 400 stationed at Swanton. Mooers and Clark conducted a regular ex-

change of information, as did the governors of the two states. There was also cooperation in getting supplies and mail from Albany to Plattsburgh. The usual time by land was five to six days, less if it could be shipped by water from Whitehall. If immediate shipping was not available, the governor ordered that it was to be sent by stage to Burlington, which was only two days from Albany, and then by water to Plattsburgh.

In New York the northern place of rendezvous was Plattsburgh, and Mooers was the supreme commander there until September. The detached militia from his entire division were alerted and met in their own localities before marching to Plattsburgh. Fortunately for the northern front, the militia responded to the emergency willingly, although not always quickly or eagerly, because crops and businesses would suffer. The first to arrive were those from the three northern counties, most of them in Miller's Eighth Regiment. The governor sent arms and ammunition as fast as possible, but he had few tents and blankets, although he did manage to send tents for 900 men early in July. Mooers found one of his early problems in the caliber of the arms he received because the cartridges did not fit them, and few bayonets were included.

Clamors for protection continued to descend upon Mooers from all segments of the border. As late as August, he was still beseeching the governor for more troops, declaring that the only answer he could give to those who pressured him was that he expected more men but could not say when or how many. By early July, however, he was able to start sending small units of the Eighth Regiment to the border towns. Major Ransom Noble of Essex County was ordered to Franklin County immediately. Noble, a tanner, left his business reluctantly and at his own request was relieved and replaced by Major Guilford Young of Troy in August. Noble made his headquarters at Chateaugay, with one company there and another at Constable. During the summer, the inhabitants, led by Gates Hoit, erected a blockhouse on the banks of the Salmon River about three miles northwest of the village of Chateaugay. It was paid for by voluntary contributions, but Hoit, one of the county's leading citizens, was able to obtain $100 toward it from the governor. It was garrisoned during part of the war until it was burned in 1814.

The rest of Franklin County was manned by its own militia, notably Captain Rufus Tilden at French Mills (Fort Covington), also under Noble. On his arrival at Chateaugay, Noble reported that Indians had set a house on fire there, but that the neighbors helped to put it out, to which Mooers responded: "From what we learn from our enemy they will not commit depredations on us if we do not upon them, yet we should be always ready and on our guard for fear of the worst."[14] During the summer, an arsenal was erected in Malone. Nevertheless, the Committee of Safety never felt adequately protected, and Mooers ultimately referred its petitions to the governor. Fortunately, most of the county for the first year and a half of the war was spared any serious threats from Canada.

In the same orders that sent Noble to Chateaugay, the two other companies of the 8th Regiment were ordered to northern Clinton County. Captain Rufus Sanford went to Champlain with a detachment of his company, leaving a few men at Chazy, while Captain John Dix went to Mooers with part of his unit. This command of the entire border by Noble was temporary and awkward, and shortly a more cohesive and permanent organization was drawn up. Noble continued to command all the militia in Franklin County, but Major Melancton Smith of the Eighth Regiment was sent to Champlain and given direction of the militia on duty in northern Clinton County. The detachments from the companies of Sanford and Dix rejoined their own units. Major Smith had full companies at Champlain, Chazy, and Mooers. General Mooers's instructions to Smith contained the admonition "to be vigilant and on the alert; suffer none of your troops to cross the Enemy's line, nor any depredation to be committed on our enemy."[15] In other words, maintain a strictly defensive posture.

It was one thing to call out the detached militia for a six-month tour, but it was something else to make them behave themselves when time hung heavy on their hands. To begin with, there were no barracks, and the men slept in tents, when they were available. Smith reported from Champlain that he could find no barracks except an old barn, although construction of barracks was under way on the edge of town. He wanted directions about clothing his men, some of whom were without shoes and shirts; if provided, they were willing to let the cost come out of their pay.

Sheer boredom and the regrets at leaving crops and businesses took their toll. Mooers had trouble with the deputy commissary of military stores, who promised Mooers he would stop drinking, but did not. From Chateaugay Lieutenant Charles MacNeil reported on Captain John Richardson, with tongue in cheek: "When we first received information that no one of us could leave our post one mile, the captain and ensign both concluded to die; but the ensign has got quite well, and we really have hopes of our captain; he begins to sip a little whiskey occasionally." Continuing his light vein in another letter, he declared: "Our company is the flower of the northern army, their activity is beyond description, they do honor to the whole globe in which they reside, their knowledge no doubt is far beyond our apprehention."[16]

Not many of the men were able to laugh at their plight, and Mooers interceded with the governor several times to improve their lot. Describing the militia as "good able bodied soldiers," he went on to say that "It would be well to keep them good natured by paying them up. Many complain they cannot live on their allowance & their pay, want both help to cloth & feed them — & besides they would be more willing to volunteer their services if it should be wanted."[17]

Smith found little to give him cheer. His command was plagued by a lack of orderliness and cleanliness, and in battalion orders he pinpointed the men who "pay no regard or respect to their Officers, but pass them with less ceremony than they do strangers. . . . That the Officers make themselves familiar with the men and are found, not infrequently associating with them as companions; by which means all command is lost & all authority despised."[18] Smith had hardly reached Champlain before some of his men wanted furloughs to go home and take care of their crops. Officers disappeared for several days at a time. Mooers urged severe measures, but public opinion would not tolerate them.

Although army regulations prescribed harsh penalities for desertion, few in the regular army suffered the maximum punishment; most deserters were court-martialed and imprisoned or cashiered from the service. Deserters among the militia were punished little if at all, because their offenses were often committed in a body. Furthermore, the legal obligations of the militia were not clarified until after the war, so that even if individual men were caught, their punishment rested upon uncertain constitutional grounds. Thus, for example, Israel Gillet in Mooers's command pleaded guilty to desertion before a court-martial. He was sentenced to be deprived of $2.50 of his wages for two months and all of his liquor ration for two weeks, and he was to perform extra drill for two hours each day for two weeks.[19]

Most militia trespasses were less serious than desertion but nevertheless disruptive of good order and, more important, of the tolerance of civilians nearby. These misdemeanors were addressed by a series of Division Orders from Mooers's headquarters. In one he regretted the failure of servicemen to attend Sunday worship or to arrive on time. In the future they were directed to be prompt so as not to disturb the others by their tardiness, "and that there be no march by fife and drum after the time of service usually begins."

On August 3, he demanded the detection and punishment of all evildoers because

> The General has been informed that some of the soldiers have been guilty of milking the inhabitant cows. He is sorry indeed that any soldier be so lost to himself as to dishonor the name and reputation of a soldier. For those that are calld out (to guard & protect the persons & properties of the inhabitants) to be the very persons to commit spoliations, destroy & pilfer, is terrible. It not only brings an odium upon the guilty but on the troops generally.

His order of August 27 dealt with similar matters:

It has reached the ear of the General that some persons whom it is suggested, even soldiers, have been guilty of purloining potatoes from the inhabitants. A soldier's pride ought to deter him from a conduct so vile.[20]

As Clinton County became increasingly a center of military activity,
Mooers fretted because there were no facilities to house the men. Apparently
no one had thought of the climatic hazards of campaigns on the northern
front. Living in tents was an acceptable temporary expedient in summer, but
few people seem to have thought ahead until necessity forced them to. The
only barracks constructed in northern New York during the summer were at
Champlain. The government had with foresight acquired property in Burlington, but even there the barracks were not completed until after the fall
campaign.

Plattsburgh, the main base in northern New York, had no barracks until
Christmas. The only military construction there was a guardhouse completed
in August. Yet as early as July 4, Mooers alerted Quartermaster General Morgan Lewis that no shelter existed for troops in the North Country, and he followed this with similar reminders. In September, he became more specific
and made his proposal directly to Dearborn. He recommended a cantonment
in Plattsburgh located two miles up the Saranac River, on the south bank.
Timber was plentiful and a rise of ground was suitable for building huts; it
was twenty-four miles to the border, with much hay, grain, cattle, and vege-
tables in between. His timing was still premature because by that time all energies were being concentrated on a large-scale "irruption" into Canada. The
location he proposed, however, did eventually become the site of a cantonment, although not until after much illness and suffering from exposure by
the soldiers.

Nonmilitary supplies were handled by a system of civilian contractors, or
commissaries, in the War of 1812. The quantity and quality of foodstuffs
varied with the efficiency and honesty of the contractors. The northern New
York front was relatively well served. Elbert Anderson was the commissary
operating out of Dearborn's headquarters, and his agent in northern New
York was Peter Sailly of Plattsburgh, who was also the collector of customs.
On the first report of war, Sailly rushed to the border with orders to prevent
all commercial intercourse with Canada, which was matched by a British embargo on goods leaving Canada. He took ten stands of arms, borrowed from
the arsenal at Plattsburgh, together with boarding pikes. In addition to the

revenue boats already at Rouses Point, he armed two revenue cutters. Within a few days he had captured $15,890 in dry goods, hardware, and glass belonging to American citizens, and stored it pending claims. He reported another $300,000 being loaded at St. Jean, but the British embargo prevented its departure.[21] Large quantities of merchandise, such as textiles and chinaware were, however, imported by merchants of New York and Boston by way of Lake Champlain. If the attempts were clandestine, the cargoes were liable to seizure and forfeiture. If they were reported openly and the goods voluntarily put under his control, Sailly stored them, and the American owners could try to establish a legal claim to them. The procedure was not a difficult one for those who could provide valid proof of ownership, such as receipts. This was the process employed by John Jacob Astor in bringing in big shipments of furs, about which more will be said later.

As for Sailly's duties as commissary, late in the summer, with word that large numbers of troops were due at Plattsburgh, he contracted for beef at three cents a pound for the men at Champlain, Chazy, and Mooers. He could find no pork in New York, and he also had to search farther afield for wheat. In December, he obtained flour for $9.86 a barrel and wheat for $1.88 a bushel. Later in the winter he was able to buy flour for $10 a barrel from Moses Catlin, a Burlington businessman with mills on the Onion (Winooski) River. He also found wheat in St. Lawrence and Franklin counties for about $2 a bushel. Most of that stayed at the posts in Franklin County, which was a part of his territory. He rented storage facilities in Plattsburgh and elsewhere, and he created a commissary store on the river in front of his house near the mouth of the Saranac River. During the winter, he suggested to the local commander, Colonel Zebulon Pike, that a guard be placed over it because, he feared, two or three saboteurs from Canada could destroy it.[22]

Meanwhile, alongside belated efforts by both sides to gear for war, several movements got under way for an armistice as a preliminary to stopping the conflict. Overlapping negotiations during the summer and fall were conducted by diplomats in Washington and London, and by Admiral John Borlase Warren from his flagship off the American coast. All of them came to nothing because of President Madison's insistence, rejected by the British, on a renunciation of the practice of impressment. But a fourth effort was made in the Northeast, and it actually achieved a three-week suspension of hostilities in that area.

When war was declared, the British minister, Augustus Foster, started for home. En route he stopped at Halifax, where he advised Prevost that the repeal of the Orders in Council should mean an end to the war and that negotiations for an armistice were the logical first step. Acting entirely on his own, but desiring to avoid an "effusion of blood," Prevost sent his adjutant general, Colonel Edward Baynes, to Dearborn at Greenbush with a set of propositions. Baynes's precise route down and back is difficult to determine, but he kept his eyes open and reported in detail about the military personalities and the troop concentrations he saw. He was received at the border under a flag of truce by Major Smith, who sent him to Mooers with an escort. In Plattsburgh he saw 400 militiamen, not in uniform and distinguished only by a military badge worn as a cockade in their hats. They had good arms and accouterments but "they did not seem to have made any progress even in the first rudiments of military drill." He concluded from the units he saw there and elsewhere that no plan was under way for invading Canada and if it happened, "from its total want of order in the organization and discipline I do not consider it as formidable or dangerous when opposed to regular and well disciplined British troops." He buttressed this opinion by his observations of the militia generally, where he found an absenteeism of 50 percent, with or without leave. Yet everywhere he thought the Americans had a very high opinion of their military prowess, "conceiving it to be in their power to pillage Montreal and to march to Quebec whenever they think proper."[23]

At Plattsburgh General Mooers and several of his officers met him in a room at the inn, probably Israel Green's. They discussed the purpose of his mission and, looking with satisfaction upon an end of hostilities, raised no objection to his proceeding on his way. Mooers even furnished a barge and escort to Burlington. There he was detained briefly because Colonel Clark was not convinced of the sincerity of Prevost, but eventually he was allowed to continue his journey.

By August 8, Baynes met Dearborn, whom he found "strong and healthy but does not appear to possess the energy of mind or activity of body requisite for the important station he fills." Nevertheless, the two men were able to agree quickly on the terms of a temporary ceasefire, its future depending on its reception by the president. Its termination, if it became necessary, would be effective four days after Prevost received notification. The motivations behind Dearborn's ready acceptance are worthy of note. He was far from ready for any campaign and, like Prevost, he thought that repeal of the Orders in Council made a continuation of the war unnecessary. Only the previous week he had been instructed by the secretary of war to launch an offensive at Niagara to relieve the British pressure on General Hull at Detroit; he wasn't ready for that either, nor had he comprehended until that time that any part of Upper Canada, including the Niagara peninsula, was his responsibility, as he explained to Eustis when he forwarded the ceasefire proposals. Baynes reported that Dearborn would "individually rejoice in such an event above all others for that the burthen of command at his time of life was not a desirable charge and that he should feel most happy in resigning it upon honorable terms." Dearborn also told Eustis that the arrangement might do some good, and that at least it could do no harm for, he wrote, "we could not act offensively except at Detroit for some time."[24]

The armistice specifically excluded Hull at Detroit because Dearborn cautiously thought he had no authority to commit the army in the Northwest; anyway, he thought that Hull's army of two thousand men was so unbeatable that it needed no protection. However, he did send word to Hull advising him to accept the ceasefire. Unfortunately, by the time the messenger arrived, and long before Dearborn could have made war at Niagara, Hull had allowed himself to be besieged by Brock with a much smaller force, and he surrendered his entire army during the period of the eastern ceasefire. Since Hull was not covered by the armistice, Prevost quite properly refused to restrain Brock "from any measures he might judge fit for repelling the invasion of the Upper Province and for compelling General Hull to retire from it."[25]

Meanwhile, Dearborn ordered his commanders in Burlington and Plattsburgh to carry out only defensive measures until further notice. The terms of the armistice were sent to Washington, where they were earnestly considered by President Madison. Several factors led him to reject it, as Eustis notified Dearborn on August 15. Madison was pinning great hopes on the negotiations he had commissioned in London, and they were not yet concluded. Furthermore, he expected a more formal commitment from the British government itself than anything that Prevost could make, and meanwhile he rejected any offer that did not promise an end of impressment. Then there was Hull, who needed a diversion such as Dearborn could make at Niagara, but Hull surrendered the day after Eustis wrote this letter.

By August 22, Dearborn received the rejection from Washington, but he postponed the notification of Prevost until supplies in transit could reach Niagara and Sackets Harbor. On the 26th, he sent Captain William Pinkney to Canada with word of the termination, explaining that the president had received no official information that would "warrant a continuance of the provisional measure that was temporarily agreed on."[26] Pinkney reached Montreal on the 30th, and the ceasefire officially came to an end four days later.

A tantalizing opportunity was thus lost for ending the war in its early stages. Both commanders thought that they were acting in the best interests of their countries. Canadian historians have been severely critical of Prevost for proposing the armistice in the first place. During the ceasefire, Prevost wrote to London that he would continue to strengthen the defenses of both Lower and Upper Canada, which "I shall probably be able to complete without any serious delay or interruption on the part of the enemy."[27] Yet his critics charge that he gave an unwarranted advantage to the Americans because he had much less material to forward and a shortage of transport with which to do it.

Dearborn has also been accused of weakly waging war by agreeing to a ceasefire. He was able, it is true, to bolster his positions more substantially because he had more to send than Prevost did. The Niagara front was reinforced with men and supplies from Oswego, and Sackets Harbor was also strengthened; both points were far stronger for the fall campaigns than any British forces opposing them. But he signed away these advantages, say the critics, by the timing of an armistice that excluded Hull; Detroit and most of Michigan territory were lost during the ceasefire.

The debate need not concern us long. Prevost seems to have had the more convincing position because his aims had the full concurrence of his government when word reached London. This is indicated by the fact that it sent Admiral Warren with similar proposals for a ceasefire in the fall, and they too were rejected by Madison because they contained no reference to impressment. As for Dearborn, there are several factors to consider. Perhaps Madison was too peremptory in rejecting the ceasefire. Almost certainly Eustis failed to delineate Dearborn's command to him. Dearborn, rightly or wrongly, was unprepared to mount any action at Niagara that could have helped Hull. As for Hull and his large army, he seemed perfectly capable, with or without outside help, of getting himself into a predicament from which surrender was the only solution. It is interesting to speculate that if Madison had accepted the ceasefire, Dearborn would have emerged as the hero of the war for bringing it to a speedy close.

With a now certain war on his hands, Dearborn, under pressure from Washington, hastened the preparations for offensive action on the Niagara and Plattsburgh fronts. Since the administration was particularly interested in the former, he put his priorities there. While the fate of Hull was still unknown, Eustis presumed that no more than a feint, even if that, need be made on Lake Champlain against Montreal. While he bolstered the Niagara front, and before any troop movements could take place to Plattsburgh, Dearborn ordered Colonel Clark in Burlington to send five companies of regulars to Plattsburgh to be posted near the arsenal and magazine.

During September, other regular troops began to arrive in Burlington and Plattsburgh in substantial numbers. The build-up was to be headed by Brigadier General Joseph Bloomfield, who arrived early in the month accompanied by Colonel Zebulon Pike of the Fifteenth Regiment. Bloomfield was now fifty-nine years of age. He had reached the rank of major in the Revolution, following which he became prominent in New Jersey law and politics. He was twice elected governor of the state. Partly because he was a Federalist, the Republican administration welcomed him into the war with a high rank for which he resigned the governorship. His first assignment was to succeed Dearborn in supervising the defenses of New York City. Apparently he was not very effective because as late as August Colonel Pike reported that "were we attacked at present we would be little better than a mob." John Freligh sourly greeted his arrival in Plattsburgh as probably "better qualified to surrender an army into the hands of the enemy than to conduct one triumphantly to victory and conquest."[28]

Colonel Pike entered the army as a lieutenant in 1799, and between 1805 and 1807 he led two exploring expeditions in the west, the first to chart the upper reaches of the Mississippi River and the second to explore the headwaters of the Arkansas and Red rivers. It was on this latter journey that he discovered Pike's Peak and was captured but later released by the Spanish, when he ventured too far into their territory.

Ordered to Greenbush at the same time as Bloomfield, he took umbrage at an article that appeared in Connecticut and New York papers which accused Dearborn's army of long "idling away their time near Albany," unprovided and uncared for. According to the article, when Pike's Fifteenth Regiment was ordered to Plattsburgh, the men refused to move until they were paid; the situation was saved only by the accidental presence of Secretary of the Treasury Gallatin who borrowed $20,000 on his personal account in Albany. According to Pike, the regiment regarded the charge as "a base calumny." The regiment was fully paid through August 31 by the regular paymaster, not by Gallatin, who appeared later.[29]

The arrival of Bloomfield in Plattsburgh produced a confrontation over rank between Mooers, a major general of militia, and Bloomfield, a brigadier general in the regular army. Bloomfield appealed to the governor, who wrote to Mooers relieving him of command of the post at Plattsburgh, especially since the militia there did not equal a major general's command. His reply to Bloomfield was more explicit. He had always felt that he would withdraw Mooers's command when either Dearborn or he himself desired it. He had no such request from Dearborn, but he was nevertheless suspending Mooers's command although technically the general was subject to Dearborn, not Tompkins, while he was mustered into the federal service. Regarding Dearborn, he was sharper: since he "seems willing to have the Command, without taking the responsibility of exercising it upon disagreeable occasions, I have concluded to assume the responsibility of exercising it, upon such occasions only. Genl Mooers accordingly will no longer interfere with you."[30] Henceforth, the ranking regular army officer commanded on the northern front. Mooers still directed the militia, but it was his sometimes thankless job to cooperate with the commanders, a procession of six of them, good and bad, during the rest of the war.

The regular force was augmented steadily during September and October, and the residents hoped that at last a decisive campaign was shaping up. However, the summer and fall on the northern front were cold and rainy. Among the men forced to sleep in tents, a variety of illnesses began to appear, as early as August in Champlain, of which more will be told later. Furthermore, Bloomfield was overcautious in his decisions and did not maintain good discipline among his troops. Therefore, the army he was gathering was sickly and had poor morale.

An important addition Bloomfield was able to make to his medical staff was Dr. William Beaumont. This young man, after teaching school for a few years in Champlain, had gone to study medicine in St. Albans in 1811. Itching for the action he sensed was coming on the northern front, he crossed to Plattsburgh to volunteer his services and was accepted as a surgeon's mate in the Sixth Regiment. When Dr. James Davis, surgeon of the Sixteenth Regiment, resigned owing to "the derangement of my domestick affairs" in November, Bloomfield recommended Beaumont as Davis' successor. A commission was issued by Madison in December, and thus Beaumont assumed his wartime position with the Sixteenth Regiment.[31]

He served conscientiously in the army throughout the war and afterwards. He expanded his medical knowledge by the vivisections which he was allowed to make on the bodies of dead servicemen. Out of this experience grew his claim to fame when, after the war, he discovered the secrets of digestion and published the results in a book whose first edition was printed in Plattsburgh. In addition to his medical career, Beaumont had an avocation in Republican politics, and he never wavered in his support of administration policy. He stated his beliefs clearly before he joined the army, in somewhat strident and self-assured tones; he was "under daily threatenings of being turned out of door for cherishing a true Republican principle. That principle is the legitimate sentiment of every real American. . . . Sooner might they remove the everlasting hills than bribe my integrity, make my faith waver, shake my belief, or divert my course from the pole star of Republicanism while reason holds her empire over the province of my intellect."[32]

Like the army, the navy in the Champlain Valley was also neglected during the first summer of the war. When war came, the two gunboats built by Woolsey in 1809 were derelicts at Basin Harbor, Vermont. In the summer, Naval Lieutenant Sidney Smith of Plattsburgh was named commander of the lake's nonexistent navy. He could get help from neither Army nor Navy departments so, on his own, he rescued the two gunboats and got them to Plattsburgh. At his own risk and with advice from Mooers and others, he repaired and equipped one, an open, armed scow about forty feet in length, and waited for orders about the other, which eventually directed its repair.

The government also contracted for 160 batteaux during the summer, and by early September, they were nearly completed at the yards at Whitehall. They were unarmed rowboats for carrying men and supplies, thirty-seven feet long and eight wide, with a capacity of forty to fifty men. Baynes saw about 100 of them at Champlain and Plattsburgh, as well as the repaired gunboat when he passed through on his mission for an armistice.

When troop movements to Plattsburgh began in September, the War Department purchased six sloops (single-masted sailing vessels) for use as transports. They were the *President,* sixty-five feet, the *Bull Dog,* sixty-four feet, the *Hunter,* sixty-one feet, and three others which do not have a part in the naval history of the lake. On September 28, Secretary of the Navy Paul Hamilton ordered Lieutenant Thomas Macdonough to leave his recently as-signed command at the Portland navy yard and take command on Lake Champlain. He was ordered to cooperate with General Dearborn but to take over the army's sloops. Simultaneously, Secretary of War Eustis alerted Dear-born to Macdonough's arrival, suggesting that "he will consult with you on the best means of defense — affording such cooperation as you may deem ex-pedient."[33] This was clearly not a very decisive order to cooperate and bore some bitter fruit later.

Macdonough had not yet reached his thirtieth birthday but he was repre-sentative of the new generation of naval commanders who received their training in the war against Tripoli. He entered the navy as a midshipman in 1800 and three years later was attached to the frigate *Philadelphia.* After it captured the *Mesboa* in the Mediterranean, he was sent to Gibraltar with the prize and consequently escaped the fate of the *Philadelphia* and its crew when it was captured. He participated in various attacks upon Tripoli and, under Stephen Decatur, assisted in the recapture and destruction of the *Phil-adelphia* in 1804. When the War of 1812 broke out, he was made first lieu-tenant of the *Constitution* before he was assigned to Portland. His rank was lieutenant, which it remained throughout the war, although locally he was designated master commandant. From that fact historians have tended to call him "Commodore," but he never gained that rank. After the battle of Plattsburgh he was promoted from lieutenant to captain, his highest rank.

Macdonough left Portland on October 5, and after a fatiguing trip by horse and chaise (cost, $75), he arrived in Burlington about the 8th. He went immediately to see Dearborn, who had come to Plattsburgh temporarily dur-ing the build-up of the army. Dearborn objected to an independent naval command, and he refused to give up the *President,* the largest and best of his sloops, although he relinquished the other five. Macdonough took them and the two gunboats to Whitehall, where he arrived on the 13th to arm and equip them. He wrote to Captain Isaac Hull in New York for stores and men;

Lt. Thomas Macdonough (1783–1825) after Gilbert Stuart. *Courtesy of State University of New York, Plattsburgh, permanent Art Collection.*

he got the former but not the latter. A shortage of seamen was to be his single most persistent difficulty throughout the war. Even the supplies were slow to arrive, largely because of the seventy-eight miles of bad roads from Albany. Nevertheless, by dint of hard work, he had some of the ships ready within a month. He converted two sloops to war vessels, but he found the other three were too old to carry guns, and they were retained by the army as transports.

On the 31st the *Hunter* under Lieutenant Smith sailed to Plattsburgh;

the *Bull Dog* under Macdonough and the two gunboats followed a few days later. The *Hunter* was armed with two twelve-pound guns and one long eighteen-pounder on a pivot; the *Bull Dog* had six-pounders and a long eighteen on a pivot; and the gunboats each carried a long twelve-pounder.[34] Dearborn finally released the *President,* which Macdonough adopted as his flagship after converting it to carry eight guns. The little fleet was far superior to the British collection of gunboats. Macdonough patrolled the lake and transported troops between Plattsburgh and Burlington. After Dearborn's fall campaign was ended, Macdonough went into winter quarters in Shelburne Bay, where he overhauled his vessels with material brought over land from Whitehall.

5

INDIANS, FURS, AND PRISONERS OF WAR

The Indians

The Indians who lived and hunted across the international border from northern New York to the upper Great Lakes were protected in this right by Jay's Treaty of 1795. As war between the two countries approached, the loyalty of these Indians became important, especially in British war planning. Americans in the Northwest had undermined their influence with the Indians by continuous take-overs of enormous parcels of their land. The British were not so much interested in their lands as in their furs and their loyalty in case of war. During the *Chesapeake* crisis of 1807, the British foreign secretary directed Governor General Craig to conciliate the tribes on the principle that "if in a contest they are not to be employed to act with us, they will be engaged to act against us, and that we are not to consider so much their use as allies as their destructiveness as enemies."[1]

This remained the basic British policy, friendship tempered by restraint. It called for the expenditure of substantial sums of money. In 1808 the military budget of the Indian Department amounted to about £5,419, and it increased substantially thereafter. Most of the money went for gifts, including great numbers of rations for the many Indians who were persuaded to remain at the forts, but also rifles, ammunition, and blankets as well as combs, mirrors, and other trinkets, sometimes numbering more than 550 different items.

The loyalty of the Indians was sought by both sides. The American aim, if war came, was to assure their neutrality on the premise that the war was between white rivals and did not concern them. The American tool was annuities to all those Indians who had had to give up their lands, including the Mohawks at St. Regis, astride the border in Franklin County, New York, and those Iroquois who had fled into Upper Canada after the Revolution. For their loyalty to the king in that conflict, they were promised lands by Governor General Frederick Haldimand. Under their leader, Joseph Brant, they settled along the Grand River on the Niagara peninsula to the number, within a few years, of about four thousand. Their poverty was slightly relieved by British distribution of presents each year, and by annuities from the United States for lands they had relinquished by treaty in New York State. To raise money for the improvement of his people, Brant wanted to sell some of his lands to white settlers, but the government believed that Indians degenerated in the proximity of settlers and forbade the sale on the grounds that the Indians held it as a lease only. This the Indians strenuously disputed.

After Brant died in 1807, John Norton tried to occupy his position of leadership, a pretension that some of the tribes refused to recognize. He was a troublesome character who Lieutenant Governor Francis Gore correctly believed was a Scotsman living as an Indian. Norton proposed two solutions to the Iroquois' problems. He wanted the British to take over the payment of the American annuities and so "break the bonds of American influence." He also asked for a new tribal home on Lake Huron. The Grand River allotment of 12 by 120 miles necessitated sprawling settlements; he asked for an area 50 by 30 miles in the West, which would encourage more compact villages. He argued that removal from the contamination of settlers and American influence was desirable, and that on Lake Huron they could keep the channels open to the Indians of the far west. He even submitted his grievances to William Wilberforce in England, who was trying to outlaw the use of liquor in the fur trade.[2]

The Americans kept close contact with the Iroquois who remained in New York. In May 1812, a four-day council was convened at Buffalo by Erastus Granger, agent to the Six Nations. The Indians promised to remain friendly to the United States, and a deputation of thirty visited their kinsmen on the Grand River "to strengthen the minds of the Indians in Upper Canada to remain neutral in case of war."[3] The British never solved the problem of the Grand River Indians before the war, although the war brought an end to the payment of American annuities. Norton and part of his people joined the British cause, one hundred responding to Brock's first call in 1812. Others stayed at home as neutrals and some even promoted the American effort. They never got their new home farther west, and when they laid claim to lands along the entire length of the Grand River, the government ruled against them.

Norton remained a problem throughout the war. Although recognized by the British as the head of the Iroquois on the Grand River, he was refused recognition by three of the tribes during the war. He was granted by the Indian Department the right to distribute supplies to his people, but he used food and liquor to try to attract a following among the western Indians, who not only accepted his largess but then collected a second quota at their regularly assigned stations. After the war the British eased Norton out by arranging a tour of England and then pensioning him off. His work for the British in the war was a mixed blessing.

On the general Indian scene the American policy of annuities was not as effective as it might have been because of continued American acquisitiveness. After the huge land cession of 1809, Captain Matthew Elliot, the British superintendent for Indian affairs at Amberstburg, across from Detroit, reported the Indians "more ripe than ever for war," and he continued: "I dread indeed that they will of themselves soon commence hostilities, and our government will, indeed already is, blamed for encouraging them." From Craig, through channels to the superintendents, repeated directives went out "to prevent a rupture between the Indians and the subjects of the United States. . . . which sooner or later would probably lead us into the being ourselves parties in the war, however much we might wish to avoid it." The Indians were to be given "clearly to understand that they must not expect any assistance from us."[4]

In spite of their belated efforts, the worst fears of the British eventuated at Tippecanoe in the fall of 1811, when Governor William Henry Harrison set out to break up the Indian concentration there. Because British-made rifles were quite naturally found in the captured encampment, American westerners confirmed their long-held suspicions that the British were encouraging the Indians to make war. Isaac Brock, the new lieutenant governor in Upper Canada, admitted his failure to restrain the Indians: "Such was their infatuation the Indians refused to listen to advice and they are now so deeply engaged that I despair of being able to withdraw them from the contest in time to avert their destruction; a high degree of fanaticism which has been for years working in their minds has led to the present state of things." Prevost was also deeply disturbed over the breakdown of British policy. He tried to refute the American charges of complicity, which the *Quebec Mercury* described as "this opprobrious system of national slander, this new species of warfare, against which neither virtue nor valour can always furnish an adequate defense."[5]

Meanwhile, Congress entered its long drift toward war. Henry Clay hoped the Indians would not fight after Tippecanoe, for "it will certainly add to our embarrassments if we have to carry on a war with them, as well as their good friends, the English."[6] A committee of the House of Representatives studied the correspondence of the secretary of war and concluded that the British had indeed excited the Indians into hostilities against the United

States. Madison touched on the subject in his war message. But both message and debate were far more concerned with the violation of neutral rights on the seas than with Indian troubles. The declaration of war on June 18 was prompted primarily by impressment and illegal blockades; the Indian situation constituted but one more grievance. The conquest of Canada, it was believed, was the best way to bring Great Britain to terms on all the issues, including the termination of the Indian menace in the Northwest.

This was the last war in which the Indians allied themselves with a foreign power against the United States. Although once wielding great influence, they no longer held a balance of power but served merely as auxiliaries to the British forces. The mere rumor of their approach terrified American civilians, and they perpetrated some heinous massacres in the Northwest. Very few served the American forces because their neutrality was considered preferable. Only in the Southwest did the Indians themselves become the object of a systematic campaign, undertaken by Andrew Jackson.

In the East the secretary of war preferred the Indians to remain neutral, but he acknowledged that the attempt to restrain them might encourage them to join Canadian Indians against the United States. Therefore he instructed Dearborn that if they were needed, they should be used only against other Indians. Although small numbers saw action at Chippewa and Lundy's Lane, and as guides, they were employed so sparingly that Madison in his second inaugural address could virtuously denounce the British eagerness to "glut their savage thirst with the blood of the vanquished and to finish the work of torture and death on maimed and defenseless captives."[7]

In Lower Canada, Prevost attached to the Voltigeurs a company of Indians consisting of six chiefs and sixty warriors, who were to be armed, clothed, and fed by the government and given presents instead of pay. The Voltigeurs were active throughout the war, including the campaign to Plattsburgh, where the approach of the Indians aroused more fears than the large army itself.

Intense undercover activity took place for the loyalty of the Iroquois at the Caughnawaga reservation near Montreal, and at the St. Regis reservation astride the border in northwestern Franklin County. Before the war the British and American commissioners had agreed that the Indians on the border should remain neutral and that troops from both sides should stay away from the St. Regis reservation. Because of the wartime fears of neighboring white settlers, the Indians were restricted in their freedom to travel and hunt. They became so impoverished that they appealed to Governor Tompkins for aid, and throughout the war they received rations from the federal stores at French Mills (Fort Covington). The contest for the loyalty of the Indians of Lower Canada continued throughout the war. The Indians themselves were deeply divided and subject to great pressures from Canada and the United States. Both sides held secret conferences and resorted to bribery in the form of cash and rations.

Mooers at Plattsburgh seems to have been the first to take up the Indian cause. On July 4, 1812, he reported to the governor that four St. Regis chiefs were in town. They appeared to be friendly and well disposed, with no desire to take up arms, but to stay at home. A few days later Mooers was reminded by the Committee of Safety of Franklin County that the people there needed protection because of their exposure to attacks by the Caughnawaga and St. Regis Indians, who were "under great pressure to take up arms for the British."[8] The committee's tone had changed somewhat from a month previously, when it urged that all Indians who sought American protection and asked for provisions must be supplied.

Late in July, Dearborn asked Mooers to be on the lookout for a "suitable character" to gather intelligence about the enemy and the Indians. When found, "Every possible precaution and discretion should be used for keeping the name of persons employed a profound secret, whether they be citizens of the United States or subjects of the enemy." But Dearborn acted on his own instructions by asking a young Indian, Eleazer Williams, to come and see him at Greenbush. Williams arrived there on August 3, and was given a warm reception and cordial hospitality. Although he found little to agree with when Dearborn appealed to him, he yielded to patriotic arguments and committed himself to raise and lead a group of intelligence-gathering agents. As a pacifist he regretfully discovered later that he was committed to the Articles of War and the war party, and he failed in his efforts to obtain changes in the terms of his employment.[9] Dearborn's only concession at that time was to bestow the grandiose titles of superintendent general of the Northern Indian Department and commander of the Corps of Observation. He is usually associated in the popular mind with the latter agency, the "eyes and ears of the Northern Army," as it came to be known.

Williams was a young, intelligent, and pious half-breed who later became the center of a controversy over his belief that he was the "lost Dauphin" of France. But in 1812, at about the age of twenty, he was still studying in Massachusetts, where he decided to become a missionary to the Indians. He had grown up at the Caughnawaga reservation in a large Indian family, although he seems to have stemmed from an Indian captive at the time of the Deerfield raid in 1704. He was probably descended from Daniel Williams, progenitor of the Williams families in Massachusetts and Connecticut. Raised as an Indian in a home where his father, Thomas, was an influential chief, he therefore knew Indian ways and language; he later gained fame as an Indian orator and he achieved his goal of becoming a missionary to the

Oneidas. During his war service, he was tormented by conscientious scruples against war and violence; throughout the period he prayed for peace, and he consistently refused to bear arms until the battle of Plattsburgh.

Dearborn's commission to Williams on August 5 offered $400 a year and two rations a day, and extra expenses for necessary travels. Dearborn also promised to help him further his education during the winter. In return he expected "perfect attention," "most ridged punctuality and integrity," "caution and prudence," and accounts to be "correctly kept and exhibited when required." On August 6, Williams departed by horse for Burlington with a letter of introduction to Colonel Clark, and another for Mooers at Plattsburgh. The latter instructed Mooers to furnish Williams with a horse and anything else he needed, again urged "the most perfect secrecy," and for the first time opened the way to American generosity to the Indians: "If any of these people should be disposed to come within our lines, they should be treated in a friendly manner, and supplied with rations."[10]

Mooers supplied him with a special passport for Franklin County and a letter to Captain Tilden at Constable. He acquainted himself with the country, met some of the Indians, and began to put together his team of "Rangers," Indian and white, including his brother John, who operated secretly under his direction. On August 24, he went to Albany and stayed up all night reporting to Dearborn. His conscience still bothered him and his journal carries the notation "Oh! That God would make all men peaceful and live together in unity." Nevertheless, he performed a very valuable service. He reported to Dearborn and Governor Thompkins; he conferred with, and undertook missions for, Generals Mooers, Bloomfield, Wilkinson, Hampton, Izard, Macomb, and Lieutenant Macdonough.

From his meeting with Dearborn, Williams went north to Whitehall where he first met General Bloomfield. After the general arrived in Plattsburgh on September 9, Williams told him about the work of the Corps of Observation. Then he rejoined Tilden for a secret conference at French Mills with some St. Regis chiefs. Tilden harangued them, gave them money and obtained their promises of help for the American cause. Williams' conscience bothered him about the propriety of detaching British Indians from allegiance to their own government. After consultation with Bloomfield he decided that it was necessary. Shortly thereafter he took two of the chiefs to Albany to be wined and dined by the governor. Yet he realistically admitted that the Canadian Indians, regardless of their protestations, were not to be relied on.

In the middle of September, three loyal St. Regis chiefs, signing their letter with an "x," sent their brother chief, Colonel Louis Cook, to Mooers with a statement of their loyalty. As evidence they appended a list of forty-eight of "the uneasy and troublesome ones" at St. Regis, together with the names of two chiefs who had joined the British. Colonel Louis stayed at the Mooers home. He needed clothing, which Mooers did not possess, and Mooers took the colonel to Bloomfield, who asked Mooers to supply the chief with the customary clothing and bill it to the assistant deputy quartermaster.

Bit by bit an American Indian policy was developed. One of its important ingredients was the rations distributed at French Mills which by December supplied 434 Indians. The chiefs usually came most often because periodically they received cash bonuses averaging $50 at a time, often distributed by Williams. In October, some Caughnawaga chiefs appeared before the Vermont legislature with land claims for which they requested annual payments. The legislature declined but voted $100 for presents and $100 for the expenses of the chiefs' trip.

In the fall, the British violated the prewar agreements by placing an armed band at St. Regis. A small detachment of American militia, using the detailed intelligence of the Corps of Observation, surrounded and captured the British force, including the first flag of the war. The British retaliated by a similar raid in which they captured Tilden and his company at French Mills. The two groups were exchanged in December. This was the only military clash in the East that arose solely out of Indian affairs.

Although supervision of all Indian relations was maintained by Dearborn at Greenbush, much of the on-the-spot work was conducted by General Mooers. After Dearborn's feckless incursion into Canada in November, he assigned to Mooers the care of all Indians in the United States on the borders of Canada between the St. Lawrence and Lake Champlain. He was to supply and pay them as agents, pay three Caughnawaga chiefs $50 each, and supervise the work of Eleazer Williams, who was "not to be absent without your explicit permission."[11] Mooers acquired a number of perplexing problems with his new authority. He coordinated the work of the Rangers with the demands of the army commanders, oversaw the rationing system and certified and found payment for the bills of the Indian service. One of his assignments was to put the St. Regis Indians who collected rations to the work of making snowshoes for the army.

He also had problems with the food rationing system at French Mills. During the winter of 1812–13, contractor W. Hastings was in charge and he complained to Mooers about the local militia commander, Captain David Erwin, who handled the actual distribution of the rations. According to Hastings, Erwin was extravagant in his issues. Mooers warned Erwin against issuing unnecessary rations, especially to any Indians who had not put themselves under American protection. He was also to avoid issuing large amounts of grain for seed. Subsequently, Erwin charged that some Indians sold the rations and used the money to buy liquor. They got drunk, and one was jailed in Malone for drawing a knife.[12]

At an Indian council in 1813 which included many Indians from Canada, Erwin reported that they wanted to continue their policy of neutrality. There were 72 war enthusiasts, but "to loos the friend ship of 350 nutral Indians for the servis of 72 compeld to serve I can not think as bee good pollicy. I have converst with the principal inhabitants and I am convinced that it would make this country a frontier."[13]

In May of the second year of the war, the Rangers received an increase in pay "to encourage them in their fidelity," as Williams described it. Williams' own bill after a year's service was $591.40. Besides his expenses it included pay at $400 and two rations at twenty cents each. It was not fully documented because Williams had lost some of his papers during Murray's raid on Platts-burgh. General Izard in 1814 suspected that some Rangers were also in the pay of the British. He temporarily stopped their monthly stipends and gave them notice that in the future their reward would be proportionate to the value of their services. No evidence exists to support his suspicions, nor do any of Mooers's papers show that he ever challenged any of the bills growing out of the Indian Service.

On the contrary, he interceded with some commanders in order to get them paid. One of his special pleadings, to the inspector general, was on be-half of Thomas Williams, the father of Eleazer, who had helped to keep the Caughnawaga Indians neutral but had consequently lost favor with the Brit-ish. Thomas came into the States, and Mooers asked for a suitable reward because father and son had "done much good by their timely and repeated interference with the hostile Indians which has probably prevented deprada-tions on the inhabitants of our Frontier is I believe unquestionable." Thomas appealed to the War Department for rations for himself and his family dur-ing the last summer of the war; he obtained them but the record is not clear how and where he did so.[14]

The role of Eleazer Williams, as it finally evolved, was to gather informa-tion and to keep the Indians at peace. Concerning his Rangers, he recorded that

> No movement made by the enemy but is known to them. The lives and lib-
> erties of the greatest personages among the enemy are often within their
> grasp and at the mercy of this secret corps of observation. Always in motion
> and activity, ready to execute the order of the government however delicate
> and dangerous the nature of it may be. . . . No appeal can be made from
> it. They are constantly exposed to martial law and to death. Their courage,
> bravery and fidelity save them — the war department often praises their dar-
> ing conduct, and rewards their services with high wages.

Understandably proud of his outfit, he also had the satisfaction of knowing that he was considered dangerous in Canada, and that a reward was offered for his capture. If that happened, he instructed his Rangers "to take and make prisoners of as many as it may be in their power of the high officers of the British army—Gen'l Prevost if possible."[15]

The Corps of Observation was pitted against British agents, who had the disadvantage of not being highly organized. After five months of war, Prevost reported having spent only £101 on the secret service of the government. Williams was fortunate in not losing any of his important agents to the British, for he knew the threat to his entire organization: "If my men are once detected they are lost." Occasionally his Rangers captured enemy agents. In 1813 one William Baker was caught and turned over to the army for disposition. After questioning, he admitted that he was a sergeant in the British 103rd Regiment. He was hanged on March 26, 1814, in the presence of the whole army. In July 1814, another was captured and induced to confess. He divulged the names of Americans, some of them smugglers from New England, who supplied the British with information about the American position and strength. He also revealed the names of British agents; the Rangers were alerted to watch for all of them. The competition for Indian loyalty ended only with the termination of the war. The accounts of some of Eleazer Williams' missions and the credit he merited for timely information are reserved for the appropriate place in the chronology of the war.

Furs

The central figure in the wartime fur trade was John Jacob Astor, but to achieve that preeminence he broke into the fur business of the Great Lakes area. This trade had been dominated by a British company whose center had been Fort Michilimackinac on Mackinac Island off the northern peninsula of Michigan, until Jay's Treaty forced a move to St. Joseph's, a Canadian island near the north shore of Lake Huron.

Before the war Astor was laying the groundwork for his vast empire. He sold quantities of furs in Europe and bought most of his Indian trade goods there. Finding British competition intolerable, he and William McGillivray, a partner in other British fur companies, formed the South West Company. It was designed to avoid destructive competition, and its sphere of influence included all the fur-trading posts in the Great Lakes area. Astor was to receive half of the profits of the firm.[16]

The South West Fur Company was a hedge against war or the closing of the trade to one side or the other. If the British were driven off American soil, they could still expect to share the profits with an American partner. Trade goods might originate in either country, but since British imported goods were cheaper and of better quality, they were to be used whenever obtainable. So little did Astor expect war, however, that late in 1811 he offered a loan to help finance the army in Lower Canada. Seeking to maintain good standing with both governments, he also reported to his friend, Secretary of the Treasury Gallatin, on the size of the armed forces in Canada after each trip to Montreal.

When the United States forbade all trade with England in March 1811, the act was interpreted as preventing the movement of Indian trade goods from St. Joseph's to Michilimackinac. Since there were not enough goods at the latter post, the Indians were angry and Astor was upset by American policy, which seemed to him short-sighted. He first applied to President Madison for a waiver but was turned down. He received a more sympathetic hearing from Jefferson at Monticello. His second appeal to the administration took place in June 1812, when war fever was mounting, and he submitted his petition as a war measure to save the goods because of the furs they would purchase. He listed his goods at St. Joseph's as blankets, coarse woolens, guns, tomahawks, and powder, and he was willing to sell them to the government if required. This time Madison agreed, and Gallatin instructed the customs officials at Detroit and Michilimackinac to receive Astor's trade goods.

Meanwhile, Prevost had been in close touch with the fur traders in Montreal, who told him they were grateful for his interest in their protection. As early as January, they had worked out their procedures in case of war: change their route via Lake Erie to one from York (Toronto) over land to Lake Simcoe and Lake Huron; arm one of their vessels of sixty tons if the enemy appeared on Lake Huron; mobilize 300 voyageurs and as many Indians to act in concert with government forces, and make all their vessels available to the government if they were needed. They suggested that the weakly held Michilimackinac would be seized and "in short they are full of loyalty and zeal, and manifest a degree of public spirit highly honorable to them."[17]

The declaration of war a few weeks later prevented the transfer of the trade goods at St. Joseph's, but more seriously it presented Astor with the possible loss of his furs at Michilimackinac. He sent a representative to alert his agents at that station. En route the messenger spread word about the war, and the British in Upper Canada first learned of it from him, even before Hull at Detroit had been notified. By a swift action the British launched a campaign that easily captured Michilimackinac on July 17, 1812, before its defenders knew that hostilities had commenced. When the facts became known, Astor was accused of deliberately warning the British. Although they did first learn of the war at the Niagara frontier through him, Astor said he was merely trying to save his furs. Some of the advantages of an international fur company now began to appear. He obtained a letter from Gallatin to his friend, Peter Sailly, collector in northern New York, which instructed Sailly to give "every facility" to Astor and other Americans to bring their own furs and other property in Canada across the border.

One reason that Astor received a friendly reception in Washington throughout the war was his willingness to loan large sums to the government. In 1813 he joined Stephen Girard and David Parish in subscribing to a big block of $16,000,000 in government stocks. Astor took slightly more than $2,000,000; he had to sell some of it at a loss before the war ended, but the transaction as a whole was very profitable to him. In 1814, at about the time he was seeking permission to send a boat for more furs, he subscribed to an additional $225,000. He also traded in treasury notes and foreign exchange during the war. Although Astor did not care for the disruptions the war was causing in the fur trade, he was a self-announced supporter of the administration. In the fall of 1812, he was sure the reelection of Madison would bring a suspension of hostilities during the winter, and peace in the spring or summer. His optimism was based on the Russian czar's offer to mediate the British-American conflict and Madison's sending of envoys to Russia.[18]

Astor personally carried Gallatin's letter to Plattsburgh, which he reached on July 2. There he waited for friends in Montreal to get him a passport, which came four days later, and Astor left for Canada. Sailly wrote to Gallatin that he doubted the Canadian authorities would allow the furs to leave the country, but if they did there would be no problems at the border. All that Sailly asked of Astor and the other Boston and New York merchants who brought in large quantities of goods during the war was that they give advance notice of a shipment and surrender it to him at the border; he would then send it to a government storage in New York, where the owners could present their legal claims to it.

Astor chose his old friend Pliny Moore in Champlain to "lodge the information in time" with Sailly. For this service and for forwarding Astor's wartime letters to Canada, Moore received no payment, but periodically Astor sent him small gifts such as "Segars" for himself and books for the ladies of his family. On July 9, 1812, he asked Moore to notify Sailly and shortly afterward the first shipment of twenty-seven bales of furs reached French Mills. It included 2,693 skins, mostly wolf but including a few beaver. These were brought to Plattsburgh and were sent for storage to New York under the protection of Deputy Collector Benjamin Graves.

Astor returned to New York but his remaining furs in Canada preyed on his mind. In October, he sent his agent, Auguste l'Herbette, to Montreal to arrange for another shipment. On November 3, he asked Moore to give the usual notification to Sailly and to direct l'Herbette not to bring any of the furs to New York, but to leave them in Plattsburgh until further notice. Shortly a huge shipment arrived at Rouses Point and was seized, as usual, at customs. With a value estimated by Sailly at $50,000, it included 20,380 martens, 46 bear, 18,000 muskrat, 525 fishers, 6,021 otter, 3,389 mink, 2,048 fox, 271 cat, and 6 wolf skins. Despite Astor's orders, the shipment was sent to New York in the custody of Ezra Thurber, inspector at Rouses Point.[19]

In February, l'Herbette was again in Canada and the shipment this time consisted of 5,214 pounds dressed beaver coating which appeared to have been used, 4,517 mink, 32 beaver, 102 otter, 35 fishes, 60 lynx, 5 fox, 9 wolf, 6 deer, and 1,490 muskrat. These were sent to New York under Inspector William Hicks. In the fall, Astor sent his nephew, George Astor, to Montreal as his agent. Late in November, Moore gave Sailly the usual notice, and subsequently another large shipment arrived that consisted of 221 bales, 9 puncheons and 1 barrel of skins. These went to New York with Inspector Caleb Luther. All the furs were released to Astor when he gave bonds for their full value. The bonds were later remitted on application in court to the government. Astor began to be suspected of bringing in goods not his own, which was never proved, and Sailly was said to have taken a bribe. Astor explained the $500 for Sailly as a payment "in lew of any claim" Sailly might face if the furs were condemned.[20]

Even after all these large shipments, he still had furs at Michilimackinac, or so Astor said. In April 1814, he went to Washington for permission to send a vessel for them. Madison agreed and Secretary of State Monroe wrote the letter of approval on condition that Prevost would "protect your property, during the Voyage, from all British and Indian annoyance."[21] George Astor went to Montreal and, through the intercession of partners in the South West Fur Company, obtained Prevost's agreement. He chartered a vessel and in November managed to bring into Erie, Pennsylvania, a large consignment. Probably some if not all of them were legally British property. Captain Arthur Sinclair, the American commander on Lake Erie who had to allow the vessel to pass, made the case against Astor most emphatically:

> It is pointedly stated in Mr. Munroes letter to me, that the extent of the permission granted Mr. Astor, was to bring away such furs and other property as had been secured to him by capitulation at the time Mackinac fell into the enemies hands. Now, Sir, I have proof positive that all such property has long since been brought away; and prisoners I have captured state to me that a messenger arrived at Mackinac from Sir Geo Prevost who stated to the inhabitants that arrangements had been made to *cover all their property*.

Mr. Astor writes me very indefinitely on the subject. He says, 'if all is right there ought to be 2000 packs but I neither know the quantity or quality.' I am informed *that* quantity will completely cover *all* upon the island. . . . You may rest assured, Sir, that Mr. Astor is taking advantage of the indulgence granted him by the President, and that species of property ceded to him by capitulation, and which property also his permission from the government extends to, has been received by him long since.[22]

Astor was never officially called to account for this or any of his other transactions. This probably stemmed from the administration's satisfaction with the retrieval of all possible property from British-occupied Michilimackinac. It was a recognition of Astor's wide influence and the financial help he was able to give the American government. But it was also a testament to the determination and skill Astor displayed in removing all the wartime obstacles in Canada as well. Equipped with the favorable intercession of high-ranking officials in both countries, there was nothing for customs officers and naval commanders to do except to allow the furs to enter the United States.

Prisoners of War

A major source of bitterness during the War of 1812 was the care and exchange of prisoners of war. Gentlemanly practices during the first months of the war degenerated thereafter into harsh recriminations and the holding of hostages in retaliation for the enemy's treatment of his prisoners.

By 1812, the principle was well established that war was an action between states, not between individuals. Prisoners belonged to the state instead of the captor. The state was consequently charged with the responsibility for their food, housing, and clothing. Agreement on details was lacking, but civilized nations generally subscribed to legal and humane practices.[23]

Prisoners of war were at first the responsibility of a very few persons. The acting British chief in the United States was Anthony St. John Baker, the former secretary of the British legation whom Augustus Foster left behind when he departed. Baker carried on as agent for British prisoners with the help of former British consuls until the American government declared him *persona non grata* for smuggling correspondence out of the country and for licensing American shipowners to trade illegally with British ports. A hiatus of several months ensued during which the British had no official agent for prisoners, until the arrival in April 1813, of the former British consul, Thomas Barclay. In time the British had agents at all the main American detention points.

For the first nine months of the war the American secretary of state, James Monroe, added the custody of prisoners to his other duties. Responsible to him were the federal marshals who, in addition to watching enemy aliens, disposed of prisoners according to instructions. The collectors at the ports received and enumerated all prisoners of war before turning them over to the marshals. The first American agent on British soil was John Mitchell, whom Monroe sent to Halifax in October. Subsequently, agents were appointed for Jamaica, Barbados, Quebec, and London. The American government completed its permanent organization in March 1813, with the naming of John Mason to the new post of commissary general for prisoners of war. Beginning in the spring of 1813, much of the formal negotiating over prisoners took place between Mason in Washington and Barclay in New York.

An informal and generous policy of exchanges prevailed through 1812 and part of 1813. The early captures were frequently paroled immediately or held at advance posts while the commanders arranged exchanges. Most of the early American captures were made at sea, and many of the men were paroled pending exchange.

The first big British capture of the war was Hull's entire army of some two thousand men at Detroit. Partly to avoid the burden of feeding and policing so many, partly because of his contempt for them, Brock paroled the militia to their homes under oath not to fight again until exchanged. He sent the regulars, including General Hull, to Quebec. Prevost released Hull and the other officers on parole, for he discovered to his delight that the general was so bitter against his own government that "I feel confident," he wrote, "his presence in the United States will have the effect of adding strength to the party there in opposition to the war, & that it will also tend to embarrass the American Government."[24] Hull's return resulted in both a noisy court-martial and an interruption of prisoner exchanges because of the misunderstanding arising over the nature of his parole.

A number of man-made difficulties periodically brought negotiations, paroles and exchanges to a standstill and occasioned hard feelings on both sides. Early in the war the British attempted to discourage the damaging activities of American privateers by holding captured privateersmen while paroling other seamen. A serious misunderstanding also arose between the two sides over the parole of General Hull and other officers, including Lieutenant Colonel Winfield Scott. Under the accepted system of the day, parolees were under the obligation not to resume military activities until formally exchanged. Prevost rejected an American proposal to exchange these officers for American-held troops from a British ship, but through a breakdown of communications American officials believed the paroled officers were properly exchanged. Consequently, Prevost issued a strong protest over the resumption of military duty by some of the officers he considered merely paroled, and he was unresponsive to an American request for further exchanges in 1813. He threatened to punish the American violators if they were ever recaptured, but the punishment was never defined. The dispute occasioned heated exchanges until nearly the end of 1813, before the formal exchange of the officers was agreed upon.

The complexities of the interning, provisioning, and eventual exchanging of prisoners of war made errors likely and charges of mistreatment by both sides inevitable. A suspicion that the enemy was cheating on the prisoners' rations was a common complaint. Although the basic rations were itemized in the formal wartime agreements on prisoners, the British in 1814 reduced theirs to the level they had employed for many years previously. After futile protests the Americans followed suit. American officials were concerned about the sufficiency of British provisions for prisoners throughout the war. A thousand gallons of vinegar and 4,500 pounds of tobacco were sent to Halifax for American prisoners late in 1813. Reuben Beasley, the agent in England, supplemented the supplies for prisoners by a cent and a half a day for soap and tobacco. He worried that American discontent in jail would encourage the prisoners to join the British army.

The British registered a series of protests against American treatment of their prisoners. According to one, the captives of Stoney Creek were marched across New York to Greenbush on rations so small that some fell behind from weakness and were beaten. Upon arrival they were kept behind locked doors and "not permitted to go out to relieve the Calls of Nature, and if any attempted to make water at a window they were immediately fired at by the Sentinels."[25]

Prevost officially complained to London about American failure to keep agreements:

Those British prisoners who have lately returned from captivity and those who are still detained have upon a long and harassing march been deprived of common comforts & needful sustenance, have been wantonly exposed to unnecessary severities and hardships, and have upon the whole experienced an extreme of refined inhumanity disgraceful to the enemy by whom it has been inflicted, and in consequences frequently fatal to the unhappy sufferers.[26]

Nine officers of the New York militia publicized their treatment as prisoners of the British by asserting that on a long march they were given only dry bread and were "subjected to insult, contumely and threats. . . . Thro' excessive fatigue and want of nourishment, many of our soldiers, whose strength was almost entirely exhausted, would sink upon the ground. They were inhumanly pricked up with the bayonet, and compelled to keep pace with the rest."[27]

Such complaints can be multiplied on both sides and are inconclusive except to indicate the bitterness engendered by the problem of prisoners of war. Their occasional inhumane treatment was probably inevitable considering the numbers involved and the great distances that had to be covered in their transfers.

Americans protested against Prevost's sending large numbers of prisoners to Halifax, and eventually to England. These movements took place during the long interruptions in the exchange program, during which facilities at Quebec became overcrowded. They also resulted from Prevost's anticipation of a worsening of the hostage problem, which is explained below, and his determination to have a plentiful supply of prisoners set aside for use as hostages if needed. Americans questioned why any prisoners should be taken to England, where exchange was so difficult, yet Beasley reported 3,368 there in March 1814.[28] Some of these were captured on the seas, but others were sent from Canada. At least another thousand were subsequently sent from North America before the end of the war.

The British were sure that American military and prison officials tried to persuade British prisoners to remain in the United States. Mason officially denied the charge on the logical grounds that he would be losing possible exchanges. Yet approximately 300 British prisoners made good their escape, usually on long marches and at an increasing tempo as the date for paroles or exchanges approached.[29] At the end of the war there was much unrest among the British prisoners, and a reluctance to be sent back to Canada from Pittsfield and Salem, where some escapes were successfully made. British agents promised their nationals pay, discharge, and land grants to persuade them to return quietly.

But the rawest nerve of the prisoner problem was struck by the British practice of holding some of their American captives as British subjects. This started in July 1812, when six Americans captured on the *Nautilus* were sent to England for trial. Captain John Rogers immediately seized twelve from a cartel ship and jailed them in Boston as hostages. The British examined their captives in England and released five of them as clearly Americans, and they arrived in Boston almost a year after their capture. The sixth was held pending further examinations, so only ten of the twelve hostages were released from confinement.

The virus of nationality soon spread widely. In the fall, when the American captives from Queenston were being put on a ship at Quebec for exchange at Boston, British officers removed twenty-three prisoners who by their Celtic accents were considered Irish. At Prevost's direction they were sent to England for trial. He acted consistently with his government's official position that British-born subjects could not become alienated, and for that principle the British had been willing to risk war in the first place. Yet in England they proved an embarrassment. They were examined closely but insufficient evidence was available to prove their nationality. Lord Bathurst, the colonial secretary, ruefully faced the British dilemma of being accused on the one hand of a lack of courage to prosecute and execute them, on the other of their unwarranted imprisonment. Late in the war the prisoners were returned to Canada with Bathurst's instruction not to imprison any others without evidence, but if it was available they were to be put on trial and executed without delay.

Meanwhile, the twenty-three had become a *cause célèbre* in the United States. When he was paroled (the Americans believed exchanged) in January 1813, Scott hastened to Washington and encouraged the administration to adopt a policy of reprisals. Under orders Dearborn set aside twenty-three British hostages in the spring and warned Prevost that they would receive the same treatment accorded the Irish-Americans. This was a blunt warning against a death sentence. The British government picked up the challenge by ordering Prevost to confine forty-six Americans as hostages for the twenty-three British, and directed that if the Americans killed any of their hostages in retaliation for future British death sentences, a double number of American hostages should be killed. The armies and fleets were to "prosecute the War with unmitigated severity against all Cities, Towns, and Villages, belonging to the United States, & against the inhabitants thereof."[30] One of the forty-six designated by Prevost was Lieutenant Sidney Smith of Plattsburgh, who was captured in June at Isle-aux-Noix with his ships the *Growler* and *Eagle*.

Unwilling to withdraw from this pointless rivalry, the War Department ordered Wilkinson to confine forty-six British prisoners and to execute as many as the British did among their forty-six hostages. Prevost's response was close confinement of a further forty-six hostages, which the Americans incorrectly heard were ninety-two. The Americans then incarcerated practically all the British officers they held as prisoners (the commissary general recorded seventy-seven), and suspended all paroles. The state of Massachusetts denied the use of its jails for further confinement, and hostages had to be transported to federal installations during the winter of 1813–14, some as far as Philadelphia. In December, Barclay warned Prevost that if the system was pursued, every British prisoner in the States would be closely confined, and he reported that 253 were already held in retaliation for a variety of British measures.[31]

Three other chain reactions developed from local situations. At its best, the holding of hostages by the Americans perhaps induced the British to be cautious in their treatment of captured Americans; no executions among hostages occurred on either side. Otherwise, this British principle of "once an Englishman, always an Englishman," which had been one of the causes of the war, continued to poison the atmosphere for the rest of the war. The conclusion of Anthony Dietz in his valuable study of the prisoners of war is that the practise of retaliation allowed "the fate of a few to determine the fate of many" by halting exchanges; that it did not achieve its goal of securing the release of the original captives, and that only generous gestures by one side brought responses in kind.[32]

In spite of the barriers to mutual trust and the systematic exchange of prisoners, and far more important than all the things that went wrong, were the formal agreements that provided for the exchange of large numbers from both sides. They were four in number and started with the appointment of John Mitchell as agent at Halifax. After first agreeing to some limited and informal exchanges of soldiers and seamen, he assumed the responsibility for making a formal arrangement with Richard Uniacke, the advocate general of Nova Scotia, and Naval Lieutenant William Miller, British agent for prisoners at the port. Since Admiral Warren, who promoted the negotiations, believed he lacked authority over land prisoners, the agreement covered only seamen. Signed on November 28, 1812, its thirteen parts specified the exchange ports, the use of cartel ships by both sides, and such matters as subsistence and paroles.

The American government never ratified the agreement, although exchanges were made under its terms. The Americans preferred to await the arrival of the new British agent, Thomas Barclay, who reached Washington early in April 1813. He and John Mason quickly agreed to some informal exchanges, and then proceeded to negotiate an all-inclusive convention. Concluded on May 12, its fifteen articles covered both soldiers and seamen and was much more explicit than the Halifax agreement on matters such as exchanging rank for rank, with a schedule of equivalents, i.e., a major general for a major general or for thirty men. The American government ratified it two days later, but the British government withheld approval pending certain amendments, which were never made. However, Barclay considered it in force, and he and Mason negotiated a few exchanges during the next several months.

As retaliation became the order of the day, the Barclay-Mason negotiations began to falter. The two men met at Georgetown in October to try to put new life into the exchange program. They reached agreement with difficulty, and it bore very little fruit. The winter of 1813–14 brought an almost

Elias Dewey's Tavern near the Canadian Border in Champlain was the site of a conference on an armistice and for the writing of two treaties for the exchange of prisoners of war.

complete cessation of exchanges while hostages and retaliation held sway.

Prevost seems to have taken the lead in trying to restore normal intercourse. In January 1814, he paroled the hostage, Brigadier General John Winder, to go to Washington with proposals for a convention on prisoners of war. The mission almost immediately produced a relaxation in the treatment of officers by both sides, and the resumption of paroles. Winder was sent back with authority to negotiate a general exchange, but the original twenty-three hostages must be included. But Winder agreed with Adjutant General Baynes at Champlain to exclude the original twenty-three and the first round of retaliatory hostages. The negotiations took place at Dewey's Tavern one mile south of the border on the road to Odelltown (Route 276) at its intersection with the direct route between Champlain and Rouses Point (now called the Bostick Hill Road). During the War of 1812, the Deweys found themselves in a kind of no-man's-land between the two armies. During one particularly tense period, the family was packed and ready to flee; a young British lieutenant, suspecting them of harboring a spy, ran his sword through several boxes and barrels. Still in existence is a mirror which, wrapped in a feather bed, received a broken corner from his probings. On another occasion,

Dewey was host to General Wade Hampton after his retreat from Odelltown. Whether happy or not about being selected, Dewey became the host for the prisoner-of-war conference in April, another in July and a meeting to conclude an armistice in between.[33]

The convention, on April 15, was to become effective on May 15, and Winder took it to Washington for approval. There it was rejected unless amended on several points, including the thorny hostage issue. Winder was sent back to get the changes, only to learn that Prevost was already carrying it out by releasing several hundred prisoners, and that the Americans had released 300 of their captives. The administration was nevertheless determined to obtain changes in the agreement, and this time Tobias Lear, late consul at Algiers and now an accountant in the War Department, was the American emissary. He and Baynes signed another convention at Dewey's Tavern on July 16, which covered all the original hostages except the first twenty-three held by the British.[34] The Americans could accept these terms more readily upon learning that the twenty-three were now held in ordinary confinement, although they were not repatriated until after the war. Under the convention large-scale exchanges were arranged during the summer and fall of 1814.

Toward the end of the year mutual recriminations once again slowed down the orderly flow of prisoners. Some of the hostage situations were not yet untangled, the Americans resented the fact that nearly a thousand American prionsers had been sent to England since late summer, while the British resented the delay in the repatriation of prisoners from some areas. Probably only the end of the war headed off another sterile deadlock in negotiations. During the spring of 1815, American prisoners were returned from Halifax and England as fast as shipping became available, and British from centers like Pittsfield as arrangements for the overland trip could be made.

The formal exchanges of prisoners were thus a consequence of four conventions, three of which were never ratified by one side or the other and two of which were negotiated in Champlain, New York. The exchanges that nevertheless took place resulted from the liberal interpretations of the agreements by agents and commanders on the spot and from the pressures upon facilities and budgets occasioned by the mounting number of prisoners. That the numbers were substantial is evidenced by the American list of 15,500 prisoners by name, a figure probably much too low in view of the prisoners that were never recorded. Mason estimated that sixty-five hundred British were taken at sea alone, although he could account for only twenty-one hundred of whom about a thousand were paroled at sea.[35]

6

THE TRAGIC FIRST WINTER

The fall of 1812, which held out prospects of great American achievements, ended in the lingering whimpers of two tragicomic campaigns on widely separated fronts. They were whimpers only by contrast with the big bang of Hull's surrender of his whole army in August.

During the summer, Dearborn, pressed by the War Department to make a diversion at Niagara in Hull's behalf, was far too late to be of help. Even after Hull's surrender he was expected to make a major effort at Niagara and something smaller north of Plattsburgh. Niagara came first.

The New York militia assembled at Lewiston under their own commander, Major General Stephen Van Rensselaer. Although he had no military experience, Governor Tompkins in appointing him sought to bring Federalist sentiment behind the war, and to capitalize upon the prestige of a political opponent. Dearborn instructed him to make a safe retreat if he were sharply attacked. Most of the regulars concentrated at Buffalo under the inspector general, Brigadier General Alexander Smyth. An arrogant man, Smyth failed to report to his superior at Lewiston and refused repeatedly to attend his councils of officers. Consequently, Van Rensselaer, under pressure from all sides for action, planned and executed an invasion of Canada without any help from Smyth and his 1,650 regulars. The stage was now set for a series of farces on the Niagara front.

On October 13, 1812, an American force crossed the Niagara River and seized the heights above the village of Queenston. Van Rensselaer managed to get about eleven hundred of his six thousand-man army across during the day. At an early stage of the battle the British suffered an incalculable loss with the death of their ablest general, Isaac Brock. However, British reinforcements arrived, and during the afternoon the tide of battle changed. Van

Rensselaer tried to get more men across the river, but the militia from New York and Pennsylvania took refuge in the theory that they were not required to serve outside the country. Consequently, Van Rensselaer stood helplessly by while a force of 900 Americans surrendered in full view across the river. The general asked to resign and Dearborn, full of "mortification" over the defeat, granted him permission The elimination of unfit generals had now started in the East.

The uncooperative Smyth was appointed to command the front, and he boasted that at last the forces were in capable hands. Dearborn urged him to develop harmony between regulars and militia, until then seriously lacking. But Smyth, who was nicknamed "Van Bladder" by his troops, had other ideas. He arranged a short armistice with British Brigadier General Roger Sheaffe, which eventually lasted from October 18 to November 19. Meanwhile he indulged his fondness for bombastic proclamations by an address to his troops which bordered on the burlesque and drew a sharp rebuke from Washington.

Choosing first to denounce the "miscarriages" of Hull and Van Rensselaer, he charged that "The commanders were popular men, 'destitute alike of theory and experience' in the art of war." From any general such an address would have seemed peculiar; from Smyth it was ridiculous because of his own lack of the qualities of leadership.[1] Smyth abandoned Fort Niagara, which did not fall to the British only because Sheaffe failed to seize his advantage. The day after the termination of the armistice Smyth sent a pointless demand for the surrender of Fort Erie, to "spare the effusion of blood." At the end of November, he launched an invasion of Canada which he then called off while several thousand of his troops were in boats ready to join their comrades across the river. His troops almost mutinied, and he was forced to change his quarters frequently because of the propensity of his men to shoot through his tent. Dearborn hastened to grant him permission to visit his family. Madison quietly dropped him from the rolls of the army, and quiet descended upon the Niagara front.

Two-thirds of the grand, three-pronged plan to invade Canada and end the war in 1812 had failed. No territory had been gained at Niagara, and an entire army had been lost at Detroit. Only one campaign remained, and Dearborn pushed preparations as fast as he could, simultaneously with the demands of the Niagara front. Beginning in September, regular army units began to arrive in Burlington and Plattsburgh, with the latter place planned as the staging area. That this effort was not to be trivial is evidenced by the fact that ultimately far more regular troops were assigned to it than Smyth had at Niagara. Yet the skeptics pointed out that Prevost was well prepared, the American numbers too few, and the season too advanced: "All this looks well on paper, I tell them; but I fear their theory will fail when they attempt to reduce it to practice."[2]

Meanwhile, the legislatures of New York and Vermont convened. Both states still had loyal Republican governors. Governor Tompkins asked his legislature for hearty concurrence in the necessity of "yielding our exertions to support the national will, constitutionally expressed, and to preserve the rights, honor and character of the American nation unimpaired."[3] Unfortunately, his party had already lost control of the Assembly, and many of his proposals got tied up in interchamber rivalry.

Governor Galusha told his Vermont legislature in October that it had become the duty of the states and of every individual "to espouse the sacred cause of our injured country."[4] The Republican legislature pledged its support to the national government by a vote of 128 to 79, established heavy penalties for traffic with Canada, freed the militia from suits during service plus thirty days, and assessed a special property tax to defray the expenses of the war.

In the midst of military setbacks and sectional tensions, national elections took place in November. Madison was the early nominee of the war faction of the Republican party. A vote for him was a reasonably clear vote for continuing the war. DeWitt Clinton of New York was willing to challenge the Virginia dynasty, which New Yorkers were sure had prevented his uncle, Vice President George Clinton, from becoming president. He actively sought war votes because he favored a more vigorous prosecution of the war. His candidacy also attracted the support of peace Republicans who disliked Madison's war-making without proper preparation, and of the nation's Federalists who had his word that he would bring about peace. His candidacy promised all things to all men.

Madison won by an electoral count of 128 to 89; a shift of twenty votes would have reversed the result. He lost part or all of every state north of the Potomac except Vermont and Pennsylvania, and was saved only by the war enthusiasm of the south and west. Federalists and peace Republicans triumphed throughout the north and Federalist strength in Congress doubled. Sectionalism, an empty treasury, and woeful unpreparedness continued to produce intense dissatisfaction. Bitter opposition to Madison and the war continued throughout its duration. It led, for example, to the oft-repeated charge that a southern administration did not desire to expand the North by annexing Canada, and that it deliberately sent incompetent or southern generals to the northern fronts, confident that they would win no unwanted victory.

Typical of Federalist attitudes toward the war were the opinions of two new Federalist congressmen from northern New York, swept into office in the election of 1812. Elisha J. Winter, who represented the northeastern counties, gleefully described the administration's quandary over proposed new taxes—if passed, risking a loss of power and if not, having to stop the war: "Poor Madison & Co. you are caught completely between Hawk & Buzzard, I envy not your happiness." He also dismissed the Russian efforts to mediate the war as "nothing more, nor less, than a trick of the administration played off to answer Party purposes." Pliny Moore agreed: "I feel no commiseration for the Hawk & Buzzard situation—let them sweat. If retention of power was the great object of the war we may expect they will continue it as long as it will favor that object. I am for one firmly of opinion that an honorable adjustment of differences might have been made before the declaration or an honorable peace now if our Administration were so disposed."

Zebulon R. Shepherd, who came from the district just south of Winters', was even more outspoken. He commented upon the likelihood that a proposed government loan would fail:

> I am not sorry on abstract ground indeed I am pleased that their resources are drying up, but these are considerations of a serious and alarming nature. . . . What then is to be our fate? I see but little help of a regenerating Spirit to save us and that only can do it. . . . My mind some how since I have been here has been deeply impressed with the depravity of the men who rule us and the certain fatal consequences of their Administration. National sins are always punished with national judgments.[5]

Despite political distractions, preparations for action on the northern front continued. The movement of troops into Canada was postponed because of the late arrival of some units during October, a month of bad weather, and the onset of General Bloomfield's illness. When Dearborn arrived in Plattsburgh on November 10, he found things in a state of unreadiness, with troops still arriving from Vermont. The regulars and some of the militia were being brought from Burlington in the army's transport sloops and bateaux, guarded by Macdonough's fleet. The militia, some of whom went across the islands to Rouses Point and joined the rest of the army there, were led by Lieutenant Colonel Edward Fifield of the Second Regiment. An officer at "Camp Plattsburgh" wrote on the 12th that "This is perhaps the last time you will hear from me at this place, if ever. . . . We march without baggage or tents, and everything we carry will be on our backs, and the Heavens and a blanket our only covering."[6]

The massed force at Plattsburgh finally started for the border on November 16, except for a small detachment left in Burlington and about 700 sick

The Pliny Moore Home in Champlain, an exact reproduction of the original that burned in 1912. Numerous British and American generals visited or stayed with Mr. Moore. A notorious partisan officer from each side died here.

and their attendants remaining at Plattsburgh. Dearborn and his suite descended upon Pliny Moore for quarters on the 18th, upon which Moore later commented: "My house was like a large hotell—all the principal officers of the Army were in it."[7] The force at the border numbered about five thousand men—three thousand regulars and two thousand militia. Between them and Montreal were about three thousand men, not more than a third being within fighting distance of the border.

On November 19 at Champlain, Dearborn formally assumed the command that he had been exercising for the past week. In the orders he declared his belief in the troops: "Their bravery and patriotism will supply any deficiency in military discipline and tactics, which time and experience will render perfect;" however, he forbade "every species of plunder or abuse of the inhabitants" in the United States or Canada.[8] More ominously, on the same day some of the militia officers told him that their men would not cross the border.

Nevertheless, at daybreak of November 20, a detachment under Colonel

Pike forded the Lacolle River and surrounded a guardhouse containing Canadian militia and a few Indians. The Americans succeeded in setting the roof on fire. The fifty men inside managed to dash out between rounds of firing and escape unhurt. Meanwhile, a second American detachment had crossed the river and, coming from the woods, fired on Pike's men in error in an exchange that lasted for thirty minutes. Both groups retreated across the river so precipitately that they left two dead, thirteen wounded, and five missing, most of the casualties resulting from their own fire.

Dearborn now had to consider his options. His men were at the border in strength sufficient to seize a portion of Lower Canada. Between half and two-thirds of his militia were apparently prepared to cooperate. Yet he had brought the whole army north without tents or other kinds of shelter and his provisions were running low, although not his ammunition. Furthermore, the season had advanced to the period when armies normally went into winter quarters. Dearborn had once told the secretary of war that Montreal could be taken with little risk. But the combination of bad weather and late season, his undersupplied troops, and the behavior of his militia made him change his mind. He later based his switch on the refusal of the militia; on another occasion he said that he entered Canada only to relieve the pressure on the army at Niagara. Eutis wrote him: "Fortunately for you, the want of success which has attended the campaign will be attributed to the Secretary at War. So long as you enjoy the confidence of the Government, the clamours of the discontented should not be regarded."[9]

The army pulled back to Champlain on November 22, and next day they marched south for Plattsburgh, leaving stored in Champlain 134 barrels of flour and 58 barrels of bread. In Plattsburgh most of the militia were disbanded, and the light artillery except one company were sent to Greenbush, closely followed by Dearborn. Of the regulars, the Ninth, Eleventh, Twenty-first, and Twenty-fifth Regiments went to Burlington under General John Chandler, while the Sixth, Fifteenth, and Sixteenth Regiments and one company of artillery remained at Plattsburgh, commanded by Colonel Pike. Militia units remained for all or part of the winter at posts from Champlain to French Mills.

Lieutenant Macdonough also went into winter quarters, in Shelburne Bay, with his little fleet. His was the only branch of the service that was able to make use of the winter to improve its fighting capabilities. In December, however, he travelled to Connecticut to marry Lucy Ann Shaler at Middletown, and returned with his bride to his Burlington headquarters. In February, he obtained fifteen ship's carpenters from New York, and in March guns and supplies were sent to Whitehall to be forwarded when the ice went out of the lake. The *Hunter* and the *Bull Dog* had their quarterdecks removed to make room for more guns, and their names were changed to *Growler* and *Eagle*. Room was made for twelve guns on the *President*, while eleven were installed on both the *Growler* and *Eagle*. With a gun on each of the two gunboats, the fleet now had a firepower of thirty-six guns. Macdonough had clear control of the lake when he sailed in the spring. He personally commanded the *President*; the *Growler* was under Lieutenant Smith, and Sailing Master Jairus Loomis sailed the *Eagle*.[10]

The army settled in at Plattsburgh and Burlington for a miserable winter. After ten days of marching and bivouacking in cold, wet weather without tents, the men needed warmth and dry quarters. They found them at neither place, although the sixteen hundred men of Burlington had a slight advantage. At least some solid barracks had been started in the area back of the bluff, but they were unheated and the plaster was still wet; yet they offered a kind of shelter that was better than the men had had for a long time.

At Plattsburgh General Bloomfield had failed to prepare winter quarters for his large force. Only after his departure were log barracks started, on November 28, 1812. Colonel Pike was left in command of about two thousand men at the post on the Saranac River, variously called Camp Plattsburgh, Camp Saranack, Cantonment Serenac, and afterward, Pike's Cantonment. Until the completion of the huts at Christmas, the men slept on the frozen ground, exposed to snow and sleet and protected only by their tents, and a thin blanket and the newly cut branches of pine trees. During December, about one hundred men died in Pike's command alone, Pike himself being sick for a considerable period, and the rate of sickness and death remained high all winter. Tradition attributes the casualties either to a severe epidemic or to the poisoning of the whiskey ration by a British spy. But exposure and neglect seem to be a more rational explanation, which Dr. William Beaumont partially substantiates with his report of having treated "a great variety of diseases."[11]

Supplies and equipment were provided by a system of private contractors, whose first interest was profit. Aside from insufficient quantities of nearly everything, their quality gave rise to a stream of complaints, especially at the bases on Lake Champlain. Pike at Plattsburgh wrote the secretary of war several times to protest against the poor quality of the supplies from Tench Coxe. When he received no answer, he folded one of the issued blankets into a large envelope and sent it to the War Department. There is no record that he received any satisfaction. The blanket, one to a man and only four by three feet, was the sole covering issued to the men during a northern winter. A similar complaint was registered by General Chandler in Burlington in March 1813. He described his blankets as four feet nine inches long and four feet wide and weighing only one and three quarters pounds. He also complained about the rations. Under such neglect, desertions were frequent and, as at Plattsburgh, morale and discipline vanished until Pike had recovered from his own illness, reorganized his men, and won their respect. The inspector general was led to instruct him: "If an officer shall mutiny, and it cannot otherwise be suppressed, the superior officer may kill or maim him while he resists. If a soldier shall mutiny, any officer or non-commissioned officer present shall seize the first musket he can lay hold of and break it over the offender's head."[12]

There were other distresses for all commanders during the winter. For example, Private Benjamin Mason of the detached militia at Chateaugay was sent to Plattsburgh in December to purchase medicine, but he deserted and a ten-dollar reward for his jailing or return to any military post failed to get any response. Far more serious because it was done on such a large scale was the smuggling of goods into and out of Canada. Military commanders were under orders to stem the flow but the practice was too extensive for the size of the force that could be committed. In Vermont smuggling was combatted by a picket guard that was kept near the border. One of its seizures was three sleighloads of wire, worth about $5,000, headed for Canada. The wire was packed in large tin cannisters, two-thirds the size of a barrel and brazed to make it tight; each cannister was set in a barrel and packed solidly in salt for concealment. More subversive was the discovery in Vermont of a quantity of undissolved verdigris, a poisonous drug, in a cask of spirits for the soldier's rations. Mr. Niles' *Weekly Register* appropriately commented that "The enemies *within* are far more dangerous than the enemies without."[13]

Close to the border in Plattsburgh, Pike felt particularly challenged by the activities of the smugglers. In January, he issued a new set of orders forbidding any travel to or from Canada without a pass from him or Chandler in Burlington because, he said, "Some members of the community have been found so void of all sense of honor—love of country, or any other principle which has governed the *virtuous* of all nations and ages, as to hold correspondence with, and give intelligence to our enemies." He then quoted the pertinent Article of War:

> Art. 56: Whosoever shall relieve the enemy with money, victuals or ammunition, or shall knowingly harbor or protect an enemy, shall suffer DEATH, or such other punishment as shall be ordered by the sentence of a Court Martial.
>
> Art. 57: Whosoever shall be convicted of holding correspondence with, or giving intelligence to the enemy, either directly or indirectly, shall suffer DEATH, or such other punishment, as shall be ordered by the sentence of a Court Martial.[14]

Even after his public denunciations he reported there was such a "thirst for gain" among the citizenry that after catching a smuggler with tobacco or leather heading into Canada, "I can find no court who will take cognizance of the transaction or person concerned." Shortly later Alexander Richards, collector of the Oswegatchie district in the Ogdensburg area, wrote to the secretary of war: "The smugglers are growing daily so bold it will be impossible to execute the laws without the aid of the military."[15] Pike found that he could not do it even with the military.

Worse than all the other troubles of this northern winter was the serious illness and high death rate among the troops. Diseases resulting from exposure had appeared among the militia at Champlain as early as September. Out of the small force stationed there after the campaign, Pliny Moore recorded on December 5 that twenty-seven soldiers had been buried to date, and his later notations showed that deaths continued all month.[16] In Plattsburgh the death rate was about 10 percent, or 200 men. They were buried in unmarked graves, presumably near the cantonment, which has led many people to search for the site of the camp. So far the search has been inconclusive and is complicated by the ravages of the river on which it was located before the flow was brought under control. If the site is ever discovered, it would qualify as a military cemetery.

In Burlington the rate was even higher—about 12.5 percent through February, by which time the deaths had almost ceased. On both sides of the lake December was the most deadly month, partly because of the accumulation of ailments from the exposures of the campaign and partly because of the severity of the weather. Dr. James Mann was troubled by the exaggerations about Burlington that appeared in public print, and he went to great pains to refute them, believing that they were made by enemies of the war in order to discourage recruitment. For example, in his book he disproved the statements that there were up to 2,800 soldiers in Burlington, and that between 700 and 800 died in four months. He also pointed out that whereas only three soldiers died in February, seventy-three died in the little town, meaning that the ailments were not confined to servicemen.[17]

Dr. Beaumont joined the service in September and found considerable illness already existing in Plattsburgh. The diseases seemed to be measles, intermittent fevers, typhus, dysentery, and rheumatism. He considered opium appropriate for all of them, with sometimes ipecac, calomel, and preparations of certain barks. As the season progressed, the men's ailments "made the very woods ring with coughing and groaning." On December 8, he described men lying in their tents, with small fires in front. The diseases were developing into pleurisy, "peripneumony," and complicated dysentery for which he believed that bleeding, opium, and ipecac worked. By that time two to five men were dying daily.[18]

When the death rate seemed to subside in January and part of February, Beaumont suspended his service to the army and started a private practice in Plattsburgh, "but," he wrote, "from sentiments of patriotism and the prospects of a Battle, I was induced to relinquish the idea and return again to the service of my country — hoping to be more useful to mankind in this than in any other situation, or in private practice."[19]

Dr. Mann studied systematically the whole range and duration of the diseases on the northern front. He was on Dearborn's staff at Greenbush, but he also served as an inspector of all the hospitals in the military district. His work included the temporary assumption of personal command of units that needed particular attention, such as reorganizing their procedures, putting an end to unsanitary practices or filling in during the emergencies following a campaign. Under one or the other of these conditions, he served for a time at Burlington, Plattsburgh, and Malone in 1813 and 1814.

On only one point do Mann's findings need to be questioned, and that is his insistence that the illnesses constituted an epidemic among military personnel. He undermined his own argument by attributing much of the disease to exposure or to alcohol. Otherwise, his comments are well worth reading, and his book is the best on the subject. Of course, allowance must be made for the relative primitiveness of all medical science in his day.

Mann found that the most prevalent ailments during the months of July through September were fevers, dysentery, and diarrhea. The men with dysentery ran a fever; one bleeding of sixteen *ounces* was the usual treatment, followed by a full cathartic of calomel and jalap. Sometimes small doses of calomel and opium every four to six hours were beneficial. Diarrhea was also best treated by cathartics. During October and November, with the change to cold, damp weather, measles constituted one-third of all the illness and, although not fatal, left the recovered patients more susceptible to pneumonia. Rheumatism also appeared, combined with diarrhea. Men over forty years of age were particularly susceptible; treatment often required the lancet, but the ailment usually yielded to calomel, opium, blisters, and warm lodgings. Mann was very critical of the "bad of policy of government" in thinking that an efficient army on a war establishment could be raised by "the small encouragement offered the soldiers." As a result, many were too old or infirm, and sick from the start. Healthy young men could get better paying jobs in safe civilian life.

During the late fall through December, a variety of pneumonias accompanied by diarrhea made their appearance; the latter was checked by opium. The pneumonias were at first not recognizable until dissections of the victims showed the "morbid states of the viscera," which led to more successful treatment. He described the characteristics of the disease in this way:

> It assumed forms highly inflammatory, accompanied not only with strong arterial action, but high degrees of *stenic diathesis,* in which the lungs were so engorged with blood, that the heart and arteries almost ceased to act, inducing at the extremities and on the surface of the body, torpidity and coldness; symptoms, bearing the semblance of a typhoid state of disease.[20]

Mann records that death often came quickly, in one to four days, apparently from suffocation. The treatment included bleeding of four to six ounces at short intervals to relieve the engorged vessels. The patient was fed brandy, wine, and soups. In extreme cases he might need a bloodletting of sixteen to thirty-two *ounces.* During convalescence, jaundice was likely to set in. If that happened, the patient was given ipecacuanha. Mann found that the large consumers of alcohol were sure to suffer the most, because the disease was made more severe by what he called "alcohol excitement." "My opinion," he wrote, "long has been, that ardent spirits are an unnecessary part of a ration." He was especially bitter about the civilians who were allowed to sell liquor to soldiers: "Sutlers unrestrained, as they frequently are, destroy more lives by these liquors, than are lost by other causes to which soldiers are exposed; and, so long as ardent spirits are permitted to be publicly sold in the vicinity of a cantonment, these evils cannot be remedied by any restrictions, under which sutlers may be placed."[21]

Mann tried in another way to explain the severity of the ailments on the northern front, which he thought approximated frontier conditions. On newly settled lands, according to him, the putrefaction of vegetable substances gives off "deleterious gases." In forested areas, the heavy fogs of lakes and rivers are slow to leave during the day. Long exposures in bad weather, alcohol, and uncleanliness contributed to the diseases of cold weather on the frontier: intermittent fevers, diarrhea, dysentery, jaundice, and rheumatism.[22]

In the midst of all this turmoil, the spring elections were held. Clinton and Essex counties were represented in Congress by a Federalist, Elisha Winter, as a result of the election of 1812. In April 1813, Federalist majorities were registered in many local elections, although statewide Governor Tompkins won reelection.

In Vermont the Republican legislature in 1812 had provided that any Vermont soldier could vote wherever he was stationed. United States troops under Major John McNeil of New Hampshire were released from Plattsburgh in time to vote in the late spring elections, and many of them did so at Colchester, the nearest polling place. The entire Colchester vote was rejected by the canvassing committee and a challenge to its action was carried to the October meeting of the legislature. The lawmakers heard conflicting testimony about the pressure applied by McNeil to vote Republican and about voting by non-Vermonters. Therefore the assembly, which the Federalists controlled as a result of the election, also discarded the Colchester vote, denying three Republicans their seats on the council. This was crucial because the election had failed to furnish a majority to any of the three candidates for governor; the legislature in October was called upon to make the choice. A Republican council and a Federalist assembly, in joint session, elected Federalist Martin Chittenden by 112 votes to 111 for Galusha. Chittenden was the son of the popular first governor of the state. During Martin's ten years in Congress, he had voted against both the embargo and the declaration of war. His inauguration was bound to have a profound impact on Vermont's attitude toward the war.

There were, however, signs of hopeful initiatives at the national level. In March 1813, the president signed an act of Congress which would, *upon termination of the war,* prohibit the use of foreigners on all American vessels. It was a real effort to make impressment no longer necessary, but the British preferred a solution of their own to the vital problem of manning their fleet.

In the same month the administration accepted the Russian czar's offer of mediation. Exploratory talks had taken place in Russia before the end of 1812. The Russians were dismayed with an American war which threatened to overwhelm their British ally, and they hoped to find a way of ending it. On the other hand, Madison had gambled on Napoleon's victory over Russia to bring Great Britain to terms. News of the great French reversal reached Washington at the same time as the offer of mediation, and Madison seized upon it. This was the action that Congressman Winter denounced as an administration trick. Nevertheless, Madison named as commissioners the resident minister at St. Petersburg, John Quincy Adams, the secretary of the treasury, Albert Gallatin, and James A. Bayard, a patriotic Federalist from Delaware. The latter two left the country in the spring, wafted by high American hopes of ending the war, but also carrying unrealistic instructions. These provided that as a precondition of peace the British formally renounce impressment; the Americans were then to work for definitions of neutral rights, a discontinuance of British fur trading on American soil and their free navigation of the Mississippi, and a mutual restoration of all conquests.

There were also signs that the administration was overhauling its military command for a more efficient prosecution of the war. Eustis was finally prevailed upon to resign from the War Department in December. James Monroe, although remaining secretary of state, was appointed temporary secretary of war with the prospect of soon becoming commander in chief of the army, a position to which he openly aspired. But a storm of protest arose, based upon both personal and sectional jealousies. Federalists had a field day, while northern Republicans made an issue of favoritism toward another Virginian. Governor Tompkins, the Republican governor who loyally supported the war, did not like the "Virginia dynasty" any more than other New Yorkers and was convinced that the party in his state could best be helped by more recognition from Washington. Consequently, Madison gave up his original plans for Monroe and in January 1813, named a New Yorker, Brigadier General John Armstrong, to the War Department.

Armstrong had served as a major during the Revolution, part of the time as aide-de-camp to General Horatio Gates. He subsequently held political office in Pennsylvania. After he moved to New York, he served briefly as United States senator. He was minister to France between 1804 and 1810, the difficult years of Napoleon's Decrees. He received and transmitted to Washington, perhaps over-enthusiastically, the famous Cadore Letter which contained Napoleon's informal promise to repeal the Decrees if the United States would hold Great Britain to account. He was later recalled at Napoleon's request. At the outbreak of war Tompkins found him available for military service if it were an independent command, and recommended him to the administration.

Armstrong was made a brigadier general and assigned to the defense of New York City, succeeding Bloomfield who was ordered to Plattsburgh. No friend of Virginians, he accepted the appointment to the War Department not out of a sense of loyalty to the administration, which he freely criticized, but in order to rescue the nation from what he considered Virginian incompetence. Originally a Federalist, he became a Clintonian after his marriage to the sister of Chancellor Robert R. Livingston. He was a skilful politician with presidential ambitions and his appointment to the cabinet was one reason why Albert Gallatin, secretary of the treasury and the ablest man in office, decided to resign after twelve years at the post. He had already clashed too often with Armstrong to be able to expect any cooperation.

In a day when the secretary of war still performed all the functions that were later assigned to a commanding general and a chief of staff, Armstrong was the strongest secretary the nation had had. At sword's point with Monroe, and never on a cordial basis with Madison, he proceeded to construct a fighting machine with which he hoped to win the war. Yet personal and political factors sometimes blinded his judgment. He dealt bluntly, sometimes harshly, with his commanders, most of whom had risen to prominence under Jefferson or Madison; but he eventually succeeded in replacing the dead wood he inherited with younger and more vigorous leadership. Even his drive and energy were insufficient to direct the kind of war that the public demanded, and he resigned under fire in September 1814.

One of the extraordinary aspects of his secretaryship was the degree to which he allowed his field commanders to change or reject his plans. Couched sometimes as proposals, sometimes as orders, they were not always feasible, and some of them deserved to be modified. But he was led into unseemly arguments at long distance which usually ended with his acquiescence. In March 1813, he suggested that Harrison invade Canada across the lake from Cleveland. Harrison had an easy job of parrying the plan by stressing the need for well-disciplined troops and absolute control of Lake Erie, both of which he lacked. Armstrong's plans for Dearborn's spring campaign will be described below.

The Navy Department also got a new head in January. Paul Hamilton had worn out his welcome and when his plan for seventy-four-gun ships was defeated and Madison told him he had lost the confidence of Congress, he resigned at the end of December. The new secretary was William Jones of Philadelphia. "As a veteran of the Revolution," writes Harry Coles, "Jones knew something of fighting; as a merchant engaged in the China trade he had acquired considerable knowledge of ships; and as a former congressman, he knew the ways of politics and politicians. With great energy and ability, Jones set about improving the organization of his department, pushing the building program, and hastening the efforts to secure control of the inland waters."[23] In other words, Lieutenant Macdonough on Lake Champlain had a new and more effective superior.

There were also military promotions during the winter. The administration had started the awkward process of weeding out the average or inefficient generals, with two down (Hull and Van Rensselaer) and several more, including Dearborn, still to go. The promotions brought to positions of leadership some younger men, but unfortunately they also elevated two others who subsequently had to be weeded out in turn. In addition to the original two major generals, six more were named, including James Wilkinson in New Orleans, Wade Hampton in Virginia, and William Henry Harrison in the Northwest. The ranks of the brigadier generals were supplemented by ten men among whom was George Izard, a Federalist from South Carolina.

Since all the evidence indicated spring action on Lake Ontario, orders went out from Dearborn for all the regulars at Burlington and Plattsburgh, together with a corps at Champlain, to move west. To the governor's protests about exposing the equipment at the Plattsburgh arsenal, Dearborn ordered most of it moved to Burlington and Whitehall. General Chandler was directed to move the provisions at Plattsburgh to Burlington. Except for calling out some militia units, nothing was done to reassure the inhabitants at the border, who believed they were being left to the furies of British raids. The northern front was, at least temporarily, being abandoned in favor of a western one in New York State.

Pike and 400 men were ordered to start the trek in mid-March. Pike's name remained behind to perpetuate his memory in the North Country that he would never see again. The military post over which he presided has been known ever since as Pike's Cantonment. Also, in December a son was born to Amos Luther of Chazy. He was named Zebulon Pike Montgomery Luther, in the spirit of the times.[24]

The rest of the Plattsburgh troops and those of Chandler in Burlington followed Pike. Press-gangs went through the countryside looking for horses and sleighs. Many still had to march, but of those who were able to ride, some froze to death rather than get out and walk. A late season and a severe snowstorm with snow three feet deep made parts of the trip a nightmare. All who got through were reunited under Dearborn in the vicinity of Sackets Harbor, more or less ready for a misplaced spring campaign.

7

A SUMMER OF SETBACKS: 1813

The season's first military activity was planned for the area bordering on Lake Ontario, and troops were collected at Sackets Harbor from Greenbush, Plattsburgh, and Burlington for the purpose. During the winter, Dearborn and the new secretary of war, John Armstrong, had corresponded concerning the nature of the campaigns of 1813. Armstrong insisted that Kingston be the prime target so as to destroy the British naval base. At first Dearborn concurred but soon urged that attacks first be made upon Forts George and Erie, on the Niagara peninsula, and then upon Kingston, to which Armstrong agreed. There were to be other changes of plans as Dearborn and Commodore Chauncey plotted their amphibious undertakings. Under the almost superstitious impression that Kingston was nearly impregnable, the two commanders selected as their objective the provincial capital of York, the modern city of Toronto.

The campaign was undertaken late in April, under the direct command of newly promoted Brigadier General Zebulon Pike, while the indisposed Dearborn watched from a ship. The town was captured without difficulty, but then an explosion of a magazine took the lives of Pike and many British and Americans. Had he lived, this scholar-explorer would undoubtedly have risen high in military or other public service. After his death, and without effective control from Dearborn, the American troops looted the town, emptied the jail, and burned the capitol buildings before evacuating the area. This needless destruction led to the British burning of the government buildings in Washington later in the war. The scene at the hospital after the explosion led Dr. Beaumont to make this gory commentary: "Nothing is heard but the groans of the wounded, and agonies of the Dying are to be heard. The surgeons wading in blood, cutting off arms, legs, and trepanning heads to rescue their fellow creatures from untimely death."[1]

In May, an expedition was launched against Fort George. Colonel Winfield Scott, captured at Queenston and later exchanged, was now Dearborn's
chief of staff and took active command of the troops. Although specifically
ordered by the president to lead the campaign personally, Dearborn was
again indisposed, so that he directed operations from his ship. Major General
Morgan Lewis, the quartermaster general, perhaps too critically wrote of
Dearborn: "He has been repeatedly in a state of convalescence; but relapses
on the least agitation of mind."[2] The British general at Fort George, John
Vincent, decided that his position was untenable and ordered the evacuation
of Fort George as well as Chippewa and Fort Erie at the other end of the peninsula. Suddenly the entire British front at Niagara was in American hands.
However, in pursuing Vincent, Brigadier Generals William Henry Winder
and John Chandler allowed themselves to be surprised and captured at
Stoney Creek.

Armstrong scolded Dearborn for allowing the British to get away, reminding him that "Battles are not gained when an inferior and broken
enemy is not *destroyed*."[3] Meanwhile, Dearborn had expressed to Armstrong
his conviction that if his health did not improve, he would need a chance for
his mind to be at ease *for a short time*. However, the administration had for
weeks felt that a change of commanders was necessary and early in July, Dearborn was ordered to retire from command pending further orders. Repeatedly he asked for a court of inquiry into his conduct, but his requests were
disregarded. Instead, he was assigned to command a military district where
active service was not necessary. Over his strong protests because he had been
personally involved, he was assigned to preside over Hull's court-martial.

Undoubtedly, Dearborn's replacement as commander of the Northern
Army was necessary. Morgan Lewis surmised that he would never be fit for
command again. Even Prevost in Canada believed that the American campaign had been ruined by Dearborn's disobedience in attacking York instead
of Kingston. Brigadier General Peter B. Porter thought that although Dearborn "had scarcely done anything which in my opinin he ought to have done
as a general, yet he was still worth all the other general officers put
together."[4] Porter touched upon the crux of the matter: who was available as
a replacement? Dearborn's age, illness, and personal shortcomings were sufficient reason for a change. But his disgrace was also a heavy price to exact for
factors beyond his control: his impossibly broad assignment; the difficulties
of invasion with green regulars and untrained militia; the obstructionism
of the New England governors; and the failures of the generals under his
command.

During the absence of the army and fleet at the Niagara front, Sackets
Harbor was defended only by units of the militia. The British at Kingston

could not let such an opportunity pass, and they attacked and briefly occupied the place on May 29. Governor General Prevost had just accompanied Commodore James Yeo to his new post at Kingston, and both were present at the attack. At first the American militia fled in disorder, but through heroic actions of the militia general, Jacob Brown rallied them and made a stand. The far superior British force was pulled out, however, to the disappointment of the Canadian public who, from the presence of the two commanders in chief, "fondly flattered themselves with a far more brilliant result," says Robert Christie. "This miscarriage with other reverses at the commencement of the present campaign, destroyed in the opinion of the enemy, the invincibility our arms had acquired the preceding autumn."[5]

Yet there had never been an intention to occupy the port permanently, but rather to disrupt its use as a ship-building center. The British accomplished this when a junior American officer, sure of defeat, set fire to the barracks and storehouses, as well as the *Gloucester* and the unfinished *General Pike*. The fires on the vessels were extinguished before they had done much damage, but the buildings were a total loss; they contained the stores captured at York as well as the canvas and many of the supplies for the *Pike*. This partial destruction of Sackets Harbor was more than was ever accomplished at the British naval base at Kingston. The Americans only once lightly attacked it.

Both British and Americans early recognized the importance of control of the Great Lakes. The British desperately needed a water highway from Montreal by which to maintain a tenuous hold upon Upper Canada; the Americans believed they must obtain control of the route in order to win their war against Great Britain. The wisdom of their emphasis upon warfare in this area is arguable because even if successful it would still leave the centers of Canadian population untouched. Nevertheless, intense rivalry developed for the control of Lakes Erie and Ontario. The British lost the race on Lake Erie, but the competition on Ontario continued inconclusively throughout the war.

Supremacy for two and a half years went to the side that had launched its latest ship, usually one that was larger than any of the enemy's. The race started in the summer of 1812, when Commodore Isaac Chauncey was sent to Sackets Harbor, and the Provincial Marine adopted Kingston as its shipbuilding center. Not until the spring of 1813 did the British Navy, after much prodding from Governor General Prevost, take over naval affairs on the lakes. The commander was Commodore Sir James Lucas Yeo; the stage was now set for an elaborate shadow-boxing between the two commodores. The fleet that was temporarily superior sailed the lake freely, while its opponents kept within their heavily guarded base until their next ship was ready, when

they sailed forth and the other side scuttled into port. Despite bold pro-
nouncements, neither commander ventured into an engagement when he
felt inferior in ships. Some idea of the fantastic lengths that the naval race
reached is the size of the last ship launched by the British toward the end of
the war: the *St. Lawrence,* a three-decker mounting 100 guns, making it the
equal of the largest vessels fighting on the ocean.

The only American naval victory of 1813 took place farther west. The loss
of General Hull and his entire army the year before had left the Northwest almost entirely undefended. William Henry Harrison, in western eyes the hero
of Tippecanoe, was made a major general with a large army on paper, and
broad authority to defend the frontiers and recapture Detroit. Secretary of
War Armstrong had no affection for him, and the two exchanged spirited
correspondence. Armstrong in March proposed an attack across Lake Erie
from Cleveland, but Harrison argued its folly, pointing out that it required at
least "3,500 well-disciplined troops and absolute control of the lake." He reminded the secretary that with his little army he now faced the whole Indian
strength of the Northwest, "directed by the skill of British officers and supported by the steady valour of British veterans."[6] Eventually it was decided
that while Harrison built up his force, every effort would be made to construct a fleet and gain control of the lake.

The race for those waters started early. During the winter, Captain Oliver
Hazard Perry was sent to Erie, Pennsylvania, and in the spring Captain Robert H. Barclay went to Amherstburg, at the western end of the lake. Despite
the tremendous difficulties experienced by both sides in obtaining supplies
and men (each captain felt he was denied sufficient help by his superior on
Lake Ontario), two fleets were constructed during the summer. Unlike their
counterparts on Ontario, they clashed on September 10, and after a fierce
and deadly battle Barclay surrendered his whole fleet of six ships. Perry recorded his victory in the famous line, "We have met the enemy and they are
ours."[7]

The way was now open for Harrison to move with his army. He occupied
Fort Malden, which was evacuated at his approach. He pursued General
Henry Proctor up the Thames River in October, captured part of the British
force, scattered the Indians, and killed their great leader, Tecumseh. Originally he had been directed to proceed against Niagara, but these orders were
changed. In effect the Battle of the Thames ended the war in the Northwest.
The Indians sued for peace, most of the troops went home, and Harrison appointed General Lewis Cass as Governor of Michigan Territory.

Harrison was the first authentic hero of the war, and he received great
ovations on his trip to Washington. Yet Armstrong would not fit him into the
military structure he was creating and insultingly assigned him to an inactive

theatre around Cincinnati. At first Harrison accepted the slight, but when he discovered that a subordinate had been given a separate command over his head, he resigned from the army in May 1814. His resignation was accepted by Armstrong, who seemed determined to check Harrison's spreading popularity and his potential political importance, and Madison did not interfere. Consequently, when the American army still faced much severe fighting and good generals were few, the services of a victorious officer were lost to the American cause by the deliberate actions of the secretary of war.

Unlike the intense activity of the year in the Great Lakes region, the Champlain Valley was at first neglected in American war plans, bypassed in favor of other fronts. The departure of the troops from Burlington and Plattsburgh in March produced anxieties along the unprotected border, reminiscent of the previous summer. Defense rested with the militia, whose effectiveness in 1813 and 1814 continued to rest on the skill of their commanders and upon the attitude of the states. Southern New England remained obdurate in refusing its militia for national service. Until fall, the militia of Vermont and New York were available along the Canadian border on both sides of the lake. Neither of the regular army commanders, Wilkinson and Hampton, however, possessed the temperament to command them in the fall campaign.

Secretary of War Armstrong had no confidence in the militia and ordered their use only if necessary. He made an effort to build a regular force large enough to meet all the requirements of the war. Early in 1813, Congress terminated the law for twelve-month volunteers, who had not come forward anyway, and provided instead for twenty regiments of twelve-month regulars. They were to be paid the same as the five-year regulars but would receive no land bounty. On paper the regular army consisted of fifty-seven thousand men, but in February only nineteen thousand were actually enrolled. Consequently, whether Armstrong or the commanders liked it or not, the militia continued to be needed for the rest of the war.

In Northern New York and Vermont, the militia were the sole defense of the country during the summer and part of the fall. They were meant to be a stop-gap until the regular forces could be built up, but even when that had been done, the regulars were kept in Burlington, not at the borders. On May 5, Captain Oliver Herrick and a company of Maine and New Hampshire volunteers arrived in Champlain to protect the area from British incursions. They stayed less than a month before they were ordered aboard Lieutenant Sidney Smith's patrolling fleet. Once again Mooers protested to Colonel Clark in Burlington that British movements could be made across the line with impunity and that not even a system of warning signals existed: "The door thrown open, the watchman asleep or lying on their oars waiting for the chief's orders."[8] The situation was only temporarily relieved when Colonel

Davis and a detachment arrived in Champlain on June 20, but they were withdrawn on July 14, and this time the Champlain Committee of Safety protested directly to the commander in Burlington.

Aside from the exposed border and the fears it engendered, the old problem of smuggling into Canada continued to harrass military and civilian officers charged with enforcing the laws. In June, Macdonough reported that many cattle and provisions were going into Canada from Vermont, usually after dark, and that rafts of timber and spars were going to Isle-aux-Noix to feed the shipbuilding industry there. At the end of the summer Captain Erwin at French Mills begged Mooers for more troops before the whole countryside was bare of provisions. He reported that a Canadian agent was there, openly contracting for supplies, and that a drove of cattle from Cornwall, Vermont, had just gone through the area. As he quaintly put it, "The host of smuglars that huver on our lines is beyond description. Since the first of August to this date their has been from the best calculation more than sixty yoak of oxen besides other beef cattle drove to Canada."9

Macdonough decided to try to check smuggling on the lake, as well as to halt the depradations of British gunboats along the line. After a strenuous winter in which he increased the firepower of his three vessels and two gunboats, he emerged from winter quarters as the master of the lake. He had experienced great difficulty in getting the guns and ships' supplies from distant points, but he never obtained the trained seamen he needed. His request in January was repeated many times thereafter: "There are no men to get here and soldiers are miserable creatures on shipboard, and I very much fear that unless I get the above (ordinary) seamen and not soldiers, there will be a dark spot in our Navy."10 Nevertheless, Macdonough found that he had to use soldiers if he was going to move his fleet.

During April, his three largest vessels went to Plattsburgh. Macdonough's own ship, the *President*, ran aground near Plattsburgh and required extensive repairs. In May, Midshipman Horace Sawyer was ordered to take a gunboat to Plattsburgh. When he entered the bay a sudden gust of wind upset it and it lay on its beam end. The crew clung to it for several hours in icy water before they were rescued by the sloop *Eagle*. Sawyer served on *Eagle* in its subsequent exploits.

Macdonough laid up his gunboats and transferred their crews to the *Growler* and the *Eagle*. Each vessel was equipped with eleven guns; the *Growler* was commanded by Lieutenant Smith and the *Eagle* by Sailing Master Loomis. They were sent to patrol the line to prevent British gunboat activity, but Smith was ordered to keep within his own lines. They got under way on June 2, and en route to his position he picked up Captain Herrick and his forty-one men at Champlain.

But the very next day, June 3, the over-eager Smith was unable to resist the flaunting of the British gunboats just over the line where the lake narrows into the Richelieu River. Early in the morning Smith signalled the *Eagle* to follow him. The pilot protested strongly, fearing the stiff south wind and the current in the river, but he was overruled. The two ships entered the river and as they approached Isle-aux-Noix ran into trouble.

Isle-aux-Noix was still primarily a military base. It was garrisoned by a detachment of Royal Artillery and six companies of the 100th Regiment under Major George Taylor. The three row galleys brought from Quebec the previous summer were manned by soldiers of the regiment. One galley carried an eighteen-pound carronade, the other two had twelve-pounders.

Each had a crew of about twenty-five and could be operated by sails as well as oars, drawing little water. They started firing on the nearer of the two American vessels. Taylor sent out two bateaux of troops and had one land on each side of the river, where there was also heavy artillery. The American ships, in trying to tack and turn, came close to shore in the narrow river. Many men were wounded and the rest were driven from their guns to find shelter. For four hours the sharp engagement continued. About eleven o'clock the *Eagle* received a twenty-four-pound shot between wind and water and sank in shallow water, the deck submerged a few inches; the British took possession. The *Growler* had its forestay and main boom shot away and, becoming unmanageable, ran around where Smith surrendered.

The British captured the crews of both ships, estimated at 100 men. None of the officers was wounded, but Midshipman Sawyer never recovered from the deafness brought on by the bombardment at close quarters. British sources list American casualties as one killed and nineteen wounded. Rodney Macdonough puts it somewhat less. The British sustained three injuries. British sources say that 108 of their men were engaged; Macdonough believes it was nearer 250. Lieutenant Macdonough later told Chauncey that "I am decidedly of the opinion that the vessels would not have been lost had they not gone so far over the line into such narrow water, where the musketry of the enemy told from either shore."[11] Meanwhile, rumors reached the British that more American ships and a three-thousand-man land force were on the way, and Taylor hurried back to Isle-aux-Noix to prepare for an attack which, of course, was never made or even considered.

After the war a court of inquiry into Smith's conduct was held at Sackets Harbor. The court found his general behavior "correct and meritorious," and although the ships were lost by going too far into the river, Smith had been deceived by his own pilot. It concluded that the boats "were gallantly defended and that they were not surrendered until all further resistance had become vain."[12]

The British captives were taken first to Quebec, where Abraham Walter, the pilot of the *Growler,* managed to escape. After a ten-day journey, he arrived back in Plattsburgh where he swore to an affidavit before Judge Henry Delord about the fate of the prisoners. At Quebec they were confined on a prison ship, examined, and eight or ten sent to England for treason trials as British subjects. Many of the rest were forced to help navigate ships to Halifax. At Quebec, Smith and Midshipman Walter Montieth of the *Growler* were at first paroled in nearby Beauport. Then they were reincarcerated, along with Dr. James Wood of Champlain, who was taken from his home while doing customs work. They were held in close confinement as a part of the forty-six hostages Prevost held in retaliation for the twenty-three held by Americans (see Chapter 5).[13]

Smith and two other prisoners escaped, crossed the St. Lawrence, and followed the Chaudière River into the interior. When they were within five miles of the border, Smith wanted to push on before dark but was overruled by the other two. During the night, they were recaptured by local militia and returned to Quebec. There they were separately and severely confined until the general exchange of prisoners in June 1814.

The British made good use of the ships they captured. On the day of the battle the *Growler* was taken to Isle-aux-Noix for repairs and a new name, the *Broke.* The *Eagle* was raised, and next day it reached the island. It was renamed the *Shannon* and with their overhauling the British controlled Lake Champlain. After the refitting, a Montreal paper understandably boasted: "Those federal and democratic *bloody pack hounds* may always rest assured of meeting a suitable reception, until they yield to our mercy, when they may expect clemency to an extent far beyond their merits."[14]

For the British, the outcome of this affair was to make Isle-aux-Noix no longer a military center only, but a naval base as well. Captain Daniel Pring was sent to take charge of the little fleet. He asked permission of Prevost to establish a shipyard there and to build two gunboats and a brig. Prevost agreed to the gunboats but delayed on the brig so that the *Linnet* was not completed until the following spring. He later approved a sixteen-gun schooner, which was finished in May. He sent William Simmons from Kingston, where he had helped with British shipbuilding on Lake Ontario, to supervise the work at Isle-aux-Noix.

The base was already protected by its insular location, and to make it as unapproachable as possible it was further defended by strong outposts radiating southward toward the border. During the winter, barracks, hospital, and storehouses were built. Yeo, who visited the site in February, found the works in good condition. For shipbuilding and repairs, a large dry dock was dug into its west side. A boat could enter it from the Richelieu, after which the gates were closed and the water pumped out by hand. The British were clearly preparing to keep control of the lake in 1814.

After his losses, Macdonough asked the Navy Department for more ships and men. Secretary Jones told him to buy and equip the two best vessels available, and four or five gunboats of the galley type. "You are to understand," wrote Jones, "that on no account are you to suffer the enemy to gain the ascendancy on Lake Champlain, and as you have unlimited authority to procure the necessary resources of men, materials and munitions for that purpose, I rely upon your efficient use of the authority vested in you."[15]

Meanwhile, an army build-up was under way in Burlington. In June, five companies of the Thirteenth U.S. Infantry arrived, with a detachment of artillery and two twenty-four pound guns. The bluffs overlooking the lake were further fortified, and a parapet of sods was erected with thirteen embrasures. Next to arrive were 700 men of the Fourth Regiment, followed by the entire Thirty-first. By July, the force included the second battalion of the Fourth, six companies of the Eleventh, the whole of the Twenty-ninth, Thirtieth, and Thirty-first regiments, two regiments of volunteers, two troops of cavalry, and two of artillery. With some 800 militia, the numbers reached more than 4,000 men, although 557 were sick and 327 absent, with or without leave. Wooden barracks were expanded between Pearl and North streets and before winter the main building of the University of Vermont was taken over to house the overflow.[16] As might be expected, the residents of the little town had great difficulty adjusting to the quartering of so many troops, many of them unruly, in their midst.

General Wade Hampton arrived in July to take command, thereby bringing a new set of problems to the Champlain Valley. Although the year of his birth is uncertain, he was either sixty-one or sixty-two years of age and known for his testiness. In the Revolution he had risen to be a colonel as one of the most daring and efficient young officers under General Thomas Sumter. He subsequently served two terms in Congress. In 1808 he entered the army as a colonel and the following year was made a brigadier general. He succeeded Wilkinson in command at New Orleans in 1809. In 1812–13 he was put in charge of the fortifications at Norfolk. During that winter, he appealed directly to the president for an active command in the north; he wanted "above all to avoid the imputation of being thought unworthy of commanding troops of my own corps, and of sharing their danger and honors." Some circumstances of delicacy, he wrote, prevented his applying directly to the War Department.[17]

In consequence, Hampton was made a major general and sent to Lake Champlain to cooperate in a vague way with Wilkinson at Sackets Harbor. He arrived in the midst of a number of problems not of his own making.

Complaining over the withdrawal of Colonel Davis' men from Champlain, the Committee of Safety wrote him:

> Understanding that the troops placed here for the defence of this post are ordered to Burlington and being menaced for these two days by small parties of the enemy appearing in different quarters in the neighborhood of the garrison, We the Committee of Safety for the town take the liberty to represent to you that in our opinion if this post is abandoned by the troops, the inhabitants will very probably not have time or means to make their escape, but must lie at their mercy — Yesterday a party of seven Indians fired on a soldier within half a mile of one of the block houses — one other party of Indians was in several inhabited houses in the adjoining town of Mooers about six miles to the west of us — Today a party of the British in uniform appeared in sight of the picket about a mile from the blockhouses — We have reason to believe they have intelligence of the march of the troops and that they will be in upon us immediately — We solicit your protection.

The next day Hampton, instead of expressing sympathy for the worried citizens of Champlain, effectively slammed the door on their hopes:

> My duties are purely Military, and extend not to the police of the Country. In a Military view, an answer to such a communication as yours, must sometimes be improper. The most that is now intended is, the private thoughts of an individual, whose good wishes extend to all his fellow citizens.
>
> You ought not to forget the extent of the American lines. That a nation engaged in an offensive war, is sometimes constrained, to direct *all its forces to one point*. The measures necessary to such an effort, can but strike you. It ought further to occur to you, that those Citizens whos[e] *choice* hath placed so near the bounds of the territory they inhabit, ought to be prepared to meet the consequences incident to their local residence; and they ought to unite their strength for the purpose.[18]

These letters are quoted to reveal not only the understandable anxieties of a typical border town, but also to introduce the character of the new commander. Mooers at Plattsburgh soon had a similar experience when he tried to introduce Eleazer Williams to him, with high praise for his intelligence activities. Hampton heartily favored making full use of Indians as warriors, a position opposed to that of both Mooers and the War Department, but he was less enthusiastic about making use of the Corps of Observation. He grudgingly agreed to pay Mooers's requisition for the Indian account but declared that he knew nothing about Indian affairs, "& I am resolved not to know" because all dealings and payments should be through one person, for the sake of accountability. He wanted the sixty warriors he had already requested for his fall campaign, however, and he would take a hundred if available. If they were any good, they would be paid the wages of federal troops, but they must clothe themselves; otherwise, "If they are good for nothing they can be discharged."[19]

Williams, after meeting Hampton, found that he "from the beginning was very unpopular with the army, and public opinion was against him." Learning that Hampton was to command the northern army, Williams brooded that it was "Strange that the Government should appoint Southern men to such responsible stations at the North. General Mooers ought to have this appointment, then Montreal would be in possession in a month. He is a brave, judicious and prudent officer, and withal extremely popular with his fellow citizens. They would follow him with the greatest cheerfulness."[20]

Hampton also tangled with Elbert Anderson, the commissary with a contract to provision troops in the State of New York whose compensation depended upon the number of rations issued. He naturally resented Hampton's determination to issue rations through his own commissaries, even after his troops later crossed into New York. Anderson protested without success to both Armstrong and the president.

Hampton considered himself a martinet. He sought to upgrade the fighting preparedness of his men for whom he entertained the utmost disdain as raw and untrained recruits. His punishments were bizarre and humiliating, but not normally extreme. The Articles of War sanctioned severe sentences, including the death penalty, but he seemed, like other commanders, to sense that public opinion would not tolerate them. The occasional deserter who was caught was sometimes shot, depending upon extenuating circumstances. Even before Hampton's arrival, Colonel Clark was complaining to Secretary of War Armstrong:

> I take this liberty, sir, to prevent so many impositions on the government as do really take place, by men of no talents for a military life procuring some friends to recommend them to the members of Congress, who bring them forward without any other knowledge of them; and when they come to be proved, many of them turn out to be lazy, drinking gamblers, and are in fact a dead weight in the army. The officers of the army have an interest in having men of industry and talents in office, it lessens their burden.[21]

Nevertheless, the first Garrison Orders, issued by Colonel Melancton Smith of the Eleventh and Twenty-ninth regiments merely chided the men on "the inattention of the soldiers to the common respects due from them to officers, their disregard to cleanliness and neetness in their dress and appearance."[22]

By mid-July, courts-martial became increasingly common. On the 13th, Benjamin Lynde was found guilty of theft and sentenced to receive "twelve bats on his naked posteriors," that is, a good spanking, and David Dickey was convicted of habitual intoxication, for which he was "to ride a wooden horse one hour two successive mornings on the publick paraid."

Other penalties reviewed by Hampton included that of Asa Hopkins of the Eleventh Infantry, convicted of sleeping on duty as a sentinel. Since he was already mustered for a discharge, he was "to have his head shaved, be marked with the letter R on each cheek and in the forehead, with Luner Costic; Drummed out of camp with a halter round his neck." (Lunar caustic was silver nitrate in stick form, used as a cautery.)

General Orders on the 24th told the sad tale of Timothy Ashley, who was convicted of disobedience of orders and mutinous conduct. He was sentenced to hard labor with ball and chain for the remainder of his enlistment; during the same period his liquor ration was to be stopped and he was to ride a wooden horse one hour every Sunday for the first two months wearing a hangman's cap, a four-pound shot tied to each foot and a label placed upon him designating his crime. There were many more sentences in a similar vein.

Life in the British armed forces, on the other hand, was a more rigorous and severely disciplined experience. The militia served under stern regulations, not always fully enforced because of public opinion; but the full penalties of a harsh code were often applied to the Canadian and British regulars. The death penalty for desertion was sometimes allowed to stand, but the record contains numerous examples of Prevost's remitting sentences. For less than death sentences, the recommendation of the court-matial was usually sustained. The 103rd Regiment of Foot, a body of regulars from New Brunswick and Prince Edward Island, had a not untypical record. Between April 22 and October 1, 1812, thirty-seven privates and corporals were court-martialed. Thirty-one were found guilty of crimes of disobedience or desertion, and six not guilty. Of the guilty, ten were sentenced to 300 lashes, nine to 200, five to 100, and the rest for less. The punishments actually inflicted included one with 300 lashes, one with 200, six with 100, and ten with fewer than 100.[23] Despite such punishments, or perhaps in order to avoid them, desertion plagued the commanders of the regular forces throughout the war. After every campaign on American soil, alarming numbers of deserters were reported. In consequence, Prevost's adoption of a defensive stance seemed to him doubly justified, for it kept his troops off foreign soil.

Prevost's main problem was not discipline, but shortage of men and supplies that had to come from England. He maintained the support of the government in London throughout the war despite his constant supplications for provisions, Indian gifts, naval stores and seamen, military reinforcements and artillery. The letters he received from London contained comments that the prince regent believed Prevost's assignment "could not have been placed in hands more worthy of receiving it;" or that he "highly approves the judicious and prompt arrangements which you have adopted."[24] Some of this sounds like London's whistling in the dark when it had nothing more substantial to offer Prevost, but the language was more extravagant than the building of morale seemed to require.

For his part, Prevost upbraided his government for its lack of instructions, reminding his superiors that he had received no orders during the first fifteen months of the war. He chided the ministers that reinforcements always arrived so late as to be indecisive. In September 1813: "The period is fast approaching when a suspension of active operations must take place." In November 1813: "The very great exertions made for the preservation of the Canadas by its population, in conjunction with the small force under my command, may eventually degenerate into indifference for the result of the present contest unless the support from the mother country is equal to the magnitude of the stake." In May 1814, he forwarded American publicity detailing the strength of their arms which he thought might make Bathurst "appreciate the exertions of the small and gallant band placed under my command by which these Provinces have, with means disproportionate, been hitherto defended against the repeated attempts of the enemy to gain a permanent foothold in them."[25]

Prevost's war effort consisted of meeting a series of apparently insurmountable crises for the first two years. Careful planning at the top, brilliant timing and improvisation everywhere, and courageous execution at the fronts help to explain the outcome. So does Indian aid and the unexpected reliability of the militia. The American shortcomings also contributed greatly to British survival. At the peace conference at Ghent, the British undersecretary of state told John Quincy Adams that nothing had saved Canada "but the excellent dispositions and military arrangements of the Governor who commanded there."[26]

By the end of 1813, Prevost had reason to be pleased with the way the war had gone in Lower Canada, but less so in Upper Canada. Good luck, a sturdy defense, and American fumbles had brought him through a dangerous year. For example, in midsummer he began to receive reports that another military build-up was occurring in the Champlain Valley. In order to gather intelligence, deter invasion by creating as much chaos as possible, and create a diversion to help Upper Canada, he sanctioned a counterstroke from

Isle-aux-Noix while he had naval superiority. This event has been known as Murray's Raid.

Late in July, Prevost sent Pring of the Royal Navy to the command on Lake Champlain and Pring chose the *Broke* as his flagship. Captain Thomas Everard came from Quebec to sail the *Shannon,* once the *Eagle.* At Isle-aux-Noix the British also had three galleys and forty-seven bateaux. Parts of the 13th and 103rd regiments boarded the small boats under Lieutenant Colonel John Murray, commandant at St. Jean. He had about 39 officers and 907 men, although American sources have persisted in recording 1,400. The orders for the campaign were to destroy all barracks and other military buildings, remove or destroy public stores and boats, but to protect private property and prevent straggling.[27]

They entered American waters on July 29. On that date Mooers alerted the Clinton County militia and appealed to Hampton for help. Although Plattsburgh citizens expected them, no troops came from Burlington. The most Hampton did was to march some men to Colchester and back; otherwise, it was business as usual at the cantonment in Burlington. On the 30th, the British armada was off Chazy, where a sloop and a Durham boat were captured. Mooers ordered out the entire militia of Clinton and Essex counties. Some of the Clinton men appeared at Plattsburgh the next morning; the militia from Essex needed more time.

On the morning of the 31st, fourteen of Plattsburgh's leading citizens begged Mooers, unless his force was truly adequate, "not to put up resistance, which could destroy the town. Order all troops not to fire — it will be a dictate of real patriotism & will save our village & property from ruin."[28] Mooers had collected about 300 militia from Clinton County by the time the British arrived at Plattsburgh.

The flotilla came on Saturday, July 31. The families of many of the leading citizens, such as the Saillys and Delords, had been sent south to Peru, Mrs. Delord approaching her seventh month of pregnancy. Most of the public stores had been sent to Burlington previously, but much still remained. The British bateaux went into the Saranac River and landed the troops on the south shore opposite the Delord and Sailly homes. They landed unopposed because Mooers took his troops westward about three miles to Thorn's Corners to wait for the arrival of more of his men. On landing, Murray pledged that no private property would be touched and that individuals would not be molested if they remained peacefully at home. Since no resistance was possible, the occupying force had its own way until it departed at ten o'clock the next morning.

During the occupation, which took place in hot weather, a perspiring Colonel Murray removed his hat and unknowingly dropped a piece of paper.

William Gilliland covered it with a handkerchief and picked it up. The townspeople who examined it believed it was written by Joel Ackley; it contained suggestions for the best way of attacking Plattsburgh and a map of the encampment at Burlington. After the British departed, Ackley was arrested.

Joel Ackley had moved to Plattsburgh from Canada in the winter before the war. He was a surveyor who had established himself as a respectable citizen, with a home on Oak Street and two daughters in the academy. When questioned by a justice of the peace, however, he admitted writing the incriminating paper. He was to receive $100 for his work and had already been paid $50. It was afterwards learned that he had been one of the most effective spies for the British for some time. They sought to defend him through a Vermont lawyer who was to be paid with some of Ackley's Canadian property. Nevertheless, he spent nine months in Burlington and Albany jails without being indicted. When no one appeared against him he was eventually released in Albany under a writ of habeas corpus confirmed by the district attorney and legalized by Chancellor James Kent. He subsequently took his family back to Canada. Only a year later he guided Major General Thomas Brisbane's Second Brigade in its advance on Plattsburgh, for which he was warmly praised by the general: "he being indefatigable in ascertaining the situation, force, and movements of the Enemy on that Occasion." After the war friends petitioned the British government on his behalf, and in 1816 the colonial secretary ordered Governor General Gordon Drummond to pay Ackley £500, less any amounts already paid him.[29]

Meanwhile, by extraordinary activity, 370 men from Essex were assembled from widely scattered rural areas and set in motion on the 1st of August, probably marching all night to reach Plattsburgh on the 2nd. The British departed the day before, perhaps on learning of their approach. Whether Mooers pulled out of Plattsburgh because he could not prevent his militia from going away, or in order to honor the civilians' request is not clear. He later explained that he did it in order to save the village from destruction.

During the brief occupation, the arsenal, a blockhouse, and several storehouses were pilfered and destroyed. Two of the latter were owned by Sailly which he had rented to the government. The contents of all three were government property; Sailly, the commissary for the region, calculated that the items burned or carried off included substantial quantities of pork, beef, flour, hard bread, whiskey, soap, and vinegar. All of this could fairly be considered public property, and its loss was figured at $25,000. Also destroyed was Pike's Cantonment, which had cost about $30,000 to construct the previous winter.

More serious was the looting of private homes. Quantities of furniture, books, clothing, cooking utensils, groceries, and dry goods, which reached a value exceeding $8,000, were destroyed or carried away. Among claims later submitted to the government were Henry Delord's for losses in his house and store of $1,079; Peter Sailly, $877 plus the two burned storehouses valued at $900; John Palmer, $380; Doctors Miller and Davidson, $1,200, and Jacob Ferris, $700.[30]

When the British left Plattsburgh on August 1, they stopped to destroy a large storehouse on Cumberland Head. From there two galleys and the bateaux with troops started for Swanton, Vermont. En route they made a brief landing at Point au Roche, and at Chazy Landing they destroyed the store of Matthew Saxe. Reaching Maquam Bay on the 2nd, they marched overland to Swanton. The barracks that had been occupied intermittently until recently were built in the shape of a crescent east of the town green. In a few hours the British burned them, the hospital, and all government property before they marched away. However, an ugly undercurrent began to enter into this freebooting enterprise. Sworn depositions went to Washington claiming rapes or attempted rapes at both Swanton and Point au Roche.

While the troops were busy at Plattsburgh, the *Broke,* the *Shannon,* and one galley sailed to Burlington, which they reached on the same day after seizing the sloop *Essex.* In the bay under the guns on the bluff, Macdonough had gathered his surviving fleet. The *President* was there, as were two sloops with carpenters working on them, one still without a mast, together with two gunboats and a couple of scows. Standing off nearly two miles, the British ships opened fire, hoping at least to destroy the three public storehouses on the wharf, and perhaps some of Macdonough's vessels as well. The fire from the big American guns was too menacing to allow a closer approach, and after an exchange of about twenty minutes, the British vessels withdrew. Macdonough sailed out to try to entice them back under American gunfire, without success.

The British sailed southward. At Shelburne Bay they captured a sloop and a schooner. Off Charlotte they took two sloops carrying flour for the American army. During the night, they sailed twenty miles farther south. All along the lake on both sides guns were fired to spread the alarm, and the militia were called out. In all, the British captured eight vessels, nearly all the merchant craft on the lake except those in Burlington harbor. They destroyed four of them and took the rest back to Canada.

Both arms of the British invasion force, apparently satisfied with the havoc they had created, headed back for the border. En route the Swanton raiders rowed into the Great Chazy River, and the soldiers marched overland to Champlain. There they committed their final destruction on August 3, by burning two blockhouses, the barracks, and a warehouse containing a quantity of hay stored for military use. They also took captive a company of Clinton County militia, who were mostly sick. These men were shortly exchanged informally for some British prisoners. During the course of the five-day expedition, sixteen men of the 103rd Regiment deserted.

The devastation in the Champlain Valley caused great consternation except among Hampton's troops, who had been safely hoarded at Burlington. The editor of *The Weekly Register* hazarded the guess that, with the destruction of Pike's Cantonment, Plattsburgh would never again function as a rendezvous for military operations. Protracted claims were submitted by owners who lost their vessels during the British raid. Horace Morgan of Chazy appealed to the commandant at Isle-aux-Noix for a return of his schooner. He said that he had been promised it back after it was used during the expedition but that it was taken to Canada instead. "It would, However, look unseemly in one," he wrote, "to Doubt your Generosity, wharefore relying upon your temper, I Submit to your Good Nature." The British were not that generous, of course.[31]

Fifteen years later Ezra Thurber of Rouses Point and Gideon King of Burlington were still trying to obtain compensation from Congress for their lost sloop, the *Essex*. This vessel, Archibald Ferris, captain, lay at Whitehall with a load of salt and nails for Plattsburgh, waiting for Ferris to be sure the lake was clear of enemy ships. On July 31, Samuel Kettletas, sailing master in the navy, and eighteen sailors arrived and insisted on hurrying to Macdonough's aid in Burlington. They wanted Ferris to sail the *Essex* and when he refused they threatened to impress the vessel. He finally agreed to go as far as he could safely. They stopped at Essex and learned that the British were at Plattsburgh, whereupon Ferris objected to going any farther. Kettletas took over the ship and left Ferris ashore, but he overtook the *Essex,* landed the sailing master and the sailors at Burlington, and set sail for Whitehall. After fifteen miles his ship was captured by the *Broke* and the *Shannon* and burned.

One of the most curious consequences of Murray's Raid involved Henry Delord. During the British occupation of Plattsburgh his fine home was occupied. The following March, Major Lewis Ritter wrote Delord from Odelltown to apologize for the damage and to send a bale of carpet. He sent the letter by way of Pliny Moore in Champlain, asking him at the same time to care for the carpet "if it should tumble into your House by an unforeseen accident." An accident occurred because, although Ritter had cleared his shipment on the Canadian side of the border, he had failed to take American customs into account. Therefore, it was seized by an American agent, and Collector Peter Sailly had the painful task of explaining to his friends and neighbors in Plattsburgh, the Delords. When sold under court order, the carpet produced $120.08. The federal government's share was one-half; one-quarter went to the officer who made the seizure, and the other quarter went

The Kent-Delord House in Plattsburgh. Home of Judge Henry Delord, it was used as headquarters by British officers during the occupation of the town in 1814.

to Sailly. He sent his share to Mrs. Delord with regrets at wounding a lady he esteemed so highly.[32]

With as much haste as was possible, Macdonough set out to recapture control of the lake. Secretary Jones had given him full authority to acquire and arm ships after the loss of the *Growler* and the *Eagle* in June. This work was not completed at the time of Murray's Raid. Shortly afterwards he acquired another sloop, the *Rising Sun,* a merchant vessel built in Essex in 1810, which he armed and renamed the *Preble.* He had his vessels ready by August 20, but he lacked men. Fifty reached Burlington on August 19, and another 200, with some officers, arrived early in September. By borrowing soldiers from a reluctant Hampton, he was able to sail on September 6. His fleet of sloops now included the *President* of twelve guns, the *Preble* and the *Montgomery* of eleven guns each, the *Frances* of six guns, and the *Wasp* with three. The latter two vessels were hired and used as armed tenders, but they sailed badly. In addition, he had four gunboats, each with one gun, and some scows.

By diligent patrolling Macdonough could now control Lake Champlain. But the British continued to make incursions into the lake, frightening valley residents with the prospects of another raid on the Murray model. One of the boldest occurred on September 7, when two sloops and three gunboats approached Cumberland Head. Mooers again called out the militia of Clinton and Essex counties. The British moved back and forth between Gravelly Point and Point au Roche. Next day Macdonough appeared on the scene and pursued them back to Canada. They made no landing, but they captured a small smuggling boat whose owner had previously concealed his cargo ashore. Macdonough told the secretary of the navy that by fleeing, the British acknowledged American supremacy. Thereafter, he patrolled near Cumberland Head, except when he was called on to convoy Hampton's army to Plattsburgh. The stage was now set for the next production of "Americans on the offensive."

8

THE HAMPTON-WILKINSON FIASCO

For several months prior to Dearborn's release from command, the War Department had been looking for a successor. It had been severely taxed to find successful generals, and the field of choice was narrow. James Wilkinson was the senior brigadier general, outranked only by Dearborn and Pinkney. Although there were many who remembered his dubious past, he was ordered to New York in March 1813, to assume command of the northern armies.

During the Revolution, Wilkinson had risen to the rank of brevet brigadier general at the age of twenty. He hitched his fortunes to those of General Horatio Gates, victor at Saratoga, and General Thomas Conway. These men involved him in a project to undermine and replace General George Washington — the Conway Cabal. Wilkinson indiscreetly talked about it and was forced to resign his brevet rank, although remaining a colonel.

After the war he moved to Kentucky, where he gained considerable political influence. Here he first began his intrigues with the Spanish in New Orleans, undertaking, for pay, to bring Kentucky under Spanish influence. Successfully concealing his activities, he obtained a commission in the army in 1791 under General Anthony Wayne. In accepting it he unhesitantly took the oath to "bear true allegiance to the United States of America." He fought in the Indian wars and was made brigadier general. But in 1792 he suggested to Spanish officials that they use the opportunity offered by an "incompetent Secretary of War" (Henry Knox), "an ignorant commander in chief" (Washington) and a "contemptible" Union.[1]

A man of some charm and ability, adroit at befriending the right people, Wilkinson during years of treasonable activities kept the respect of important personages such as Thomas Jefferson. He seemed to thrive on intrigue and was always in need of great sums of money. As commander of the army for many years after 1796, he could charge the Spanish high prices for his advice and information, and as governor of Louisiana Territory after 1803, he could continue fishing in the troubled waters of the Southwest.

It was perhaps inevitable that Wilkinson should be drawn into Aaron Burr's vague plot for conquest or empire in that area. Wilkinson was a party to the plans but deliberately betrayed them to advance his own career, at the same time demanding a reward from the Spanish in Mexico for *saving* their lands. He testified against Burr at a trial in which Burr was exonerated of the charge of treason; Burr's charges of Wilkinson's complicity were generally believed but impossible to prove. Congressional inquiries into his role were made in 1807 and again in 1810. Finally, in 1811, he was tried by a court-martial, which brought seven charges and twenty-five specifications against him. He was publicly accused of treason, neglect of duty, and waste of public money and supplies. Insufficient evidence was available to prove the charges, and the court concluded that "General Wilkinson appears to have performed his various and complicated duties with zeal and fidelity, and merits the approbation of his country."[2]

Wilkinson's sword was restored to him and in anticipation of war he was ordered to New Orleans early in 1812 to prepare the defenses of the Southwest. Although he demanded more troops, he wanted nothing to do with Major General Andrew Jackson and his Tennessee militia who, after mobilizing and travelling a great distance, were in consequence ordered home by the secretary of war. In April 1813, Wilkinson performed his one decisive act of the war by seizing Mobile in a part of West Florida still held by the Spanish. At fifty-five years of age, he was not an active campaigner, and he was ill for considerable periods during the war. He had hoped to enjoy the climate and the relatively simple command at New Orleans for the duration, but was made a major general and tantalized with the prospects of another Saratoga in his future if he would take over Dearborn's command. Reluctantly he accepted. He delayed his departure from New Orleans, travelled leisurely, and reached Washington at the end of July 1813. He and Armstrong spent eleven days discussing the Canadian campaign. Wilkinson was given to understand that General Wade Hampton at Burlington would be subject to his orders, but Armstrong made somewhat different commitments to Hampton. He was told that his assignment was intended to be a "distinct and separate command," available only for joint operations with Wilkinson.

Wilkinson assumed Dearborn's command in August, arriving at Sackets Harbor on the 20th. As one military historian has put it, "Age and infirmity gave place to age and fatuity."[3] A comedy of errors ensued which nullified the campaign and ended the military careers of the two principals. Wilkinson and Hampton were bitter rivals who failed to cooperate, and Armstrong muddied the waters with his personal intervention. Armstrong was a skillful politician but a mediocre general who failed to obtain Hampton's cooperation and who wrangled with Wilkinson for a month over the objective of the campaign. He insisted that it be Kingston, but finally gave way to Wilkinson's counterproposals of a *joint* expedition from Plattsburgh and Sackets Harbor against Montreal. After he had lost confidence in Wilkinson, he did not replace the general; nor did he call off the campaign after its success appeared unlikely.

In Wilkinson's behalf, it may be pointed out that the staff he inherited contained several elderly and incompetent men; that considerable time was needed for organization; that Hampton tried to resign just as Wilkinson was getting under way; that Chauncey's indispensable naval support was slow and uncertain; and that he was intermittently ill from ague and fever brought on by exposure. His biographer believed that he used opium, a stock remedy of the day, for his ailments, and that it might account for his unstable judgment and his credence of enemy apparitions.[4] In any case, Wilkinson was incapable of providing sustained and inspiring leadership for a difficult campaign.

Even before reaching Sackets Harbor, Wilkinson notified Hampton of his assumption of command. He asked for a full report of Hampton's force and equipment at Burlington for "our effectual cooperation in the common cause of our country." This was a bad start with the touchy Hampton. Two weeks later Wilkinson complained to Armstrong that he could not get an answer out of him: "I hope he does not mean to take the stud; but, if so, we can do without him and he should be sent home."[5]

Hampton was not reserved with Armstrong, however. He reminded the secretary of his reluctance to take command under Wilkinson until he had been assured that he would have "a distinct and separate command," and that his force would not be taken from him or put under a superior officer after he had trained the raw recruits. He suggested a combined campaign and after the juncture of the armies, seniority would operate. He thought that Wilkinson's letters made it abundantly clear that his command "has sunk within that of a district." There was only one thing left for him to do, and that was to resign: "I can neither expect to render a service to my country, nor preserve my reputation."[6] Armstrong rejected the resignation and attempted to smooth over the distinction between separate and independent commands.

In view of the enmity between the two generals, Armstrong decided to go to Sackets Harbor and try to mediate, or at least handle the communications between them. He arrived on September 5, and oversaw the military preparations while Wilkinson made an extended recruiting trip. Even after Wilkinson returned on October 4, Armstrong remained for several weeks, supervising preparations for a complex two-pronged operation entrusted to antagonistic generals.

On September 1, Armstrong urged Hampton to make a prompt movement against Isle-aux-Noix, St. Jean, and Chambly, choosing which side of the lake he wished. Hampton was initially receptive because he had expected action before the end of the season, and the fact that the orders came from Armstrong, not Wilkinson, preserved the fiction of a separate command. He consulted Macdonough about a joint operation against Isle-aux-Noix but the naval commander, badly hurt by his losses in the Richelieu three months previously, vetoed the project. Consequently, Hampton told Armstrong that his plans were "impracticable" and that an attack on Isle-aux-Noix was out of the question because of its great strength and its difficult approach. His campaign, instead, would go across the plains of Acadie, bypassing the island. He declared that he would have fewer than four thousand effectives and he thought the enemy force numbered more than five thousand. Armstrong acquiesced.[7]

During the first half of September, intense activity took place in Burlington and Plattsburgh. In the latter place Hampton ordered the preparation of a hospital. Yet after having the men under his command all summer, Hampton had the nerve to tell Armstrong that they were "totally destitute of the least instruction. Too much must not be expected from us."[8] He requisitioned 400 militia from Mooers, who wondered why the request had not gone to the governor. Mooers told Tompkins that Hampton was obviously planning to make a "vigorous movement," but he feared the consequences if a large force was not committed to it, and he knew of none: "I do not believe Canada is so easily taken as General Hampton and some others expect. I feel anxious for the campaign—a defeat would be ruinous to this frontier & an eternal stigma." John Freligh of Plattsburgh echoed Mooers's concern about the small size of Hampton's force, believing that twenty thousand men would be required to take and hold Montreal. Mooers decided its aim was no more than a feint to cover a bigger operation westward.[9]

Leaving General Parker in command of a small garrison in Burlington, Hampton sent his army to Cumberland Head between the 10th and 16th of September, and on that date Hampton himself arrived. A vigorous impressment of horses was made on Grand Isle in order to mount the dragoons, and oxen were brought in to haul the heavy baggage. The huge movement went smoothly because, he said, "With McDonaugh's aid have put a stopper on the lake which ensures tranquility while my preparations are going on."[10] For this portion of the campaign, Macdonough's job was to prevent the British fleet from entering the lake. During the next stage, he convoyed the boatloads of men who rowed north from Cumberland Head on the 19th. They were off Chazy Landing by midnight and lay on their oars in bateaux, embarking soon after sunrise. They rowed up the Great Chazy River to the rapids and disembarked near Champlain village. The cavalry and artillery went to Champlain by land. Hampton's entire force of about four thousand men included militia, a squadron of cavalry, detached artillery with ten guns, and eight regiments of regulars. Two more regiments, the Tenth and the Thirty-second, were en route from New Hampshire.

In Canada the militia had been called out en masse, and once again all the roads and bridges near the border were obstructed. At Champlain two detachments of American troops rushed straight from their landing place to surprise the British outposts at Odelltown, but they lost their way. On the same day the whole army crossed into Canada to a depth of about three miles from Champlain. They were harassed but no engagement took place. Hampton did not need long to learn that the driest summer on record had left no water for either man or animal.

Calling his officers together that night, he asked for their advice. Because of the drought, "It was not a time to hesitate," he wrote Armstrong, and "there was but one voice," and that was for a pull back and an approach to Montreal through the valley of the Chateaugay River.[11] The army returned to Champlain on the 21st. Armstrong concurred with the decision but regretted that Hampton had not at least reached St. Jean. Hampton and his men left Champlain on the 22nd for Chazy. From there they marched a hot, fatiguing forty miles along the north bank of the Little Chazy to Four Corners, the village that is better known as Chateaugay, New York. They erected tents south and west of the site of the later railroad station, while Hampton, his staff, and black servants stayed in a tavern. During his absence, he left Brigadier General George Izard in command of a regiment at Plattsburgh, while General Thomas Parker remained in over-all command in Burlington.

Hampton's withdrawal from Clinton County again left the area exposed to enemy attack, and the clamors for protection mounted. The Third Brigade of the Division of Vermont militia (all the men from Vermont's Franklin County), were mustered by the federal government and marched to Champlain under Lieutenant Luther Dixon, leaving their own forty miles of border exposed. Since it was harvest time, all but 300 departed without leave. Among them was twenty-year-old Silas Gates, who went to St. Albans. Private Alva Sabin and Captain Asahel Langworthy's rifle company were sent to bring back Gates and the other deserters. When they found him, Gates at first appeared to be acquiescent, but then he ran away and Sabin shot him at twenty-five yards. Sabin was indicted for murder and tried in December; both then and a year later a hung jury saved him, but the case was not closed until December 1815. Sabin later became a Baptist preacher in the town of Georgia, went to the General Assembly and finally to Congress.[12]

The border still seemed to be relatively unsecured. Late in September, Melanchton Woolsey, former collector on Cumberland Head, complained that some British officers had wandered into his property, saying they were looking for General Parker. He thought some line must be drawn because during their visit the British saw the entire American camp nearby. The militia at Champlain tried to act belligerently, but their efforts were not very effective. Early in October, they attacked a British picket near the lines. The action brought forth a furious blast from Major J. Perrault, who had emerged as the best-known partisan fighter on the Canadian side of the border:

> Citizens of Champlain! — I am happy that humanity should still have so much power over me so as to inform you that should any of the militia of Champlain, be found hovering this side of the line, I will let loose upon your village and inhabitants, the Canadian and Indian force under my command. You are probably aware that it has been with greatest difficulty I have till now withheld them. But your cowardly attack at midnight, of a small picket of ours, has torn asunder the veil which hid you from them. — So beware![13]

In order to check Canadian boldness, Hampton at distant Four Corners ordered "a petty war near Lake Champlain." He explained to Armstrong that "what I am aiming at is tranquillity on the road, by kicking up a dust on the lines," in other words, a diversion to help his own campaign.[14] Colonel Isaac Clark in Burlington was ordered to make a raid into Missisquoi Bay, that part of Lake Champlain which expands into Canada east of the Alburg Peninsula. On October 12, he led 101 men by boat to the area of Philipsburg and Caldwell's Manor, where he ran into a militia force of about the same size under Major Joseph Powell. When Powell asked for a parley, he was ordered to the rear of the American line, and when his men prepared to charge, their captain and several men were shot. The rest surrendered, and a relief force marching to their aid was frightened into hasty retreat.

Clark took away 101 prisoners, leaving one British dead and eight wounded, of whom two later suffered amputations. Clark had no losses. He also took away horses, oxen, bedding, and wearing apparel. He returned to Missisquoi Bay on October 27 and drove off 90 head of cattle, apparently smuggled from Vermont, but the British saved about 170 head by driving them to Yamaska. Residents around the bay were in constant alarm, and many sent their movable property inland to Stanbridge and Dunham. It was the British counterpart to the American dilemma at Champlain.

Pliny Moore's journal starkly records the situation at Champlain:

Oct 28—Br. 300 here cmd by Maj. Perrault
Nov 2—Br. 1000 came out & robbed civilians
Nov 14—50 cavalry arr, stayed one night & dptd.
Nov 16—50 Br. soldiers & 3 off.[15]

American response was always belated to large raids because the militia had to be called out from rural areas and marched to the scene of trouble. Anticipating problems late in October, Parker in Burlington asked Mooers to support Macdonough with bateaux and to call out the militia. Mooers mustered Miller's regiment on October 29. Mooers wrote the governor about the invasion of the 28th and thought the British fleet was also coming; he feared for the safety of supplies at Plattsburgh. On November 3, he wrote Hampton to beg for troops; he told the general that since his departure the militia had been called out three times and that civilians were moving away in despair.

After the large raid of November 2, Pliny Moore told Parker:

It is now a war of the rifle & militia against the citizens & the declared purpose of some of their Commanding officers (whose views & feelings are very different from the Army) is to brake up the Alliance—the confederacy as they are pleased to term it & several I believe who have been sent here for our protection have been heard to say that they wished to see this Village sacked & burnt & it seems as if the measures pursued were calculated to that end.[16]

Ezra Thurber in Rouses Point echoed Moore's sentiments when he asked Mooers to persuade Parker to stop the American militia's raids across the line: "Can it accomplish any good on the general scale of national affairs. The fact is, us that lives on this frontier must pay for it—retaliation is determined on by the enemy." He said that a British guard of forty men had searched his house, threatened to make him a prisoner, and made him fearful of staying near the border.[17]

Luther's Third Brigade of Vermont militia saw a shadow of events to come when the newly chosen Federalist governor, Martin Chittenden, spoke to the Vermont legislature about the militia: "I have always considered this force peculiarly adapted, and exclusively assigned for the service and protection of the respective states." On November 10, he ordered the militia to return to Vermont with General Jacob Davis, whom he sent for them. He pointed out that "an extensive section of our own frontier is left unprotected" and the citizens "exposed to the retaliatory incursions and ravages of an exasperated enemy."[18]

Davis was arrested and held at Plattsburgh until he gave security of $5,000 to appear before the federal district court in New York City. Some of the rank and file went home quietly, but eighteen officers sent their governor a vigorous refusal. They considered his authority over them suspended during the war, and his order they regarded "with mingled emotions of pity and contempt for its author, and as a striking monument of his folly." They felt the order was "an unwarrantable stretch of executive authority, issued from the worst of motives, to effect the basest purposes. It is in our opinion, a renewed instance of that spirit of disorganization and anarchy which is carried on by a faction, to overwhelm our country with ruin and disgrace."[19]

Hampton, safely removed from this squabble, had been warned by Armstrong to proceed no farther than Four Corners "until you have advice of our movements," meaning Wilkinson's preparedness for a combined campaign.[20] Having been joined by some additional units, Hampton and his five thousand men waited twenty-six days for further word from Armstrong. In the interval he built a second blockhouse at Chateaugay named Fort Hampton, but more often Fort Hickory in honor of Andrew Jackson. It was four miles northeast of the village and a half mile south of the border. He also repaired the road to Plattsburgh and kept 400 wagons and 1,000 oxen in motion to bring supplies.

De Salaberry's 150 Voltigeurs and 100 Indians paralled Hampton's route to Four Corners and harassed his outposts at that station. Then the Canadians pulled back to block the road along the river. On October 19, Hampton finally received word that Wilkinson was ready at Sackets Harbor for his part of the campaign. The orders directed Hampton to move to the mouth of the Chateaugay where it enters the St. Lawrence, and there join forces with Wilkinson. Hampton moved out on October 21, leaving fifteen hundred militia, who refused to cross the line, to guard the stores and the road to Plattsburgh. All of his men were still in summer uniforms which were beginning to get threadbare, although the fall season had arrived with frosts and rain.

General Izard was detached early in the morning to clear the road along the Chateaugay. He did this successfully, so that the main body of the army reached the junction of the Chateaugay and Outardes rivers the next evening. Izard had taken a blockhouse near the present village of Ormstown, which Hampton expanded and used as a base. Meanwhile, the Canadian forces were gathering to block his progress. In addition to the Voltigeurs, they included part of the Canadian Fencibles, and a battalion of Select Embodied Militia under Lieutenant Colonel George Macdonell, who had made a wild dash by water and land from Kingston. Their total numbers were 1,590 men, fewer than a quarter of them militia and Indians, the rest almost entirely French Canadian regulars. They faced odds of four to one against them.[21]

De Salaberry decided to make his stand on the left bank of the river, about six miles below Hampton's position. He rapidly fortified it with breastworks and blockhouses, and he abatised the approaches. On the evening of the 25th, Hampton sent Colonel Robert Purdy of the Fourth Regiment and three regiments across to the right bank of the river in order to approach the British position at one of the fords. After an all-night struggle through swamps in the dark, repeatedly misled by his guides, he had only progressed six miles and was not near the fords by morning. Just after he left, Hampton learned of the quartermaster general's orders to construct huts for ten thousand men for the winter on the Chateaugay below the border. He immediately pondered the purpose of the campaign if the men were expected to winter in New York State. Since Purdy was already in motion and his own troops ready, he decided to proceed as planned.

Next morning he set the main army in motion, led by Izard. As he approached the abatis he listened for Purdy's firing at the ford, which would tell him he had engaged his opponents, but no sound arrived from that direction. At about ten o'clock the first shots were fired at Izard's lead party, and the ensuing battle lasted until three o'clock in the afternoon. Meanwhile, Hampton halted his movements until he knew Purdy's whereabouts.

At about eleven o'clock Purdy's men floundered out of a final swamp and faced a company of Chausseurs, with two companies of Macdonell's battalion on the way. By noon, Purdy's force was retiring before what it considered a large army of opponents. Sending word of his reverse to Hampton, he was told at two o'clock to retire four miles and cross the river to rejoin the main army.

Hampton waited until two o'clock to move. Then he ordered Izard to advance on a formidable abatis, where a sharp fire was exchanged. For the next hour the Canadians' success resulted almost entirely from their heavy firing and the sounding of bugle charges in all directions, which apparently misled Hampton into thinking his opponents had vast numbers. Realizing that he could expect no help from Purdy across the river, he ordered Izard to retire three miles to the point reached by the baggage train, where he made camp. In the last stages of the fight, Governor General Prevost arrived to witness the event. He had not had far to travel because the battle site was only thirty-five miles southwest of Montreal.

Purdy was not yet out of the swamps. Pursued closely as well as being fired on from the opposite bank, he pulled back in disorder to Round Point, where he and his men spent another wet, dangerous night. He rafted his men across the river for treatment by Hampton's surgeons, only to learn that

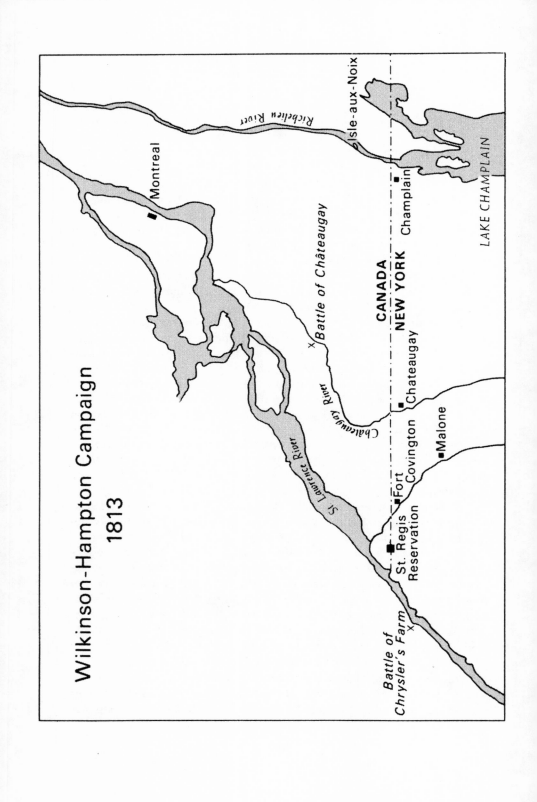

Wilkinson-Hampton Campaign
1813

Montreal

Richelieu River

Isle-aux-Noix

LAKE CHAMPLAIN

Champlain

Battle of Châteaugay

CANADA
NEW YORK

Châteaugay River

Chateaugay

Covington

Malone

St. Lawrence River

Fort

St. Regis
Reservation

Battle of
Chrysler's Farm

the main army had already retreated beyond that spot. He ordered the construction of a floating log bridge over which 100 men under Major Josiah Snelling crossed under fire and caught up with Hampton's rear, carrying the wounded with them. Most of Purdy's men forded the river and rejoined the army next day, although some of the fatigued and sick did not catch up with it until it reached Four Corners. Purdy later made an understandably bitter report of the action by accusing Hampton of being "under the influence of a too free use of spirtuous liquors," of interference, and of "the capriciousness of his conduct and the total want of steadiness in his intentions."[22]

Hampton remained at his base until October 28. He called a council of his officers and probably again heard what he wanted to: unanimously they favored withdrawal to save the army, and either go into winter quarters or prepare to fight elsewhere. Consequently, he marched his men back to Four Corners, beginning on the 28th and arriving on the 30th. The casualties of the expedition are still in dispute. Hampton said they were no more than fifty. Other knowledgeable sources give a range of from fifteen to seventy killed, twenty to thirty-three wounded, and sixteen to twenty-nine prisoners.[23]

A torrent of dispatches flowed between Hampton, Wilkinson, and Armstrong during November. A complication in the smooth flow was caused by the departure of Armstrong from Sackets Harbor before the Wilkinson expedition got under way. On November 1, Wilkinson finally started out by boat, but he did not know until the 6th that Hampton had retreated. Thus he fatuously proposed a change of plans on the 1st for Hampton either to threaten faraway Chambly or join him at the confluence of the Grand and St. Lawrence rivers. On the same day Hampton sent Armstrong his second resignation, "when I can neither feel security nor expect honor." On the 4th he gave Armstrong his reasons for pulling back, including the scarcity of supplies and the coming of winter, which was producing sickness in his troops, but especially that he had been kept "dangerously in the dark" about Wilkinson's movements.[24]

Meanwhile, Wilkinson was with great difficulty manouevering his eight-thousand-man army from Lake Ontario into the St. Lawrence, dodging British traps among the islands, and being subjected to fire from the shore. Yet on November 3, he asked Armstrong to notify Hampton of a new junction point (St. Regis), desiring Hampton to hear it from the secretary "as he has treated my authority with contempt, & has acted exclusively under your orders . . . that I may be saved the hazard of a second insult, for I need not say to you . . . that in this case my feelings shall be silences, and that I will humiliate myself to make the most of this pretender."

On the 6th, when he learned of Hampton's retreat, Wilkinson wrote him direct that "I am destined to and determined on the attack of Montreal, if not prevented by some act of God," and asked Hampton to join him at St. Regis if he was not in force to meet the enemy by himself, and to forward two or three months of supplies from Plattsburgh. On the 8th, Hampton assured Armstrong that "With these measures what can be accomplished by human exertion, I will attempt, with a mind devoted to the general objects of the campaign," but on the same day he refused to meet Wilkinson at St. Regis because Wilkinson's supplies were so low. However, he would try to open a route to Caughnawaga or any other point Wilkinson might name, from Plattsburgh to the northward.[25]

In the next few days, Wilkinson received a taste of hell himself. Edging his way through the river obstacles, he saw his men suffer agonies in open boats in cold, wet weather. He cleared the border and on November 10 stopped at Chrysler's farm on the north bank of the river. Learning of a British force approaching from the rear, he sent General John Parke Boyd and two thousand men on the offensive. The force he went out to meet was 800 men under Colonel J. W. Morrison, who had slipped out of Kingston and raced to overtake Wilkinson's army. Boyd's force was routed by Morrison at the battle of Chrysler's Farm on the 11th. The Americans lost 102 killed, 237 wounded, and about 100 taken prisoner, while the British loss was 22 killed, 48 wounded, and 12 missing.

Next day, when Wilkinson learned that Hampton refused to join him, he called a council of officers. Battling illness he, like Hampton, probably heard what he hoped to when the officers voted to call off the campaign and go into winter quarters. Congressman Winter later commented that "Wilkinson took the most plausible way, to persuade us that he was Victorious, which was—to arrive at a certain point was his object, and having accomplished that, in opposition to the views and exertions of the enemy, he thereby gained a victory of them."[26]

Hampton was still bombarding Armstrong with messages, attempting to explain his actions. On the 12th, he wrote concerning his men at Four Corners that fatigue, sickness, and bad weather "have deprived them of that spirit, which constituted my best hopes." Next day, however, he wrote equivocally that the inspector general, Henry Atkinson, would try to force a communication with Wilkinson at St. Regis. "The disposition of the enemy's force," he said, "must determine our success. . . . All that is possible, however, shall be attempted." Whether Hampton had not yet made up his mind what he would do or was not quite ready to say is not clear.[27]

However, between the 8th and the 12th Hampton took his army back to Plattsburgh. On the 15th, he notified Armstrong that his troops were going into winter quarters and he intended to go south, asking permission to leave the military district; he also accused Wilkinson of being inconsistent and of making ugly insinuations in his letters. From this point onward, charges and countercharges were exchanged as each general attempted to place the blame for his own failings on the other. Of the two, Wilkinson's accusations were the more strident. Pointing out how lightly Montreal was garrisoned, he mourned, "What a golden, glorious opportunity has been lost by the caprice of Major General Hampton." Two days later he wrote of Hampton: "He chose to recede, in order to co-operate."[28]

On the 17th, Wilkinson wrote directly to Hampton, sending general orders for him to return immediately to Four Corners with every effective man and one month's supplies. At first Hampton agreed to march back to Four Corners, but since he had discharged all the militia, three thousand barrels of provisions would be left unprotected in Plattsburgh. Next day Wilkinson changed the orders to Hampton's sending only certain units to Four Corners to protect the stores there. On the 26th, Wilkinson flatly blamed the failure of the campaign on Hampton and sent an aide-de-camp to arrest him in Plattsburgh on charges of "disobedience of orders." The trial was to be held in Plattsburgh, and Hampton was to return there if he had departed.[29]

Warned by a friend, Hampton pressed a steamer into public service and left on November 23 for Whitehall and straight through to Washington. Eleazer Williams tried to reach a balanced assessment of the man by recording: "In fact he lacked judgment, and adhered too much to ignorant and evil advisers, but he is in the main, a brave, and good officer, who wishes to sustain the honor of his country." William Duane, later Andrew Jackson's secretary of the treasury, could not be objective about Hampton for he said, "I would not trust a corporal's guard nor the defense of a hen-roost to him against any equal number of men. His obliquity of mind and judgment would sacrifice anything military placed under his command."[30]

At first Armstrong intended to call a court of inquiry into Hampton's conduct, but in the spring the president decided to accept the general's resignation. Perhaps his wealth and political following helped him escape the court-martial that conduct like his had brought to others. Furthermore, Armstrong had shifted the blame for the fiasco on Wilkinson and had begun to prepare for his court-martial. Hampton returned to private life in South Carolina and became one of the wealthiest planters in the country. He lived to the age of eighty-four years.

The chief memorial to Hampton in the North Country is the Plattsburgh Air Base, which is merely an extension of the cantonment he started in November 1813. He preempted much of the land on the peninsula which separates the Saranac River and Lake Champlain and started the construction of barracks and other facilities. The timber on the property was used on the buildings and the fences provided fuel for the winter. The owners, Pliny

Moore and Levi Platt, petitioned for a year and a half for payment from the government. The issue became involved with New York's relinquishing jurisdiction and with the belief, stated by the secretary of war, that a permanent military post should be nearer the border. In February 1816, Congress finally acquired the property in Plattsburgh; meanwhile, it had become the site for three large forts in 1814.[31]

Wilkinson was reduced to frustrated denunciations of Hampton for the rest of the winter. Not yet aware that he too was under suspicion, he began as early as November to propose grand plans for taking Isle-aux-Noix and Montreal, but inconsistently he also hoped to winter in Albany and leave Izard in command. Hampton had already designated Izard as his successor in Plattsburgh. Izard reported that the supply situation was chaotic and the streets of the town filled with vast quantities of public stores. As acting quartermaster general he appointed Colonel Melancton Smith, whose first undertaking was to get supplies off to Wilkinson in his winter quarters. Unaccountably, Wilkinson ordered Izard and the portion of the army that had not gone to Burlington to join him at French Mills. Again, the Plattsburgh front was to be abandoned.[32]

The supplying from Plattsburgh of Wilkinson's troops had collapsed under Hampton's quartermaster. Added to the other miseries of his men was, consequently, a shortage of provisions. He had taken them three miles into Salmon River and chosen French Mills for his winter quarters. The vanguard arrived on November 13, two days after the battle. The settlement included a grist mill, a saw mill, a blockhouse, and a few houses. To honor General Leonard Covington, who died on the 13th, he named the blockhouse Fort Covington, and the town later took the same name. The blockhouse could not hold all the sick and wounded, and the overflow was sheltered in tents and shanties. Huts were begun, but very few were completed in the next month. The hardships of the recent campaign immediately began to be manifested. Thousands of men had spent much of the previous twelve days in open boats on the St. Lawrence, exposed to November winds, rain and frost. The makeshift shelters were completely inadequate to protect the men from the onset of illness.

Wilkinson settled down for the winter in the Harrison mansion in Malone, eighteen miles away, whence he was borne in a litter by eight men. There he ordered the acquisition of buildings to serve as a hospital for 450 men, but many of the sick still had to remain at French Mills because of sheer numbers: one-third of his 6,000 men were unfit for duty at one time. His army was literally disintegrating around him: The desertion rate was high of men who started for home or Canada. Leaves and discharges reduced the ranks. Corruption was rampant at French Mills, where officers trafficked in supplies and with the British, or carried the deserters and dead on the rosters, pocketing their pay.

Wilkinson still had time to grieve over Hampton's escape, and he told Armstrong in December: "I will not charge this man with traitorous Designs, but I apprehend in any other Government, a military Officer who just defeated the object of a campaign by *Disobedience* of orders & then, without authority, furloughed all the *efficient Officers* of the Division he commanded on a national Frontier, in the vicinity of an Enemy, would incur heavy penalties." Nor had he lost any of his bombast on other matters. He promised Plattsburgh citizens immediate protection when they petitioned him for it: "Devoted to the service of our common country next to its independence and honor, it is a duty, as pleasing to me as it is solemn to afford all the protection in the power of the troops I command, to the persons and property of my fellow citizens." He was as good as his word and sent units from Burlington and his own army. He also had time to dream of great military ventures in the future for, he wrote, "I am desirous the troops under my command, should not eat the bread of idleness."[33]

The troops whom he did not want to be "idle" were experiencing great anguish during that terrible winter. Dr. Mann arrived in Plattsburgh early in December to put the hospitals, "now in extreme disorder, under some regulations."[34] He found heavy casualties already occurring among the men from diseases similar to those of the previous winter. The troops were still living in tents while the barracks were being built, and meanwhile construction of the hospital was neglected in the rush for materials. It was being built of planks and boards rather than logs, which the surgeon general, Dr. James Tilton favored, because the logs would need to be hauled from a distance whereas the planks were available from nearby sawmills.

Mann pushed on to Malone, where the need was even greater, and reached there on December 15. He found that the academy, arsenal, and two private houses had been appropriated as hospitals. Within 10 days he had 250 men in individual beds, warm even during the coldest weather. He noticed an improvement in the men as soon as they were able to move from the tents at French Mills, where large numbers were still incapacitated because of the lack of room at Malone. By February 1st, he had 450 sick at Malone and another 200 at French Mills. Between January 1st and February 9th, admissions at Malone numbered 380, deaths 20. Mann quoted a morning report in December of a 160-man unit in which 75 were sick: 39 with diarrhea and dysentery, 18 pneumonia, 6 typhus, and 12 with paralysis of all the extremities. He had great difficulty keeping up with the flow of the sick from French Mills, which surpassed the hospital's capacity, supplies, nurses, and washwomen. He was particularly distressed that so many arrived from French Mills without their papers, beds, or blankets, noting that six died in transit from the cold.[35]

The men at French Mills were not properly housed before the first of the year, and they had only a month to enjoy their relative comfort. Armstrong ordered the place abandoned and Wilkinson's entire army moved to Plattsburgh and Burlington. The destruction at French Mills was started on February 3. The new huts were destroyed, 328 small boats were sunk or burned, and nonportable stores were burned or dumped in the river, although quantities of supplies were left behind in the haste to get away. Brigadier General Jacob Brown and two thousand men were ordered to Sackets Harbor; the rest went to Plattsburgh except for the sick and wounded, who were to go to Burlington. The 50-mile trip was hardest on the 450 casualties. They were sent in sleighs successively put in motion so that when the first arrived in Plattsburgh, the last were leaving Malone. Snow or rain fell for the entire journey; six died, but some others actually showed improvement. Twenty of the sickest men were left behind where they were taken prisoner by the British. However, they merely had to sign paroles, and most of them eventually showed up at the hospital in Burlington. Wilkinson made the trip by sleigh, walking briefly when his legs would support him.

Hardly had Wilkinson's army left Franklin County than the British moved in. They raided Constable and carried off 100 sleighloads of public provisions sent out from Plattsburgh. Then strong detachments moved into Malone and Chateaugay, where they found hundreds of barrels of pork and flour. The troops and the Indians were kept under tight rein and private property was respected. After the Malone raid, about sixty Irish troops deserted and said that half of their regiment would do the same if they got a chance.

Whether from the first or a subsequent raid on Chateaugay, the British looted the Masonic rooms, and the Masonic jewels and a carpet were stolen. Gates Hoit followed the troops to the vicinity of Cornwall and left a note for the commanding officer. The note was forwarded to a lodge in Montreal and subsequently the Montreal brothers presented Chateaugay with jewels and a carpet more valuable than the stolen ones. One of these jewels is now a part of the collection of the Grand Lodge Museum in New York City.[36] Hoit, who had been one of the stalwart defenders of the county throughout the war, was given $300 for his secret services by Congress in 1832. The second raid into Chateaugay brought a plea for protection to Wilkinson in Plattsburgh. He sent a strong detachment which, however, reversed direction and returned to Plattsburgh when they learned that the British had pulled back. Franklin County had to learn to live with the British for the rest of the war; fortunately, the severe actions of 1814 took place on other fronts.

Dr. Mann accompanied Wilkinson's casualties to Burlington, "a new heaven and a new earth," as he called the facilities. He reached there on February 16, when half of the sick had already arrived and had joined 160 of Hampton's casualties. He called it the best regulated hospital on the northern front, with clean, bright, and well-ventilated wards. He added to the facilities by taking over twenty rooms in the barracks and instituted the whitewashing of walls with lime and water. A fresh coat of sand was applied to the floors daily; bunks were removed and cleaned after every occupancy, and the straw of the sacks was burned.

Mann remained in Burlington for five months and brought it to a peak of cleanliness and efficiency. At one period during the winter he had between 700 and 800 patients in 40 wards adminstered by 8 surgeons and surgeon's mates. March was the most sickly month, with 931 admissions and 29 deaths. The dead from January through April numbered ninety-five men. The diseases were similar to those of the previous winter, and he instituted heavy bleeding, aided by cathartics, calomel, and opium in small doses, or blisters on the chest. He learned from experience that too long or copious use of acetite of lead brought complications and eventual death, but he also discovered that he could obtain cures for syphilis of long standing by the use of nitromuriate of gold.[37]

Thus the dreary winter wore on for sick and well alike. There were other problems than sickness, however. In December, a damaging British raid occurred at Derby, Vermont, where public storehouses and barracks were burned. This is the event that led the Plattsburgh leaders to ask for protection from Wilkinson. Then there was always smuggling, which continued unabated all winter. In December, Sailly declared war on the buying of Canadian horses and the paying for them with steers and cows: "I would not be justifiable, Sir, however inclined I might be, to Countenance the exportation of Cattle to Canada on any pretext whatever." From Vermont came the report that 120 yoke of oxen had "gone over" to the British to help transport their military stores, which Hezakiah Niles called "very neighborly."[38] The military forces at Burlington and Plattsburgh were in no condition to pursue smugglers, and Macdonough had gone into winter quarters at Vergennes.

9

THE THIRD TENSE SUMMER: 1814

During the winter, a promotion elevated George Izard to the rank of major general and Alexander Macomb to brigadier. In each case they were recognitions of military qualities displayed in previous campaigns, and each was a sign of progress in the administration's weeding out of the old and unfit in favor of the young and vigorous.

Izard at thirty-eight years of age had had a military education in Europe. His army career started in 1797, but he resigned in the cut-backs of the Jefferson years. During the War of 1812, bad luck followed him in the form of frequent transfers, usually against his own judgment. From the defense of New York City he was orderd to Hampton's command in 1813, where there were few honors to be gained, especially at Chateaugay. He succeeded Wilkinson at Plattsburgh, only to be ordered away shortly before the big battle.

At thirty-two, Macomb was one of the youngest generals in the army. He served a brief tour between 1798 and 1800; in 1801 he was back in the army to stay. He went through West Point in its first class and then served as chief engineer for seven years in the south Atlantic area. Before the war he was made adjutant general of the army; when hostilities began, he succeeded after many petitions in getting a field appointment. He was in command of the army units at Sackets Harbor during the first winter, took part in Dearborn's spring campaigns at York and Niagara, and in the fall went with Wilkinson down the St. Lawrence.

After Wilkinson brought his army to Plattsburgh in February, he sent Macomb to command the Burlington brigade. It consisted of the Ninth, Twenty-first, and Twenty-fifth regiments, while the rest of the army, except the sick, remained in Plattsburgh. Nathan B. Haswell, acting commissary in Burlington, left a record of a soldier's daily ration at that time: 1½ pounds of beef or ¾ pound of pork, 18 ounces of bread or flour, and a gill of rum, whiskey, or brandy; with every 100 rations also went 2 quarts of salt, 4 quarts of vinegar, 4 pounds of soap, and 1½ pounds of candles.[1]

All winter Wilkinson had Napoleonic dreams of conquest. Disregarding the condition of his demoralized and disease-ridden army, on January 7 he thought he could take either St. Jean on the Richelieu or Cornwall on the St. Lawrence. On January 16, he went to ask Governor Tompkins for a thousand militia for his plans, which now were aimed at Kingston and Prescott in Upper Canada: "Charge me not with caprice for thus suddenly varying my plan of operations," he asked Armstrong. Only two days later, although Tompkins had agreed with the Kingston-Prescott project, Wilkinson now thought a direct attack on Montreal was better![2]

Whether in an effort to retrieve his sagging reputation or not, he decided to pursue the Montreal plan. This prompted Congressman Shepherd to write: "Debility often produces awful spasms which are the precursors of dissolution & death and we may with reason calculate that the same causes in the body politic will produce the same effects as in the human body."[3] Nevertheless, Wilkinson brought his entire force of four thousand men from Burlington and Plattsburgh to Chazy and Champlain, an enormous enterprise in itself; this was accomplished just after the middle of March. From Chazy he sent Macomb and a detachment across the ice in sleighs to Swanton, and from there on the 22nd, they raided Philipsburg on Missisquoi Bay.

Macomb was also sent on a scouting mission to gauge the possibility of taking Isle-aux-Noix over the ice. The British, fearing such an effort, had been keeping the ice broken all around the island. Wilkinson in consequence apparently intended to bypass the island and campaign down the west side of the Richelieu. Macomb remonstrated as vocally as a subordinate officer could, pointing out what a strong British defense and roads deep in snow and mud could do to an invading army. Eleazer Williams, whose corps had been ordered to scout the island and the stone mill at Lacolle, also warned against the campaign, but he recorded in his journal: "The General could not see any hindrances to his intended invasion. The honor of the army *must* be retrieved."[4] A council of officers considered three routes and picked the one by way of the mill.

The first objective, Lacolle Mill (modern Cantic, Quebec), lay on the south bank of the Lacolle River, with a blockhouse on the north side. The Mill was actually a three-story stone fortification, a strong outpost for Isle-aux-Noix five miles away. It had eighteen-inch walls and heavy timbers in the windows with loopholes for muskets. The approach from the south was flat and half inundated by the melting snows, while the roads were blocked by fallen trees. It was manned by 200 men, mostly regulars of the Thirteenth

Regiment, but during the engagement several hundred reinforcements managed to reach it and swell its defenders to nearly 1,000 men.

On March 30, Wilkinson put his army in motion. Since some of the units had eight miles to go, it was afternoon before the engagement could begin, and to complicate matters, ignorant guides led the army astray. Sergeants were ordered to fire on any who tried to desert. Macomb attempted to bring up an eighteen-pound cannon, but the ground was too soft. The best he could do was bring into the action 12-pounders and 5½-inch mortars. From 250 yards, their fire was ineffective, and the mill remained unharmed. Even the musket fire from 150 yards was inaccurate except during the British sallies from the mill or the arrival of reinforcements. The fire from the mill was so galling that Wilkinson could not bring himself to order a charge. After two hours the attack petered out, and about sunset the army pulled back to Odelltown for the night, and to Champlain next day, where it remained for a week.

The losses in this futile engagement were, for the British, ten dead, forty-six wounded, and four missing. American casualties were 13 dead, 128 wounded, and 13 missing. During the retreat, Julius Hubbell's law office in Chazy (the present public library) was used as a temporary hospital. Yet attempting to put a bold face on the whole operation and in spite of the fact that the secretary of war had admonished him against an incursion into Canada, Wilkinson wrote him: "So small an affair does not merit so tedious a detail, but it warrants the remark that it will produce a degree of self confidence, of reciprocal trust, of harmony and friendly attachments in this corps highly beneficial to the service. It is a lesson of command to the officers, and of obedience to the soldier, worth a whole year's drill of empty parades." In general orders on the same day he proclaimed that "The affair of yesterday is honorable to the troops, and gives them a title to the thanks of the general and their country."[5]

Wilkinson's days were already numbered. Actually, Armstrong had removed him from command on March 24, but he did not receive the letter until he was back in Plattsburgh from Canada. He was told that a court of inquiry would be held at Lake George on April 25. The president of the court would be General Izard, and it would contain two brigadiers and two colonels; Wilkinson could object if the size was too small. He proclaimed his outraged innocence to an Albany friend on April 9: "I confess to you, that, after four or five years of remorseless persecution, during which painful period, my character has been mangled and lacerated throughout the nation, I reluctantly obtrude myself on the public, to refute those modern slanders and . . . the continued menaces vomited forth by certain public prints."[6]

Wilkinson turned over command of the Northern Army to Brigadier

General Macomb as the ranking officer in the absence of Major General Izard, who was at Lake George for the court-martial. Wilkinson started south on April 19, and went to Lake George, but absented himself from the proceedings. He objected to the small court, the junior rank of its members, and the fact, he said, that he did not yet know the charges against him. Izard and three other members of the court appeared, but the fifth did not, so the trial was called off. Armstrong then told Wilkinson to choose Philadelphia, Baltimore, or Annapolis as his residence and to await further orders, but he tarried at Lake George until the middle of May, then proceeded leisurely to New York. There he was served with an arrest warrant and the charges against him. He went to Washington late in June and managed to get the restrictions on his residence removed. The secretary of war had no option but to postpone the trial until high-ranking officers had concluded their summer campaigns; although it was caused by himself, Wilkinson chafed at the delay in obtaining justice.

The court-martial was finally scheduled for January 3, 1815, at Utica. It consisted of thirteen generals and colonels, with Major General Dearborn, much against his will, as president. Owing to the lack of accommodations at Utica, the trial was rescheduled for the courthouse at Troy on January 16. Martin Van Buren, a civilian, was named as a "special judge-advocate," but Wilkinson objected and won his point.

The four charges and seventeen specifications were all connected to the northern front in 1813–14 and included items such as delays, poor tactical judgment, neglect of provisions and stores, and scandalous drunkenness, and willful lying. They were poorly worded and not specific, and the court found him not guilty on March 21. Lurking behind the decision was the unformulated conviction that others should share the blame for the collapse of the campaigns in 1813. However, in the postwar reduction of the army to ten thousand men, the aging general was given no place, and his military career was at an end after forty years. He spent the next year exculpating himself in three volumes of memoirs.

Back in the North Country, Macomb inherited a demoralized and sickly army. As late as May 17, men died at the Burlington hospital. Macomb asked Governor Chittenden to call out the militia to serve at Burlington and Vergennes. Perhaps he wished he had not because he found that "The difficulties made by them on being collected for muster was truly ridiculous & I deem it my duty to say that no reliance can be placed on them as a source of defense." A month later it was the same: "With respect to the militia I have only to remark they did not give us even an opportunity of mustering them and they very soon discharged themselves."[7]

Macombs's command was of short duration, however, because Izard ar-

Maj. Gen. Alexander Macomb (1782–1841) in 1825. Plaster life mask by John H. I. Browere. *Photograph courtesy of the New York State Historical Association, Cooperstown, N.Y.*

rived on May 1 and took over. He made his headquarters on the New York side of the lake, leaving Macomb in charge of the brigade at Burlington. Among the other problems he inherited from the Wilkinson regime was the necessity of constructing a fortification somewhere on the lake. On March 4, Wilkinson and Major Joseph Totten of the engineers had reconnoitred Rouses Point, looking for a place for a heavy battery that would keep the British fleet in the Richelieu. Wilkinson's repulse at Lacolle taught him the difficulties he would have in building and maintaining a fortification so near the border, and he began to favor Point au Roche. Totten, however, vetoed that site because there was no harbor or suitable place for an encampment. This unfinished business awaited Izard's attention.

In May, Armstrong ordered Izard to plant a heavy battery either at Rouses Point or at the mouth of the Lacolle River. Izard demurred because Ash Island and the Lacolle were in British hands, while the Rouses Point site offered no room for defensive work in its rear and would be very hazardous to occupy. Instead, on his own and despite Totten, he selected a location on Cumberland Head and during July he installed a battery of four eighteen-pounders, with a redoubt on the high ground to its rear. Known as Fort Izard, it proved useless in preventing the British fleet from entering the lake, which is too wide for effective cannon fire, and it was never used although the guns were mounted for a few weeks. More important, he started the construction of three forts at Plattsburgh.[8]

Izard also had a disorderly army to try to whip into shape. When he arrived on May 1, he found only two thousand raw, ill-clad, and poorly disciplined effectives. Many were one-year men about to be discharged. The dragoons were without clothing, their arms were useless, and they had not been paid for months; riflemen had not been paid for more than a year, and desertions were common. There were even desertions among troops en route: of 100 recruits at Greenbush, 26 deserted on the road to Whitehall. Izard's southern prejudices also emerged; he reported the annoyance of his officers and men when a detachment of Negroes arrived with the New England troops, and since his men objected to doing duty with them Izard organized them as "a sort of Pioneers."[9]

Both Macomb and Izard complained about the quality of their officers, Macomb finding them "totally destitute of military discipline & pride." Learning of the punishment of soldiers privately by whipping, Izard in general orders told his officers to put a stop to the practice, and admonished them: "The officer of every grade is not only the leader of men, entrusted to his charge in the hour of battle; but should be their protector, guardian and friend, in the repose of camp or quarters." At first Armstrong merely clucked at conditions, but he finally told Izard to accept the resignations of "all officers whose past conduct gives no pledge of future usefulness."[10]

The officers were not the only troublemakers. In both Burlington and Plattsburgh, the rank and file, unpaid and idle, found time to get into mischief. In March, all of them were moved a mile out of the village of Plattsburgh to the cantonment. Even then, they tore down fences between the two sites. Suits and remonstrances preoccupied the authorities on both sides of the lake. In Burlington, rumors circulated among the townspeople that the army intended to burn certain houses in the village. A meeting of officers on May 20 prepared a public denial of the report.

Soldiers were not the only offenders because civilians sometimes vented their disgust with the military. Six justices of the peace in Plattsburgh issued a warning in May against the "disorderly practise of discharging firearms" in the village as "absolutely hostile to the public safety."[11] Civilian-military tensions continued high all summer and culminated in Colonel John Fenwick's letter to Judge Henry Delord in Plattsburgh, less than a month before the British invasion:

> Very great irregularity exists amongst some of the inhabitants of the Village & I can scarcely believe such persons can be Americans. Even in times of peace discharging of fire arms is not allowed where any police is established & in time of war it must be attended with serious consequences. Alarms are created, the soldiery may be irritated, & in themselves attempt redress. This remark may apply in the case of this day. One of my men was wounded this morning by a musket ball discharged by some licentious or ill disposed person. I pray you, sir, to cause enquiry to be made in this case. As a magistrate I will assure myself you will conceive it your duty to suppress such acts. As the father of a family & a good citizen you will equally feel bound to protect both, who cannot walk the streets of Plattsburgh without exposure & risque of losing their lives. Besides, it is in violation of the orders of your magistracy, declaring it a breach of the peace, & also of a Genl Order which I shall enforce. I understand my Patrol was threaten'd a few nights ago.[12]

There were also problems with the military stores. An inspection in March uncovered the fact that horse meat was labelled as prime beef, that hard bread, beef, and pork were not edible, and that brine was leaking from the barrels. In August, when provisions and clothing were sent to Whitehall for safekeeping, Peter Sailly commented that it was "scattered" by others' orders than his own; some of it went to the forts in barrels as part of the defense works, and some was stolen or allowed to spoil.[13]

Hopeful signs were also not lacking. The most promising development was the productive winter Macdonough had spent at Vergennes. This village of 835 people lay seven miles up a winding Otter Creek, and Macdonough built a shipyard at the foot of the falls. There was an abundant source of water power on the river, plenty of timber nearby, and usable veins of iron at Monkton, a few miles away. At or near the falls were eight forges, blast, and air furnaces, rolling mills, wire factory, grist, saw, and fulling mills. Before the 1814 campaign the works produced, among other items, a thousand thirty-two pound cannon balls.[14]

On January 28, Secretary of the Navy Jones directed Macdonough to build about fifteen gunboats or a ship and three or four gunboats. At all costs, he said, "The object is to have no doubt of your commanding the lake and the waters connected, and that in due time. You are therefore authorized to employ such means and workmen as shall render its accomplishment certain."[15]

Macdonough chose to build a ship because sailors were hard to obtain and fifteen gunboats would require more men than one ship. Eventually, he built both as he heard about the British construction at Isle-aux-Noix. He was fortunate in having the services of Noah and Adam Brown, who had constructed Perry's fleet on Lake Erie the year before. They thought they could have the ship done in sixty days, but they outdid themselves and completed it in forty. Timber was still standing on March 2, but the keel was laid on the 7th, and she was put into the water on April 11. She still had no guns, anchors, cables, or rigging because they had not arrived. Orders were slowly filled, the roads were bad, and heavy loads were out of the question. One consignment at Troy was put together for eighty teams, but they still left three heavy cables behind. Much of the shot came from Boston, but some of it was produced at Vergennes. By May, the necessary supplies had arrived but not the men. The *Saratoga*, 143 feet of fighting ship, carried 26 guns of heavy caliber: eight 24-pounders, twelve 32s and six 42s.

Macdonough and the whole North Country knew that a naval race with the British was under way, but they felt exposed until Macdonough could finish his fleet. Fearful of an incursion by the British fleet before Macdonough was ready, Wilkinson asked the governor of Vermont for help from the militia. The governor ordered out 1,500 men, 500 of whom he sent to Burlington, and 1,000 to Vergennes to guard the fleet. Macdonough apparently found them a mixed blessing. The militia guard room was above his office in the village. One day a careless discharge of firearms sent a bullet through the ceiling which nearly hit him. Outraged, he told the commander: "If you will take your militia home I will take care of the fleet. I am in more danger from your men than from the enemy."[16] Macomb eventually replaced most of the militia with regulars, except for Captain William Munson's company from the adjacent town of Panton.

Macdonough needed trained seamen, not more militia. He appealed repeatedly to the Navy Department and was often referred to the army. He suspected that the men were being sent in reply to Chauncey's more strident demands for Lake Ontario. Macdonough's recruiter at the New York shipyards signed up about thirty; another fourteen came from Marblehead and Salem, and twenty-seven from Boston. During April, Macomb sent 270 soldiers to help man the fleet; they went reluctantly, and Macdonough was unhappy over the necessity of using landlubbers at all. Nevertheless, his needs were growing. He was still constructing gunboats and converting other vessels to military use. He had launched the *Saratoga* and was about finished with the refitting of the steamboat *Ticonderoga* from civilian to military use.

Late in May, Izard ordered Macomb in Burlington to provide another 100 men, but Armstrong gave Izard a stern lecture:

> The call of the Navy for soldiers as substitutes for marines or seamen, or for the protection of ships building or built or laid up to avoid the enemy, are becoming frequent & producing a very considerable diversion from our field strength, and if yielded to without the most distinct understanding that the supply is temporary & will be withdrawn whenever wanted for military purposes, will extinguish all effort on the part of that Department to furnish itself. . . . Be explicit therefore with Captain [sic] Macdonough, otherwise he will expect from you this campaign as much if not more aid than he had the last one from General Hampton.[17]

Izard passed on these strictures, but Macdonough reminded him that he had constantly importuned his own service. Izard reluctantly allowed his previous assignment of troops to stand but deplored the "injustice to the men and the mortification to their officers" of using army men in the navy. He felt that he had no alternative because if Macdonough had had to stay in Otter Creek another week, Plattsburgh would have been out of bread. However, he switched to volunteers in order to remove as much dissatisfaction as possible, but he soon found that "some officers whose principal importance in the army consists in the talent of being dissatisfied with everything have discouraged their men from coming forward."[18]

Because of the fear of a British raid before Macdonough was ready to cope with it, attention was also given to fortifying the mouth of Otter Creek. Macdonough's absence allowed British ships to interfere with traffic between Plattsburgh and Burlington — Izard said they "sculk behind the islands."[19] If Otter Creek, though narrow, was deep enough to float Macdonough's fleet, it was also capable of admitting British ships. Consequently, in mid-April, Wilkinson met Governor Chittenden at Vergennes in order to consider the needs, and then Wilkinson and Macdonough picked the site for a battery where the creek entered the lake. Known as Fort Cassin for one of Macdonough's trusted officers, its guns would come from the navy, and the engineers and men would be provided by Macomb in Burlington. It was ultimately armed with seven twelve-pounders on ship's carriages.

The worst fears were realized on May 9, when Captain Pring entered the lake. His winter at Isle-aux-Noix had also been profitable, and he was able to sail with the new twenty-gun brig *Linnet*, six sloops, and ten galleys. He had also had difficulty in manning his fleet, and at one point Prevost brought some naval officers to Isle-aux-Noix to persuade them of the needs. Nevertheless Pring, like Macdonough, was forced to use army men to meet his shortages.

Pring anchored behind Providence Island from the 10th to the 13th. During this period, by questioning some Americans in a small boat he first learned about the size of the twenty-six-gun *Saratoga*. More determined than ever to try to enter Otter Creek and destroy the ship, he set sail on the 13th and anchored off Split Rock. Next morning he was off the mouth of the creek. Meanwhile, the alarm had spread, and militia calls went out on both sides of the lake. Macomb received the warning on the 10th and sent fifty light artillery men under Captain Arthur Thornton to man the battery, while Lieutenant Stephen Cassin supported him with sailors. From a distance of two and a half miles, Pring opened a bombardment on Fort Cassin which dismounted one gun and slightly wounded two men. The guns of the battery responded with such vigor that Pring was deterred from approaching any more closely and after about an hour and a half sailed away. The fort saved Macdonough's small fleet and gave him the opportunity to complete his work.[20]

On the same day, on his way north, Pring sent three galleys up the Bouquet River to the falls at Willsboro, looking for public property which he did not know had been moved. Lieutenant Colonel Ransom Noble had gathered the Essex County militia the day before, and at the incursion of the galleys he marched for the mouth of the river. He caught one galley in such heavy fire that it had to be towed away, but he sustained two wounded men in the action. The British proceeded on their way back to Canada, stopping long enough at Rouses Point to destroy the public stores of provisions maintained by Peter Sailly and Elbert Anderson.[21]

One of Pring's benefits from the raid was information about the *Saratoga;* by summer the British were hastily building the biggest war vessel ever to sail on Lake Champlain, with Simons still in charge of construction. Meanwhile, Macdonough sailed out into the lake on May 26, and immediately controlled it. His fleet consisted of the ship *Saratoga* of twenty-six guns, the schooner *Ticonderoga* with sixteen, the sloop *President* with ten, the sloop *Preble* of nine, the sloop *Montgomery* of six, and six gunboats with two guns each. The gunboats were seventy-five by fifteen feet, manned with forty oars. The *Frances* and the *Wasp*, used during the previous season, had been disarmed and returned to their owners because of their poor sailing qualities.

Macdonough patrolled the lake all summer and thus was able to help suppress rampant smuggling operations. Throughout the conflict massive trade with the British in Canada and overseas was carried on by the New England states and New York. Before the war, British troops in Spain and Portugal had depended upon the United States for foodstuffs. This trade was continued after 1812 under licenses issued by the British admiralty to large numbers of American ships. The licenses were openly bought and sold by brokers in the large American cities. They served to pass the ships through the blockade free from British capture. British admirals and governors also issued licenses for trade with Nova Scotia, New Brunswick, Newfoundland, and the British West Indies. Large quantities of English manufactures were imported into the United States and substantial sums of American currency found their way into Canada. The Maritime Provinces prospered as never before; the commercial states of New England also profited from their sale of manufactured goods in the South, and their market for foodstuffs abroad.

The most flagrant trading with the enemy occurred in the valleys of Lake Champlain and the St. Lawrence. During the summer of 1814, Izard graphically described the situation:

> From the St. Lawrence to the ocean an open disregard prevails for the laws prohibiting intercourse with the enemy. The road to St. Regis is covered with droves of cattle, and the river with rafts destined for the enemy. The revenue officers see these things, but acknowledge their inability to put a stop to such outrageous proceedings. On the eastern side of Lake Champlain, the high roads are found insufficient for the supplies of cattle which are pouring into Canada; like herds of buffalo they press through the forest making paths for themselves. . . . Nothing but a cordon of troops from the French Mills to Lake Memphremagog could effectively check the evil. Were it not for these supplies the British forces in Canada would soon be suffering from famine, or their government subjected to enormous expense for their maintenance.[22]

The few agents charged with halting this traffic in New York included four at French Mills, one each at Malone and Chateaugay, five at Chazy and Champlain, and Ezra Thurber and five sailors with a revenue cutter at Rouses Point. They faced armed and determined smugglers who either avoided or overpowered the agents sent after them. They attacked a party of customs officers at Georgia, Vermont, and a British detachment seized the collector at Alburg and took about $1,000, of which $700 was collections. The smuggling of cattle was the most pervasive activity, because British contractors paid $10 to $12 a hundredweight. They were brought from downstate New York and from all over Vermont and New Hampshire. Sailly commented: "I foresee that all the cattle of Vermont and eastwardly, will find their way to Canada, and I fear our own troops hereafter may suffer the want of meat."[23]

In the fall, seven farmers from Chateaugay drove thirty-three head of cattle toward Canada. Near the border they were overtaken by the collector of customs who, with three assistants, drove the cattle sixteen miles toward Plattsburgh. Then a party of ten armed men from Canada attacked them and started for Canada with the men and cattle. Finally, they were overtaken by American citizens acting as volunteers, and the cattle were delivered to the collector in Plattsburgh. Some idea of the scope of the smuggling activities may be obtained merely by looking at the numerous advertisements in the Plattsburgh paper of goods captured and auctioned by the federal government.

More immediately threatening than the traffic in foodstuffs were the repeated attempts to supply the shipbuilders at Isle-aux-Noix with the materials they needed. On June 28, Sailing Master Elie Lavalette intercepted two spars that were being towed near the border. One was eighty-five and the other eighty feet long, and they were obviously intended for the British *Confiance*, whose construction was in the planning stages. On July 7, Midshipman Joel Abbott captured four more spars near the border, and from their size they appeared to have been cut for a mainmast and three topmasts. On the 23rd, two American gunboats captured a raft with planks and spars valued at $5,000 to $6,000, together with twenty-seven barrels of tar. Macdonough kept the tar but gave the rest to the collector, who sold it to the quartermaster's department, and it was used to help build the forts and batteries at Plattsburgh. These interceptions delayed the completion of the *Confiance*, but only temporarily; a detachment of marines finally secured the necessary masts.

New York State, but not Vermont, experienced a radical change of political direction in the midst of all the military events. As late as February, the Federalist assembly in New York, in replying to Governor Tompkin's message, savagely attacked the federal government. The governor remarked that "the Assembly had too much Massachusetts leaven in it to do any thing favourable to the support of the country."[24] The election in May changed all that, however; whether from the steady devotion of the governor or a belated rallying around the flag, the Federalists were turned out of office in massive numbers. The newly elected assembly would have a Republican majority of 36 in a body of 112, the state senate a Republican lead of 20 in a body of 32. Republicans swept the boards in Plattsburgh and Peru, although not in dependably Federalist Champlain. Federalist Congressmen Shepherd and Winters were voted out of office after only one term. In addition, New York's new congressional delegation would contain twenty-one Republicans and six Federalists, whereas only two years previously the proportion was almost exactly the reverse.

The Madison administration had other favorable omens in this third year of the war. One of them was the breaking of the long deadlock with the British over prisoners of war and hostages, which is described in Chapter 5. A curious offshoot of the negotiations for this achievement was an abortive attempt at another armistice. When Baynes visited Pliny Moore during the winter he made some unrecorded remarks which Moore passed on to his friend, John Freligh of Plattsburgh. Freligh thought them so important that he wrote his congressman, Elisha J. Winter: "Judge Moore informs me he had considerable conversation with Adjutant General Baynes on the subject of an armistice, and had the satisfaction to learn from that gentleman that the Governor in Canada stood ready to enter into one at any time the Government of the United States should think proper to make the proposition."[25]

Winter communicated this letter to Monroe who on March 1st wrote General Winder, back in Montreal after his parole for the prisoner-of-war negotiations, to learn whether Baynes spoke with authority, and to ascertain Prevost's views. To Winder's query, Prevost replied that Baynes' talk was of a private nature and unauthorized by him. But Prevost chose to interpret Secretary of State Monroe's letter as a definite offer of an armistice, which he was glad to accept. Baynes would be his deputy, with full powers of negotiation at Champlain or any other meeting place.

Winder was Monroe's intended negotiator of an armistice, but he became involved in American efforts to amend the agreement on prisoners and Monroe named Colonel Ninian Pinkney to arrange an armistice. Pinkney was not conversant with the circumstances, and his instructions were incomplete. Consequently, the talks between Baynes and Pinkney at Dewey's Tavern on May 1st were postponed pending clarification from Washington, and were never resumed.

While he was in Champlain for the talks, Baynes again visited Judge Moore to try to find out how his earlier remarks could have been interpreted as an offer of an armistice. "The Judge assured me," wrote Baynes to Prevost, "that no communication from him could have sanctioned such an assertion . . . and added that from the liberal sentiments which appeared to influence your conduct, and the general tenor of my conversation, he had no doubt that you would feel inclined to renew the armistice which had been so wantonly and improvidently rejected by the President, but that it could not be expected that any overture of that nature would again originate with Your Excellency."[26] Thus three months of intricate maneuvering came to nothing, largely because of the new British determination to launch offensive operations during the summer.

Alongside these pacific developments, the border warfare continued with all its accustomed bitterness. Colonel Clark was sent to the Vermont line in March both to check the smuggling and to be ready for retaliatory strikes. He raided to within six miles of Isle-aux-Noix, captured a British advance guard, seized arms and ammunition, and retired safely.

At about the time Clark went to his new assignment, Lieutenant Colonel Benjamin Forsyth and 300 men of the Rifle Regiment were sent to northern New York. Forsyth's career during the War of 1812 had unfolded on the New York frontiers. He served with both the Dearborn and Wilkinson campaigns, was twice promoted, and gained a soaring reputation as a partisan officer. His successful raids and harassments of British positions made him a wanted man by his opponents, but his boldness and impatience with restraint led him into trouble in 1814.

During the spring he seized a notorious spy named Perkins at his residence in Odelltown and brought him across the line, although he had been ordered to take Perkins only on American soil. The British retaliated by seizing Elias Hamilton and holding him until Perkins was released. Izard sensibly released Perkins, calling the episode "one of the many instances in which Forsyth's indiscretion proved embarrassing."[27]

On June 28, a small party was sent to Odelltown to try to entice a British detachment into an ambush. All was going as planned but Forsyth, who led one part of the ambuscade, prematurely came out of concealment before the trap was ready to be sprung, and started firing. The British fired and retreated, but one of their shots mortally wounded Forsyth. He was taken to the home of Pliny Moore, where he died the same day and from where he was buried with military honors the next day. Izard thought Forsyth was "gallant but eccentric and irregular"; since he could not possibly announce that one of the Americans' war heroes had died because he failed to follow orders, no serious inquiry was ever held.[28]

The death of Forsyth made the British bolder than ever. On July 18, about seventy Voltigeurs and Indians attacked a picket guard of twenty Americans in Champlain under Lieutenant Charles Shelburne of the Fourth Regiment. Although he repulsed the attackers, he was wounded three times but recovered. His other losses were three dead and three others wounded. The next day two British patrols met and attacked each other, killing seven of their own men.

Forsyth's counterpart as a partisan fighter on the Canadian side of the line was Captain Joseph St. Valer Mailloux, variously misspelled Mayhew, Mahew, Maheu, Mayo. His outfit was the Frontier Light Infantry at Odelltown. He had Indians operating with him and his raids had long terrorized the border. In their anger over Forsyth's death, Americans selected Mailloux as the vehicle for their revenge. On August 10, a party of sixteen of the Rifle Regiment under Lieutenant Bennett Riley crossed the line and lay in waiting

until Mailloux and an Indian passed by. Riley called out to Mailloux to escape, but a volley from his men probably killed the Indian and certainly
wounded Mailloux in several places. He was carried in a blanket to headquarters in Champlain, but second thoughts persuaded the commander that if he
died there the British would suspect neglect or foul play. Therefore, they
transferred him to the basement of Moore's home, where British surgeons
were allowed to treat him. There he remained until his death one week later.
His body was sent back to Canada with the honors of war.[29]

Forsyth had maintained lax discipline over his men of the First Rifle Regiment. After his death, command of the unit passed to Major Daniel Appling who, Izard thought, overdid the discipline. By tolerating the private
punishment of enlisted men by officers, he lost numbers of them by desertion to Canada, and Izard again ordered an end to private punishments, as
he had done in May.[30]

Meanwhile, the American seasonal build-up occurred in the Champlain
Valley during the spring and summer. By the end of August, Macdonough
had completed four more gunboats for a total of ten. On July 23, the keel of
the brig *Eagle* was laid and she was launched on August 11. When she later
joined the fleet she carried twenty guns. Recruiting of seamen in New York,
Boston, and Newport was unproductive, and Macdonough commented: "It
was with great reluctance that Genl Izard furnished me with men from the
ranks, but I presume he will spare me about forty more for marines for the
Brig."[31]

Izard's force also slowly increased in size. When he assumed command
on May 1, he counted only two thousand effective troops, but by mid-June it
was three thousand. Before the end of August he had forty-five hundred
men at Chazy and Champlain. Another 400 were working on the forts at
Plattsburgh under Colonel Fenwick, and 200 were completing Fort Izard on
Cumberland Head. Except for the hospital, Izard denuded Burlington of
regular troops in June. He brought over Macomb's entire brigade of five regiments to Cumberland Head, where they camped until the end of July. Then
he brought his whole force together at Chazy and Champlain. Macomb's
men moved in boats to Chazy Landing, while Brigadier General Daniel
Bissell's brigade marched overland from Plattsburgh. Macomb's included the
Sixth, Thirteenth, Fifteenth, Sixteenth, and Twenty-ninth regiments while
Bissell's contained the Fifth, Fourteenth, Thirtieth, Thirty-first, Thirty-
third, Thirty-fourth, and Forty-fifth. Macomb's men went to the Great
Chazy River to guard the ferry landing and mills, but a week later an outbreak of measles made him change the camp to the Little Chazy. The men
had no diversions, were mostly idle, and became discontented while they
waited for they knew not what.

The seeds of personal disaster were planted in August for two of Plattsburgh's leading merchants. Regulars in the army had not been paid for
months and were beginning to show mutinous behavior, which could not be
tolerated on the eve of a British invasion. Officers, who received a cash allowance for rations, needed regular paydays in order to eat; enlisted men, although fed by the army, wanted cash for various necessities and, always,
tobacco.

Macomb pleaded with Henry Delord and William Bailey, who operated
the Red Store, to extend credit to both officers and men; they would be re-
paid as soon as the men were paid, which he expected daily. The partners
were in a dilemma. Other merchants in town had refused Macomb, prefer-
ring to preserve their stocks and believing that a mutiny might bring the
army to its senses. But Bailey and Delord reasoned that if they helped to
maintain the army's morale, their business might be better protected in a
time of trouble, and they could still collect at a future day. Personal and patriotic impulses also influenced their decision. So they began granting credit
to the troops in and around Plattsburgh, as well as to naval personnel. Their
investment appeared as secure as the United States government itself.

Although he had a sizable army gathered near the border, Izard realized
that no offensive operations were being planned for that season by the War
Department. Believing that the Plattsburgh front and Lake Champlain were
under control and that the action of the season was taking place at Niagara,
he suggested his transfer on July 19. His letter crossed one from Washington
dated July 27, ordering him westward with his troops. Only then did Izard
begin to get word of the concentration of a huge force across the border.

The British build-up was made possible by the defeat and exile of Napoleon in April. Some sixteen thousand hardened veterans of Wellington's
campaigns in Spain were thus freed for assignment elsewhere, and during the
summer they began to arrive in Canada. The colonial secretary's secret instructions laid out the blueprints for a new offensive: "Should there be any
advanced position on that part of our frontier which extends towards Lake
Champlain, the occupation of which would materially tend to the security of
the Province, you will if you deem it expedient expel the Enemy from it, and
occupy it by detachments of the Troops under your command, always however taking care not to expose His Majesty's Forces to being cut off by too
extended a line of advance."[32] This last warning probably reflected the unhappy memory of British failure to subdue a much smaller country at the
time of the Revolution, and especially of the catastrophe that befell Burgoyne when he tried to lead an army to Albany.

The British plans for campaigns on all the lakes were well developed before the Americans realized their danger. Prevost received Bathurst's secret

instructions in July in which he was ordered to undertake offensive operations all along the front as soon as the reinforcements reached him. The troops arrived continuously all summer. Prevost despatched some to the Niagara front, where he told Drummond to seize the initiative, with his ultimate objective at Sackets Harbor. Because the British lacked clear control of Lake Ontario, these troops were forced to march 250 miles from Kingston to Niagara.

Prevost organized many of the new troops in the Montreal area. He debated between striking along the St. Lawrence and Lake Ontario, or up the Champlain Valley. He wrote to London early in August that it would be impossible to collect his forces before the end of the month; that in any case, control of neither lake could be counted on before September 15th. But in the same month he was prodded by a dispatch from London: "If you shall allow the present campaign to close without having undertaken offensive measures against the enemy you will very seriously disappoint the expectations of the Prince Regent and the country."[33]

There is no evidence that Prevost was enthusiastic over his new orders. As the commander throughout the war, he had known instinctively that a threatening campaign by the British would at last call forth a maximum war effort from the Americans. He was also acutely aware of the importance of control of the lakes as a guarantee of the success of any land campaigns. But he no longer exercised sole control over naval affairs in Canada.

Commodore Sir James Lucas Yeo, British commander on all the Great Lakes, was so absorbed with his naval race on Lake Ontario that he tended to let Lake Champlain take care of itself. He allotted very little in stores and men to the British base at Isle-aux-Noix. He was on uneasy terms with his subordinate there, Captain Pring, and with Prevost himself, but Prevost was being pressed by his government to launch an offensive. He resented orders for military action before effective naval support was available on either lake. Referring to "the vacillating communications I have received from Sir James Yeo," he viewed the situation on Lake Ontario as too uncertain before October to risk the sending of a large invading force, which must travel by water. He was thus forced to rely upon the *Confiance* to give the British control of Lake Champlain.[34]

Prevost had every intention of avoiding Vermont, for as he wrote to London, "Vermont having shewn a decided opposition to the War, and very large supplies of specie daily coming in from thence, as well as the whole of the Cattle required for the use of the Troops, I mean for the present to confine myself in any offensive Operations . . . to the Western side of Lake Champlain."[35] Prevost was impatient to launch his attack because of the lateness of the season. He was upset when he learned that the *Confiance* would not be ready before September 15. He decided that the invasion could not wait and that undoubtedly the cautious naval officers could be hurried a bit. So he marched for the New York border, upon receipt of the news that the *Confiance* had been launched on August 25.

So well did Prevost guard his secret that Izard was unaware of the threat until early August. Then he wrote a series of appeals to Armstrong for a change in his orders. On the 11th he warned:

> I will make the movement you direct, if possible; but I shall do it with the apprehension of risking the force under my command, and with the certainty that everything in this vicinity but the lately erected works at Plattsburgh and on Cumberland Head will in less than three days after my departure be in the possession of the enemy.[36]

On the 20th:

> I must not be responsible for the consequences of abandoning my present strong position. I will obey orders and execute them as well as I know how. Major-Gen'l Brisbane commands at Odeltown; he is said to have between 5 & 6,000 men with him; at Chambly are stated to be about 4,000.[37]

Unaccountably, Armstrong did not change the orders, and the hapless Izard started his departure from the North Country with four thousand men on August 27, and completed it on the 29th. After consulting with his officers, he chose to go by way of Utica because of the exposed terrain across northern New York. His progress was slow because of the oxen he used for his train. He spent the first night at the Au Sable River, the second a few miles south of Elizabethtown. He lingered two days at Lake George, to wait for a change of orders that never came, on September 4 was at Glens Falls and Schenectady on the 7th. He took with him the Fourth, Fifth, Tenth, Twelfth, Thirteenth, Fourteenth, Fifteenth, Sixteenth, and Forty-fifth regiments plus light artillery, dragoons and all the surgeons of the entire army.

Meanwhile, a curious contretemps developed over the calling out of the militia. In mid-August Mooers, hearing an invasion was imminent, offered to muster them, but Izard told him there was nothing to justify his alarm, although a battle was probable eventually and the nearest companies might be told to stand by for future orders. Mooers fumed to the governor that a few companies were ridiculous and that several thousand men were needed. A week later, when Izard did request a call-up, Mooers, for whatever reason, replied that he had no authority to do so except in case of an invasion. Izard then appealed to the governor, who told Mooers he approved of his earlier offer and was surprised that Izard had rejected it; but he assured Mooers that he had the authority and if he had not already done so, should order out the militia immediately. Mooers did so on the day the British crossed the border.[38]

Izard marched out to a disappointing future. If it was battles and military fame he was seeking, he arrived too late at the Niagara front. Heavy fighting started early in July when Major General Jacob Brown seized Fort Erie on the Canadian side of the river. British Major General Phineas Riall established a line on nearby Chippewa River which Brigadier General Winfield Scott smashed on July 5. Twenty days later Brown engaged Riall and Lieutenant General Gordon Drummond at Lundy's Lane, near Niagara Falls. A savage five-hour battle ended in a draw, although the Americans retired from the field. Casualties on both sides were heavy: for the Americans, 853 and for the British, 878.

Brown's army fell back on Fort Erie, which was invested by the British during the whole month of August and half of September before an American sortie destroyed the British batteries and forced Drummond to withdraw. The front that Izard reached in September had already gone through its worst spasms, and the rest of the season was spent in desultory and inconclusive skirmishing.

The other important front of the year was Chesapeake Bay. General Robert Ross and four thousand veterans from Europe were expected to make a diversion on the eastern coast in support of the British army in Canada. Admiral Sir Alexander Cochrane planned an expedition to retaliate against the American destruction of York during the previous year. The troops landed and marched inland toward Washington. At Bladensburg, Maryland, they met and defeated a force incompetently led by General Winder. Unopposed, they marched into Washington on August 24, and remained there overnight. They burned all the government buildings, including the president's house and the Capitol, before retiring. It was Secretary of War Armstrong, however, who bore the brunt of the criticism for the city's weak defenses, and under pressure he resigned on September 3. He was succeeded by James Monroe, who for a second time became acting secretary.

The British were not through in the Chesapeake. In mid-September they attacked Baltimore, attempting in an advance by land and bombardment from the sea to capture the place and destroy its shipping. They failed because of the city's sturdy defenders. When the American flag was still flying over Fort McHenry the next morning, an observer, Francis Scott Key, was stirred to write the "The Star Spangled Banner."

Aside from the sacking of Washington, the only unqualified British achievement of 1814 was the easy occupation of the eastern third of Maine. They pinned great hopes on being able to back up their demands at the peace conference, which finally convened in August. In the east they wanted two border changes: in Maine, where they wanted an all-British route between Quebec City and Halifax, and in northern New York to give them a foothold on Lake Champlain and control of the entire length of the St. Lawrence River. Their expectations of achieving the latter rested with the approaching battle of Plattsburgh.

10

THE BRITISH OCCUPATION OF PLATTSBURGH

When Izard marched out of the North Country on August 29, his command devolved upon General Macomb, who experienced a brief panic when he realized the threat he faced. He knew that a huge British army was poised just north of the border, but estimates of its size ranged from seven thousand to fourteen thousand. He immediately asked Eleazer Williams for intelligence reports every ten hours. He summarized his situation as "everything in a state of disorganization — works unfinished & a garrison of a few efficient men and a sick list of one thousand. . . . Happen what will you may rely that the garrison will do its utmost."[1]

Actually, dysentery, diarrhea, and typhus had reappeared in Izard's army during August, and he left 921 sick men under the care of Dr. Mann at Plattsburgh when he departed. Consequently, Macomb was able to count on only nineteen hundred effective regulars to stem the horde of veterans of the war in Europe.

As soon as Izard's protection was withdrawn at the border, the inhabitants were subjected to small forays from Canada. Marauding Indians irritated and frightened Americans more than the threat of a large British army. For example, a single drunken Indian appeared at Pliny Moore's door in search of rum and money. Then he tried to put his hand into the pocket of Silas Hubbell, the lawyer. Such incidents, Moore protested to General Brisbane, were a nuisance, especially disturbing to women and children. Julius C. Hubbell also complained about rampaging Indians, especially a band of 300 who terrorized Chazy, took old spelling books out of the schoolhouse, and pulled and ate onions in his garden.[2]

The expected invasion began on August 31 when Brisbane crossed the border with one wing of the army and camped on the north bank of the

161

Great Chazy River. The rest of the army and Prevost himself entered New York next day. In a proclamation aimed at detaching Americans from their government, Prevost promised "the peaceable and unoffending inhabitants" that they could expect "kind usage and generous treatment." Then he denounced his real enemy: "It is against the government of the United States, by whom this unjust and unprovoked war has been declared, and against those who support it, either openly or secretly, that the arms of his majesty are directed." His promise of redress for any violence to persons and property was kept in the main, and looting and illegal seizures were kept at a minimum.[3]

Panic spread throughout the Champlain Valley, and Dr. Beaumont sardonically described the scene in Plattsburgh:

> The people are all frighten'd nearly out — out, did I say? rather into their
> *wits* — if they have any — moving everything off — under the expectation that
> all will be burnt or destroyed — poor souls, many of them, love & uphold the
> British — censure & condemn our own Government — complaining they have
> no protection — neither will they take up arms to defend themselves —
> Indeed I pity their depravity — but dont care much for their losses — if they
> should maintain any.[4]

At the last minute, an unaccountable change of command occurred on the British side as well. On September 1, Captain George Downie, arrived at Isle-aux-Noix to take command from Captain Pring, who had been in charge for more than a year. Downie had been serving on Lake Ontario under Yeo, and the only explanation for the shift seems to be Yeo's incompatibility with Pring.

Prevost was determined not to make a decisive move before the fleet was ready, and he was deeply irritated that, with all summer to prepare, the ships were not finished. He was aware that the *Confiance* was far from complete, but he began to write the commander daily to hasten preparations, *after* his army was already in the United States. Yet the *Confiance* was not put into the water until August 25, and when Downie first saw her, she still lacked much of her equipment, including items such as locks for the guns, which appeared unobtainable.

Nevertheless, in order to insure Prevost's supply line as he moved south, Pring with some gunboats occupied Isle La Motte on September 3. He paroled the militia he found there and installed a battery of three long eighteen-pound guns opposite the mouth of the Little Chazy River, where army supplies were to be landed. Pring then waited on the island for the rest of the fleet to join him.

On the day the British crossed the border, Macomb asked Mooers to provide troops for the Chazy Road to watch the enemy and mark its route. He
hoped the militia would give the invaders a "warm reception," and meanwhile he declared that he had plenty of arms and ammunition for a siege.
Without waiting for further authority from the governor, Mooers called out
the militia of Clinton, Essex, and Franklin counties. In his division orders he
warned the men to behave themselves: "Attention & good order are expected
by the major general & he would feel mortifyd to hear of any depradations on
the inhabitants or ill usage to any one, as the object in calling militia out is
for the purpose of repelling the enemy & protecting the citizens in their persons & property."[5]

A few days later sweeping authority to call out the men of the whole military district arrived from the governor, and Mooers immediately levied on
Saratoga, Montgomery, and Schoharie counties. Owing to the lateness of the
call and the distance, only a few of these men arrived before the battle, the
rest being still on the road. In consequence, the militia Macomb could count
on came from the three northern counties of New York—General Daniel
Wright's Fortieth Brigade. The Essex County units were given a rousing send-
off of speeches, music, and tears. The first of the levies arrived so promptly
that they were able to take positions along the line of the probable British advance by September 2. Septa Fillmore, tavernkeeper of Chazy, rode off to
battle without taking time to be fully dressed. The British did not burn his
tavern, apparently because it displayed a masonic sign, but they cut down his
orchard and seized or destroyed much else, for which he never received compensation.[6]

On the 31st, Macomb asked Governor Chittenden for the Vermont militia. Adhering to his earlier stand that they could not serve outside the state,
Chittenden appealed to General John Newell of Charlotte for volunteers
instead. Newell quibbled about the lack of a direct order, and Chittenden repeated the request. Ultimately, General Samuel Strong of Vergennes assumed command of the volunteer troops and crossed the lake at their head,
but the delays meant that his men could not reach the front until after the
British had arrived in Plattsburgh.

Meanwhile Macomb, given the precious gift of time because of Prevost's
leisurely movements, became the center of a whirlwind of activity. Defeatists
on his staff urged him to safeguard his men and stores by retreating southward but Macomb, although acknowledging that his forts might hold out
only until reinforcements could arrive, was determined to stand or fall with
his fortifications. One of the first things he did was to send a detachment to
rescue several bateaux of government provisions Izard had left at Chazy. He
dismantled Fort Izard on Cumberland Head and brought its garrison into

The General Mooers House in Plattsburgh as extended and bricked over c. 1821. Used as headquarters by General Macomb during the battle of Plattsburgh, it still contains a cannonball in an interior wall.

Plattsburgh. He made his headquarters in a yellow wooden house on Bridge Street which Mooers owned but did not occupy until after the war. It still stands and it contains a cannonball in an inside wall, received during the battle.

Macomb gathered his entire force around the works in Plattsburgh. They totalled about 3,400 men, but some 1,400 were sick or otherwise unavailable to him, such as 250 men on duty with the fleet. The core of his army was the Sixth, Twenty-ninth, Thirtieth, Thirty-first, Thirty-third, and Thirty-fourth regiments, totalling 1,770 men. In rushing completion of the forts, he divided the work among several details, telling the men they must defend their own work "to the last extremity." In general orders on September 5 he announced: "The eyes of America are on us. . . . Fortune always follows the brave. The works being now capable of resisting a powerful attack, the manner of defending them the General thinks it is his duty to detail, that every man may know and do his duty."[7]

The forts upon which he placed so much reliance were three in number and lay in approximately a straight line across the narrow peninsula that separates the winding Saranac River from the lake. They were large earthen fortifications, graded so that the approach from the north was a steep upward climb and heavily abatised. Their southern approach was less carefully prepared, and therefore more vulnerable if opponents could manage to get in their rear. They were, however, heavily fortified with guns that could fire shot up to forty-two pounds.

At the time Macomb assumed command, two of them had not received their permanent names, and were known only as redoubts, but he named them before the battle. Redoubt #1, the later Fort Brown which was named to honor that American general's successes at Niagara, stood just above the river and presents the only remains of the battle in Plattsburgh today. Its completion and defense were assigned to Lieutenant Colonel Huckens Storrs and parts of the Thirtieth and Thirty-first regiments. The largest of the three stood in the center of the peninsula and had been named Fort Moreau by Izard after the noted French general exiled by Napoleon, who lived for nine years in the United States. It was entrusted to Colonel Melancton Smith of Plattsburgh and the Sixth and Twenth-ninth Regiments. Redoubt #2 stood near the banks of the lake; it was called Fort Scott, also for a successful officer at Niagara. It was commanded by Major Thomas Vinson and occupied by the Thirty-third and Thirty-fourth regiments.[8]

Two outposts were also constructed. About sixty rods south of the lower bridge over the river, a blockhouse was manned by Captain John Smith of the First Rifle Regiment with a detachment of his own company and convalescents of the Fourth Regiment. Near the point where the river enters the lake, another blockhouse was garrisoned by a detachment of artillery under Lieutenant Abram Fowler. Major John Sproull was sent to the bridge over Dead Creek with 200 of the Thirteenth Regiment and two field pieces. Dead Creek then entered Plattsburgh Bay far to the eastward of its present mouth. Lieutenant Colonel Daniel Appling, with 100 riflemen and New York cavalry, was sent north of the bridge to obstruct the State Road.

On the 5th, Macomb also ordered 720 sick men to Crab Island, still under Dr. Mann. During three days of wet weather, they slept in tents on the wet ground, until straw could be brought from Grand Isle. Eventually, roughly planked hospitals were erected. The men were supposed to be moved to Burlington, but the transports were all busy ferrying war stores. When the lake calmed enough, many of the invalids were transported by open boat in small detachments.[9]

Macdonough brought his fleet into Plattsburgh Bay on September 1. He picked the site because he knew that a north wind that brought the British southward would create problems when they tried to tack into the bay; he also knew that a confined battle space was better for him than open lake because it would allow him to exploit his superiority in short-range guns (carronades). Within the bay he formed his ships in a line running roughly from northeast to southwest (see map, p. 182), in which the *Eagle* was at the north end, next to it the *Saratoga,* then the *Ticonderoga* and the *Preble.* The *Eagle* was opposite a line somewhat to the south of the mouth of the Saranac River, while at the other end the *Preble* was anchored about a mile and a half northerly from Crab Island.

Each ship had springs, or hawsers, attached to its bow anchor and extending the length of the vessel to the stern. The vessel could be turned by hauling on the port or starboard spring, and stern anchors were provided for use in an emergency. The ten gunboats were placed in groups of two or three, about forty yards west of the vessels. The line was formed a little more than half way from the village to Cumberland Head. For good measure, a six-pound cannon was placed on the north tip of Crab Island for the invalids and wounded to operate if the opportunity appeared. The *President* and the *Montgomery* were being used as transports. On the day of the battle, the latter was in Burlington while the *President* was twenty miles south of Plattsburgh, with its guns ashore and repairs being made to the ravages of a storm four days earlier.[10]

The British objectives of their campaign have occasioned wide differences of opinion among American historians, many of whom have assumed without evidence that, like Burgoyne, Prevost was headed for Albany and New York City. Macomb thought that the campaign was meant to extend only as far as Crown Point and Ticonderoga, but he did not give his reasons for thinking so. Prevost never intimated that it was designed for any object except Plattsburgh. The peace conference had already been in session for nearly a month, and the British knew they needed some quick, last-minute victories to bolster their demands at the conference table. The colonial secretary's instructions to Prevost also had a bearing on objectives; they dealt with "any advanced position on that part of your frontier which extends towards Lake Champlain, the occupation of which would materially tend to the security of the Province," always being careful, however, "not to expose His Majesty's Forces to being cut off by too extended a line of advance."[11] In other words, get a foothold on Lake Champlain so as to be able to demand its demilitarization and, possibly, a shift in the boundary. A campaign which stopped at Plattsburgh met the requirements, as well as the predilections of a defense-minded governor general.

The size of Prevost's army has also produced widely varying opinions.

Every figure from seven thousand to fourteen thousand has been used by British and American writers. The high number was favored by Captain A. T. Mahan and Benson J. Lossing. Macomb on September 2 told the secretary of war that the approaching British army numbered eight thousand men. But after the battle he reported that a British force of fourteen thousand had occupied Plattsburgh. However, he explained that the figure was "as given by a Clerk in the Adjutant Genls Department and confirmed by the many Deserters." This phrase is heavily lined out, whether before the report left Plattsburgh or after its receipt in Washington it is impossible to say. At any rate the letter, which is primarily responsible for a long-standing but erroneous tradition, has for its authority only the repudiated estimate of a clerk and of deserters.[12]

Two well-known students of Canadian affairs believed that seven thousand British troops reached Plattsburgh. The American historian, A. L. Burt, used that figure. Writing much earlier the British historian, Charles P. Lucas, arrived at the same number. He also believed that Prevost left another four thousand men at the boundary as a reserve. It is possible that the belief in this border reserve accounts for the use by historians Theodore Roosevelt and Julius Pratt of the figure eleven thousand to describe the British forces. William Wood, the Canadian editor of the British documents of the war, states that some ten thousand troops were assigned to the Plattsburgh campaign, and that seven thousand of them actually reached Plattsburgh. Of the lot, Wood was the most accurate.[13]

The unassailable figure is clearly stated in the report from Plattsburgh on September 8, 1814, of the British adjutant general, Major General Edward Baynes. A total of eighty-two hundred officers and men were at Plattsburgh in three brigades; twenty-one hundred more were manning outposts between the village and the border. One week later, Baynes's report of the retreating army in Odelltown, which had apparently withdrawn most of its outposts, showed a total of 9,785 present, with 460 still on outpost duty. It is quite possible that these reports have eluded researchers for the simple reason that they appear in the archives only once, under a date in April 1815, nearly seven months after the Plattsburgh campaign.[14]

The reduction in the traditional size of the British force does not materially lessen their overwhelming preponderance, which was four to one in relation to Macomb's effective regulars. The British troops were largely Napoleonic war veterans under experienced officers. They were organized into three brigades under the general command of Baron Francis de Rottenburg, a Pole who entered the British army in 1794. He had directed the forces of Lower Canada between 1811 and 1813, and briefly administered the province in 1813 during Prevost's absence at the front.

The First Brigade was led by Major General Frederick Robinson, son of the Loyalist, Colonel Beverley Robinson of New York. The major general had fought in southern France under Wellington and was twice severely wounded, once in the face. His units included the Twenty-seventh, Thirty-ninth (646 left on outpost duty), Seventy-sixth and Eighty-eighth (548 on outpost) regiments of foot.

Major General Thomas Brisbane led the Second Brigade. He had also fought in southern France in 1813–14, and was wounded at the battle of Toulouse. His units at Plattsburgh were the Thirteenth, Forty-ninth, Meuron's (446 on outpost), the Canadian Voltigeurs, and the Canadian Chausseurs.

The Third Brigade was headed by Major General Manley Power, who fought under Wellington and then with the Portuguese army. His brigade included the Third, Fifth, Twenty-seventh, and Fifty-eighth regiments. The three brigades made up the entire British force except the 200 Indians who accompanied them.

The British apparently entered New York in two wings, the right into the village of Champlain and the left down the Odelltown road (Route 276). This wing camped just below Dewey's Tavern, and the officers stayed there. According to family tradition, when a soldier was flogged for insubordination, others brought beef brine from the tavern to cleanse his wounds. The two branches of the army remained in their camps to get organized and allow more time for the navy's preparation. Finally, dismayed at the rapid passing of the campaign season, Prevost ordered an advance. From this point on, it would have been better for his future reputation if the governor general had remained in Canada and left the campaign to his seasoned generals. It is hard to see how Macomb in his unfinished forts, few militia, and no Vermonters yet in sight could have withstood a swift attack immediately after the British first entered the country, with or without their fleet. Instead, Macomb was given eleven more days to make his preparations.

The British moved on September 4, the left wing probably through Cooperville for a junction with the right wing at Honeymoore's Corners. The army remained overnight in Chazy at the cantonment about a half mile north of the village. Hubbell's law office was used as a headquarters and several officers billeted themselves in his home, paying for their food and lodging in gold. Prevost and his staff stayed in Alexander Scott's fine home. All three of these buildings are still in use. A group of soldiers wanted to be shown some Yankees, whom they had been led to believe were small people. When Philip Honsinger, 6 feet 7 inches tall and weighing 260 pounds, was presented to them, they were overheard to say, "If the Yankees are all like him, the Lord deliver us from fighting them."[15]

A Hubbell family tradition, which found its way into one of the books of Ernest Thompson Seton, related how Mrs. Hubbell, a daughter of Pliny

Law office of Julius C. Hubbell in Chazy, occupied by the British army as headquarters going to and returning from Plattsburgh.

Moore, saw her uninvited guests off with the comment: "Good-bye, sirs, for a very little while, but I know you'll soon be back and hanging your heads as you come." The angry reply she received was: "If a man had said that, I would call him out; but since it is a fair lady that has been our charming hostess, I reply that when your prophecy comes true, every officer here shall throw his purse on your door step as he passes." During their retreat she reminded them, and they kept their part of the bargain.[16]

Some British officers pressed Moses Mooers and his horse into service to show them the main route south. As he described it, "The road was filled in with trees and they were mad at me because they thought I had misled them, but I hadn't. A lieutenant rode my horse. He was very gentlemanly and gave it back to me, and fifty cents for my services."[17]

The Alexander Scott Home in Chazy, used by General Prevost as his headquarters going to and returning from Plattsburgh.

The route had been obstructed along the State Road (now Route 9) by Appling, who had been sent out for that purpose. The west road to Chazy was reconnoitered by militia units of Miller's regiment beginning on September 2, and part of the Essex County militia beginning on the 3rd. The British had not yet arrived in Chazy, and their route from there southward was still unknown. However, by the 4th, militia units were out on the Beekmantown Road, and Aiken's Company spent the night near West Chazy. This group had come together as volunteers only the day before and was composed, except for the officers, of school boys of about sixteen years of age. The captain was Martin Aiken and the lieutenant was Azariah Flagg, both of whom were prominent young men in the village; sixteen boys were in the company. During their exuberant service, they captured the imagination of the North Country; Eleazer Williams wrote of them on the 6th: "There is no corps more useful and watchful than the one under the command of Captain Aiken and Lieut. Flagg."[18]

Lester Sampson's Tavern in Ingraham. The settlement around it was once known as Sampson's. The British left wing camped near it on the way to Plattsburgh.

The British moved south on the road to Plattsburgh on the 5th, apparently intending to take the whole army by that route. The systematic obstructions caused a change in plans, however; units that had not yet left Chazy were ordered to take the west road toward West Chazy. The subsequent route of the left wing under General Brisbane is easy to trace: it camped on the night of the 5th at Sampson's Tavern (Ingraham), left several hundred men on outpost duty on Vantine's farm, and marched south next day unimpeded except for the blocked roads until it reached Dead Creek bridge.

The exact route of the right wing under Generals Power and Robinson is impossible to determine because of the multiplicity of roads they might have chosen. As far as is known, they made only one encampment that night. The scanty evidence indicates that they followed the main road to West Chazy but skirted the village by turning south on the Ketcham Bridge Road to its junction with the main road north from Beekmantown to West Chazy (Route 22). Their camp lay astride the town line on the farm of Miner Lewis and stretched up Route 22 toward West Chazy. The inhabitants of the area spent a tense night and either fled or hid, although the British troops were kept under strict control. The only clash occurred about midnight when the Essex County militia, which had transferred to Beekmantown Corners, sent out a patrol that met a similar British group.

The army was on the march early on the morning of the 6th, having impressed all the teams they could find. Henry Dominy had driven his into the woods for concealment, but his hired man, John Hamilton, gave the game away. Hamilton was taken along to drive and collect the wounded. After performing this duty for a while, he managed to evade his captors and drive the team back to the Dominy farm. After the war he tried to get a pension for his war service, but the family laughed at him "for trying to get a pension for helping the British."[19]

Some British officers arrived at the door of the Reverend Stephen Kinsley, who lived near West Chazy, and asked for breakfast. After the meal, the minister invited them to remain for prayers. Politely and attentively they listened to him pray that "the enemies of our country may be sent back with shame to their own country." Afterwards one of the officers remarked, "I think you haven't much faith in your prayer, sir." Kinsley replied, "I have *full faith* that you will go back with shame to your country."[20]

The marching British unexpectedly divided north of Beekmantown Corners, the larger number proceeding directly south on the Barber Road, while the others turned east on an old road just north of Silver Creek, then south on the Ashley Road to East Beekmantown. The whole right wing had been expected to come through East Beekmantown, and consequently all the skirmishes on September 6 occurred on that route. General Mooers had taken personal command of his 700 militiamen on the 5th, and they camped that night in East Beekmantown. In the evening he sent his adjutant to Plattsburgh for help. Macomb ordered Major John Wool with 250 regulars and Captain Luther Leonard with two cannon to march for Beekmantown, "to meet the Enemy and give an Example to the Militia."[21] Leonard held back because he had not had the order direct from Macomb and consequently arrived late. Wool and his men departed at midnight and were in East Beekmantown by sunrise. He had been in the army since 1812, was shot through both thighs at Queenston, had fought well under Hampton and would behave valiantly at Plattsburgh. He later became inspector general of the army and had a prominent role in the Mexican War.

Wool took a position near the Ira Howe house, which still stands where the Ashley Road joins Route 22 just north of East Beekmantown. Women and children fled to the woods, hid in the cellar or, like Sarah Howes, took her children and valuables down to the creek. Her son Nathan, in the militia, went AWOL in his worry about her, and was dishonorably discharged as a result.[22]

Mooers sent Major Reuben Walworth and a detachment up the Ashley Road to destroy the creek bridge, but it was too late. The British interrupted Walworth, wounding and capturing two of his men. He pulled back to Wool's position, and there a serious skirmish took place. Several British were killed and wounded, and the Howe barn became a temporary hospital. Wool and his regulars contested the rest of the way into Plattsburgh by forming, firing, and pulling back to a new position. Mooers and the main body of the militia stood in East Beekmantown, but at the British approach many of them broke and ran away. Some of them stayed, however, some were rounded up and persuaded to make another stand, but others went straight home. In the East Beekmantown area, Dr. Benjamin J. Mooers, nephew of the general, was binding up the head of a wounded soldier when he found himself between two armies. He quickly finished the job and spurred his horse to safety.

The next stand by the Americans was at the top of Culver Hill, so-called because all the adjacent land was owned by the Culver family. As the British marched up the hill, in perfect formation and filling the road, Lieutenant Colonel James Wellington of the Third Buffs, no relative of the duke of Wellington, contrary to local belief, made a prominent target. Militiamen behind a stone wall fired and killed him instantly. He was temporarily buried in a garden at East Beekmantown. Ensign John Chapman was also killed in this stiff engagement. The wounded were taken into the Daniel Culver house on the west side of the road for treatment. The skirmish did not last long; Wool was eager to pull back before the British on the Barber Road could get in his rear.

Snipers harassed the British for the next two miles. The Barber Road and the Beekmantown Road contingents of the right wing were reunited at Smith's Corners, opposite today's Super 87 Drive-In Theatre. Wool, the militia and, at the last minute, Aiken's Company made their final stand at Halsey's Corners, named for the Reverend Frederick Halsey, chaplain of Miller's regiment, whose stone house still stands west of the corners. Captain Leonard had finally arrived with his small cannon, and the British were met with a withering fire. St. John B. L. Skinner, one of Aiken's company, remembered that Leonard's first shot cut a swath through the middle of the perfectly marching column. The second similarly failed to interrupt its machinelike precision, but the third, a shower of grape shot, caused momentary confusion. The bugles sounded a charge, the men discarded their knapsacks and rushed the battery.[23] The Americans pulled back toward the village. In this confrontation, British Lieutenant Robert Kingsbury was mortally wounded, taken to nearby Isaac Platt's home, died there, and was buried in Platt's garden.

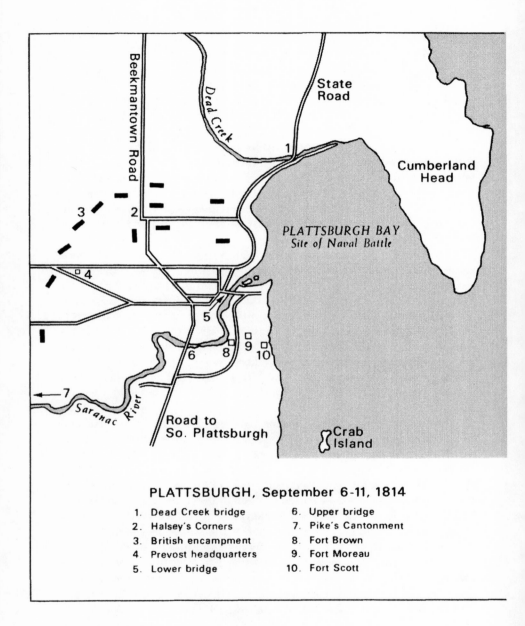

PLATTSBURGH, September 6-11, 1814

1. Dead Creek bridge
2. Halsey's Corners
3. British encampment
4. Prevost headquarters
5. Lower bridge

6. Upper bridge
7. Pike's Cantonment
8. Fort Brown
9. Fort Moreau
10. Fort Scott

Meanwhile, the left wing had spent the night at Sampson's. The local commanders of a company of New York Dragoons, Lieutenants Matthew Standish and Roswell Wait, dressed as British officers and reconnoitered within British lines. Returning to their unit, they led a charge against a picket guard which fled, but the whole army came alive. Otherwise, the night at Sampson's was uneventful, and on the 6th the army marched smoothly as far as Dead Creek. After sabotaging the roads, Appling had fallen back to join Sproull at the bridge. A storehouse and huts had been erected on the sand ridge between the creek and the lake, and there the two officers attempted to employ the delaying tactics that were being used on the right wing at Halsey's Corners.

On breaking through the barrier at the bridge, British troops were fired on by some of Macdonough's gunboats which had moved in close to shore. The gunboats were sent in hasty retreat, however, when the British brought some of their own artillery to bear, killing one American and wounding three including Lieutenant Silas Duncan of the *Saratoga*, who lost his right arm as a result. The British left and right wings joined forces somewhere near the modern intersection of Boynton Avenue and Route 9 in Plattsburgh, and started marching on the village, which they occupied as far as the Saranac River on the same day. All the American troops scrambled for the two bridges. The militia crossed the Upper (South Catherine Street) Bridge and tore up the flooring after all were across, using it as a breastwork. The Lower (Bridge Street) Bridge was a closer call. Removal of the flooring was done under severe fire, the workers covered by Aiken's company which took post in the sawmill above the bridge. The British were discouraged from crossing the river by bridge or ford by the vigilance of both regular and militia units along the south bank.

Most of Plattsburgh had fallen on the first day, but it had been a costly enterprise for the British. They lost three officers killed and several wounded, but their soldiers' casualties were about 100. The American losses totalled about forty-five.

That night Mooers, from his headquarters in South Plattsburgh, wrote to the governor in despair over the behavior of his men: "A portion of the militia have entailed an eternal disgrace on themselves, many of whom have left the ranks and gone home." In his division orders after the battle, he praised the work of some of the militia and of Aiken's company, but then: "The general regrets that there are some who are lost to patriotism and to honor, after coming forward in obedience to his call, fled at the first approach of the enemy, and afterwards basely disbanded themselves and returned home; thereby disgracing themselves, and furnishing to their fellow-soldiers an example of all that brave men detest and abhor." Macomb agreed in part with this assessment when he wrote: "The militia . . . except a few brave men, fell back most precipitately in the greatest disorder." In the same letter, however, he concluded the "The Militia behaved with great spirit after the first day and the volunteers of Vermont were exceedingly serviceable."[24]

The British laid out their encampment in a huge arc north and west of the village, extending from the lake shore around to the Saranac opposite the former site of Pike's Cantonment. Prevost made his headquarters at the Edward Allen house which stood in the triangle now formed by Broad and Cornelia streets. Generals Power and de Rottenburgh had their headquarters farther west on what is now Route 3, in homes that are no longer standing. Brisbane chose the home of Samuel Lowell, which still stands at 98 Boynton Avenue. By tradition, Lowell's wife concealed a keg of British gold on the premises, and in the hasty retreat the British forgot to look for it. Lowell was able to build a finer house after the war.

After the British arrival, Macomb still had several days to work on the forts. The British, while waiting for their fleet, constantly probed the bridges and fords. On the first day their sharpshooters occupied the dwellings along lower Broad and Margaret streets and fired across the river at close range. Macomb ordered hot shot fired at them, and one by one they burned to the ground. The courthouse was destroyed, perhaps by some other means, but the private dwellings and businesses number fifteen, not including out-buildings.[25]

The invaders also made great efforts to erect some batteries. They had dragged sixteen guns on carriages from Canada which included long and short-range guns, howitzers, and mortars. Prevost decided that he needed more and sent to Isle-aux-Noix for two eight-inch iron mortars and two iron twelve-pound guns. These did not arrive in time to be used during the battle.[26] Four batteries were placed: on the lake shore north of the mouth of the river, on the steep bank back of Broad Street, near the cemetery, and in the big bend of the river on what is now White Street. At least two emplacements were made on Delord's Point, and the wonder is that they did not attract enough American fire to destroy the homes of Delord, Dr. Davidson, and Peter Sailly.

As soon as word of the invasion reached the villages of Vermont, whether or not the call for volunteers had yet reached them, an outburst of enthusiasm occurred. Tuesday, the 6th, was the date of the annual state elections. After the voting in St. Albans, a fife and drum were heard and volunteers were asked to fall in. Eighty did so and immediately marched for the sand bar to South Hero. One prominent young lawyer was swept off the bar and was saved only by his horse. Requisitioning small boats for the crossing from South Hero to the New York shore, the unit reported to Macomb on the 8th

and was ordered to join General Strong at his headquarters at Pike's Cantonment. Men from Georgia also crossed the sand bar, in wagons after dark. The
wagons became tangled in the logs and stumps that had drifted on the bar,
and the men found themselves up to their armpits in water trying to un-
tangle the mess.[27]

In Middlebury the excitement on the 6th was intense, and nearly 200
men rushed to volunteer. Units left for Plattsburgh as soon as they could be
outfitted. The sum of $295 was collected from the townspeople to pay for
ammunition and equipment. Men and boys worked all night in Horatio Seymour's law office in Middlebury to make cartridges. Afraid of using candles,
they worked in the dark and next morning the floor was blackened with
powder, leading one to exclaim: "We certainly have been in more danger
here to-night than any of our volunteers will be in at Plattsburgh."[28]

Apparently the only Vermonter to have second thoughts was a man from
Essex. He started for the lake shore, his zeal pushing him ahead of his companions. Soon he began to hear heavy firing in the direction of Plattsburgh.
Those whom he had outstripped met him in rapid retreat toward home. He
explained breathlessly that "he had on his best Sunday shoes & his wife would
feel *dreadfully* if he spoilt them, so he was going back to change them."[29]

They crossed the lake in every kind of vessel that would float. Many did
not make it in time for the battle; this was true of the detachments from
Highgate, Shoreham, Ira, and Clarenden, for example. But the men from
Orwell arrived as the British were retreating, and without orders pursued
them and surprised their rear guard at Chazy. From Colchester came thirty-
seven, Huntington twenty-five, Jericho forty-three, Shelburne twenty-five;
the list is long. They totalled twenty-five hundred by the time of the battle
on the 11th, with many more en route. In the haste of their departure, some
came without arms or other equipment. Since many of them arrived at the
mouth of the Salmon River, William Gilliland, the large property-owner
there, interceded with Mooers to get the arms they needed.

Macomb greeted many of the arrivals and sometimes personally issued
arms and ammunition. He gave them pep talks about the kinds of activities
he thought they could do best. He greeted General Strong by handing him a
piece of evergreen as an emblem of the Green Mountains. He sought at least
to build morale since he lacked the time to weld his disparate forces into an
army, but he also told Mooers he hoped he was keeping his men on the move,
harassing enemy pickets: "They should not be idle. And more particularly
should they be prevented from destroying their ammunition by firing at tar-
gets. The practice is most unmilitary when so near the enemy & besides we
have not so great a quantity of that article to be expended in useless firing."[30]

Skirmishes occurred daily, although Prevost's big guns remained silent until the morning of the 11th. When Wool reached Fort Moreau on the 6th, he found it incapable of being defended because it was so crowded with troops, baggage, tents, and supplies that the guns could not be serviced. When Macomb's attention was called to the situation, he ordered the excess troops and supplies moved out.

One American raid was particularly bold. The British were constructing a battery at the bend in the Saranac River, only 500 yards from Fort Brown. In the middle of the night of the 9th, Captain George McGlassin and a party of 50 crossed the river and, by the subterfuge of noisy charges appearing to come from two directions, frightened off a work force and covering party of 300, spiked their guns, and retired without casualties. During the same day, three boys of Aiken's company were nearly captured while they were obtaining supplies from a barn within enemy lines.

Eleazer Williams, working closely with Macomb, experienced a rise in his "war spirit" by the 5th, and although he had always refused to take up that "carnal weapon," he did so now and carried it through the battle period. He devised a trick with which to frighten Prevost, and Macomb commissioned him to execute it. Crossing to Burlington, he obtained from Colonel Elias Fassett a letter announcing falsely that Governor Chittenden was marching for St. Albans with ten thousand men and that five thousand more were on the move from St. Lawrence and four thousand from Washington counties. The letter was deliberately allowed to fall into British hands and probably hastened their retreat after the battle.[31]

After the arrival of the British, Macomb paraded the whole of his small force at each guard-mounting in order to exaggerate his numbers to his watching opponents. The visibility of this operation was enhanced when, nightly, he burned the barracks, warehouses and stables which lay between his forts and the British. The night before the attack he allowed some suspected spies to overhear the false information that Izard's army was nearby and that the woods contained ten thousand concealed militia, with more due the next day. After these "suspicious fellows" were seen crossing the river to the British position, Macomb spent the night covering all the roads leading to the forts with leaves and freshly planted evergreens, while opening new roads leading southward away from the forts.[32]

11

THE BATTLE OF PLATTSBURGH

The two armies and Macdonough's ships waited five days for the arrival of Downie's fleet, which was still not ready because of the *Confiance*. Downie's manpower was adequate, but just barely. He had plenty of sailors for the large vessels; the Thirty-ninth Regiment provided much of the crews of the twelve gunboats, and about seventy men from the Third Battalion of the Canadian Militia were distributed in three of them. The gun crews of the *Confiance* first went to their stations on September 8, although supplies for equipping her guns were still lacking.

Nevertheless, the fleet moved out from Isle-aux-Noix on the 7th, but in the movement southward the *Confiance* grounded as she came out of the Richelieu. She was floated again without damage, and the fleet joined Pring at Isle La Motte on the 8th. They remained there for the next two days while work went forward on the *Confiance;* her last carpenters left the ship at Cumberland Head just before the battle. The gun crews had their first practice on the 9th, and on the evening of the 10th, navy and army officers met at Chazy Landing for an elegant dinner served on casks covered with boards and fine table cloths.[1]

Meanwhile, Prevost tried to advance the date of the fleet's sailing by every sharp word he could think of. Downie told him on the 7th: "Conceiving that the moment I can put this ship in a state for action, shall be able to meet them." Next day Prevost, in urging more haste, laid out his plan for a joint operation:

> I only wait your arrival to proceed against Genl. MaCoombe's last position on the South Bank of the Saranac. Your share in the operation in the first instance, will be to destroy or capture the Enemy's Squadron if it should wait

179

for a contest, and afterwards cooperate with this Division of the Army, but if
it should run away and get out of your reach, we must meet here to consult
on ulterior movements.[2]

On the same day Downie replied emphatically that

I stated to you that the Ship was not ready — she is not ready now, and until
she is ready, it is my Duty not to hazard the squadron before an Enemy, who
will even then be considerably superior in force.

On the 9th, Prevost told him he had postponed moving on the forts, but
"I need not dwell with you on the evils resulting to both Services from delay."
On the same day Downie wrote Prevost that he expected to sail on the 10th;
however, contrary winds prevented him from doing so. Bitingly, Prevost
pointed out that he had had his troops in readiness for an attack since six
o'clock that morning, and that "I ascribe the disappointment I have experienced to the unfortunate change of wind and shall rejoice to learn that my
reasonable expectations have been frustrated by no other means." This correspondence is important not only because it reveals the relations between the
two services just before the battle, but also because it was the navy's prime
evidence in a subsequent court-martial.

Downie finally sailed on the morning of the 11th. He knew the size and
disposition of his opponent within Plattsburgh Bay, but he relied on his superiority to assure him a victory, and his advantages were numerous. He possessed only eight guns more than Macdonough, but they were considerably
better at long range, while Macdonough's numbered more carronades, terribly destructive at short range, like a shotgun firing slugs. Downie had about
100 more men in his ships' complement, and his total tonnage was about 200
more than Macdonough's. The *Confiance,* with its thirty-seven guns, could
fire a broadside only ninety-six pounds short of the long-gun broadside of
the entire American fleet, and the *Linnet* exactly made up the difference —
the two ships equalled the long-range firepower of the entire American fleet,
and the British still had the *Chub* (formerly the *Growler*) and the *Finch* (once
called the *Eagle*), with eleven guns apiece.*

Unaccountably, Downie rose to Macdonough's bait by engaging him *inside* Plattsburgh Bay. His long-range superiority would have made it possible
to pound Macdonough into submission from a distance without suffering
from his huge carronades. Stopping off Cumberland Head, he reconnoitered
Macdonough's position in a small boat, then led his fleet into the bay. His

*See the Appendix for the ships, crews, and firepower of British and American ships.

original plan had been to sail the *Confiance* past the *Eagle* with a broadside, and take his position opposite the *Saratoga*. The *Chub* and the *Linnet* were then to engage the *Eagle*, while the *Finch* and twelve gunboats would take on Macdonough's lesser vessels, the *Ticonderoga* and the *Preble*. Perhaps he forgot that Macdonough also had gunboats, ten of them. In any case, his plans went immediately awry.

The favorable wind that brought Downie from Chazy complicated his efforts to tack northward into the bay, and he had to maneuver in the face of an opponent who was poised in fixed position. Downie's plan almost inevitably meant a battle in two segments: *Eagle*, *Saratoga*, and seven gunboats against *Confiance*, *Linnet*, and *Chub* at the north end of the line, while *Ticonderoga*, *Preble*, and three gunboats faced *Finch* and four gunboats, the other eight British gunboats never joining the battle. Meanwhile, small boats containing British subjects from Canada rounded Cumberland Head to witness the fray, while the shores of the head were lined with curious Americans. Just before the start of the battle Macdonough and his officers on the *Saratoga* knelt on deck for prayer.

A general engagement opened at about nine o'clock. The *Confiance* was forced to anchor prematurely under fire at 350 yards while still attempting to maneuver into a better position. The *Linnet* and the *Chub* came up to confront the *Eagle*; as the *Linnet* passed the *Saratoga*, she loosed a broadside which caused no serious damage, but a ball broke the coop containing a gamecock, which flew into the rigging and crowed defiantly. The crew took this as a good omen and cheered lustily.

In addition to eight inactive gunboats, Downie also quickly lost the services of two of his large vessels. Fifteen minutes into the confrontation, the *Chub* had her sails and rigging so badly damaged that she drifted out of control through the American lines and surrendered. An American gunboat eased her close to the western shore of the bay. On the other end of the line, the *Finch* was so damaged by the *Preble* and the *Ticonderoga* that she drifted out of line and struck a reef off Crab Island. The invalids fired their six-pounder and forced her to surrender also. However, the *Preble* was likewise so severely cut up that she ran inshore under her own sails. The *Ticonderoga* was thus left alone to face the fury of four gunboats whose crews tried repeatedly to board her. Her guns were fired by pistol flashes when the matches for the firing pieces became useless, and the *Ticonderoga* remained in action throughout the battle.

At the other end of the line the *Eagle* was receiving the full fire of the *Linnet* plus partial fire from the *Confiance*, although the original plan had not envisaged the need for the *Confiance* to divert any of her fire away from the *Saratoga*. Severely shot up, the *Eagle*'s commander, Lieutenant Robert

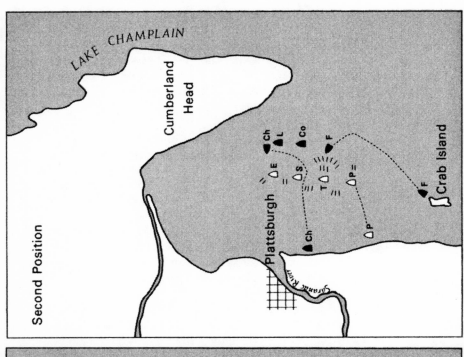

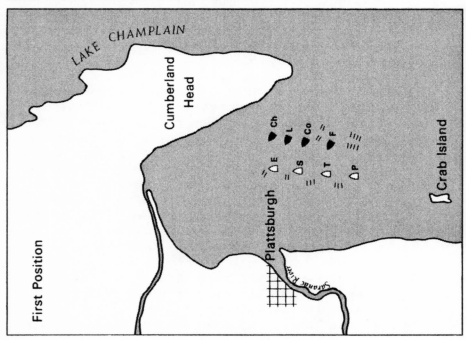

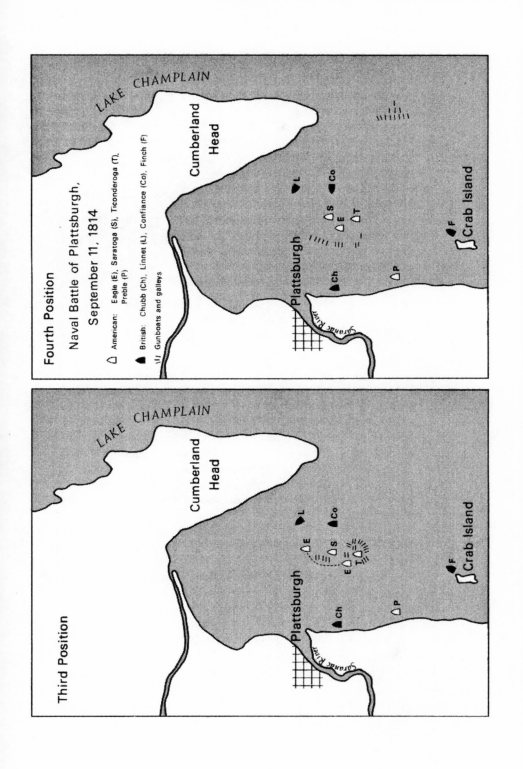

Third Position

Fourth Position

Naval Battle of Plattsburgh,
September 11, 1814

△ American: Eagle (E), Saratoga (S), Ticonderoga (T),
Preble (P)

▲ British: Chubb (Ch), Linnet (L), Confiance (Co), Finch (F)

⫫ Gunboats and galleys

LAKE CHAMPLAIN

Cumberland
Head

Plattsburgh

Saranac River

Crab Island

"Naval Battle of Plattsburgh, September 11, 1814." Painted by Julian O. Davidson, student of M. F. H. De Haas, in 1884. *Courtesy of Key Bank N.A., Plattsburgh, N.Y.*

Henley, cut her cable at about ten thirty and drifted to the rear of the *Saratoga*, where he could bring fresh batteries to bear on the *Confiance*. While this was going on, the *Saratoga* was receiving the combined fire of the *Linnet* and the *Confiance*. Quite early in the battle Downie, who was standing behind one of his guns when it received a shot from the *Saratoga*, was killed instantly. Macdonough was knocked down twice, once remaining senseless briefly, and his ship twice caught fire. Amid all this turmoil Macdonough managed to make some of his ship's sightings and firings because his first lieutenant was sick ashore and his second lieutenant, Peter Gamble, was killed early in the engagement.

The *Saratoga*'s starboard guns by now were nearly all out of action, and only four of those on the *Confiance* still functioned. Macdonough let go his stern anchor, cut his bow cable and winded his ship to bring the port guns to bear. The *Confiance* tried clumsily to execute the same maneuver but she got stuck at right angles to the *Saratoga*. The *Saratoga*'s broadsides were so terrible and unanswerable that the crews on the *Confiance* refused to return to their posts. There was nothing to do but surrender, which was done at eleven o'clock. The *Linnet* tried to hold out but a broadside from the *Saratoga* forced her to strike her colors also, at eleven twenty. During the battle, the *Confiance* received 105 round shots in her hull, the *Saratoga* 55. Macdonough's ship was so badly damaged that it was two hours before he could take control of the surrendered British vessels.

Macdonough at first ordered his gunboats to pursue the fleeing British gunboats but changed the order to one of assistance for the *Confiance* and the *Linnet*, which were nearly ready to sink. A few of the British gunboats fought well but most of them fled long before the end of the battle. Their commander escaped while under arrest preparatory to trial and although never caught, he was dropped from the naval list. Shortly Pring, who commanded the *Linnet*, and the commanders of the three other vessels came under a convoy guard to turn over their swords to Macdonough, but the American, praising their fine qualities, refused the swords even though the men were his prisoners. On the day of the battle he sent an eloquent message to the secretary of the navy: "The Almighty has been pleased to grant us a signal victory on Lake Champlain in the capture of one Frigate, one Brig and two sloops of war of the enemy."[3]

The human cost of this terrible pounding was, among the Americans, 4 officers and 48 men killed and 58 wounded, for a casualty rate of 13 percent. The British lost 5 officers and 49 men dead and 116 wounded, a rate of 18 percent. The battle was heard or watched by many people on Grand Isle and elevated areas on both sides of the lake. Julius Hubbell of Chazy, who witnessed it from Cumberland Head, remembered that "The firing was terrific, fairly shaking the ground, and so rapid that it seemed to be one continuous roar, intermingled with spiteful flashing from the mouths of the guns, and dense clouds of smoke soon hung over the two fleets."[4]

Hubbell was allowed to board the *Saratoga*, where he saw the dead neatly stacked and the seams full of blood. He found the *Confiance* "absolutely torn to pieces" and mutilated bodies in all directions. Simeon Doty, a militiaman from Alburg, confirmed the destruction and bloodiness of the scene on the day after the battle. From the number of reminiscenses it is easy to visualize a constant procession of the curious peering through the wrecks of both fleets.

While all this was taking place on the water, a much different tempo was adopted on land. Simultaneously with the first firing of the guns in the bay, at about nine o'clock, the British land batteries opened up for the first time in a massive bombardment which quickly silenced one of the American blockhouses. But speedy troop movements were another matter.

General Robinson had been notified the day before that he would lead the attack across the river at the fording place near Pike's Cantonment. For that purpose he would have both his own First and Power's Third brigades, some four thousand officers and men. Robinson obtained Prevost's agreement to his moving to the ford at daybreak the next morning, the 11th. But next morning the order to march was not forthcoming; instead, the men were told to cook breakfast as late as eight o'clock. Impatient to be on the move, Robinson says he finally obtained from Prevost an hour for the advance to the ford: ten o'clock! Meanwhile, the naval battle was raging.[5]

At the prescribed time the two brigades started for the ford, guided by members of the quartermaster general's staff. But the guides took the wrong road, and after retracing many steps they finally reached the ford but, says Robinson, "a full hour of precious time had been irretrievably lost by the unfortunate mistake." On the opposite bank about 400 American militiamen were guarding the crossing, but in the face of withering fire several British companies forded the river and dispersed the Americans in all directions. The companies were ordered to halt on the south bank until the entire army was across. Four battalions were already formed when a message from Prevost ordered an immediate retreat because the British fleet had surrendered. Robinson describes the scene: "Never was anything like the disappointment expressed in every countenance. The advance was within shot, and full view of the Redoubts, and in one hour they must have been ours. We retired under two six pounders posted on our side the Ford in as much silent discontent as was ever exhibited."

This account of the engagement by its commander differs markedly from the traditional American accounts, largely based on Macomb's report to the secretary of war.[6] Robinson omits mention of two attempts to cross the river by Brisbane's division, at the lower and upper bridges in the village which, Macomb says, were repulsed by the regulars. Macomb also mentions "an immense number" of scaling ladders with which the British planned to assault the forts. Robinson is undoubtedly accurate in saying that his men were ordered to form on the south bank before advancing, and that their retreat was the result of an order from Prevost. Macomb is therefore guilty of exaggeration when he reports that Robinson's army "were either killed taken or driven back" by the "brave Volunteers and Militia," although he is accurate in claiming the killing or capturing of a whole company of the Seventy-sixth Regiment. The local folklore must be discarded that the British pursued the fleeing militia more than half way to South Plattsburgh. Robinson says that he could see the forts in the distance. An advance upon them would not have detoured by way of South Plattsburgh, several miles to the south.

The land battle at Plattsburgh has often been considered trivial compared with the explosion on the lake, and Macdonough has overshadowed Macomb in all of the subsequent commemorations. It is, however, easy to underestimate the deterrent effect of thirty-two-year-old Macomb's sturdy defense. In contemplating the reduction of the American forts, for example, Prevost considered the cost too high before the fleet arrived and, counting on a naval victory, he felt such a loss of life was unnecessary. After the defeat on the lake he wrote the Colonial Secretary: "This unlooked for Event depriving me of the Cooperation of the Fleet without which the further prosecution of the Service was become impracticable, I did not hesitate to arrest the course of the Troops advancing to the attack, because the most complete success would have been unavailing, and the possession of the Enemy's Works offered no advantage to compensate for the loss we must have sustained in acquiring possession of them."[7]

His conclusions are at variance with those naval historians who believe that British possession of the forts and their huge guns would have made Macdonough's position untenable in the bay *prior to the battle,* but that during the fight they might have indiscriminately hit the British fleet as well. That Macdonough believed he might be in danger from the shore batteries is evidenced by the fact that after the battle he moved his ships toward Crab Island, well out of range of the land guns.

The British batteries continued in action until a ceasefire was ordered at about 3:00 P.M. Thereafter Prevost's order for an immediate retreat was set in motion. The ordnance began to be pulled out at dusk, and the entire army was on the move an hour before daybreak the next morning. Every piece of ordnance was taken back as well as much of the ammunition and stores, by the use of carts and wagons. When they broke down, their contents were destroyed on the spot. The lack of transport forced the abandonment of shells, fifty thousand cartridges were destroyed, and other munitions were hidden in the lake off Chazy Landing. Much was also sent in boats, but one sloop loaded with ordnance sank off Isle La Motte.[8]

The retreat was hasty, and many Americans were convinced that the main reason was Prevost's fear of being cut off below the border by swarms of militia; Prevost himself confirmed this reason in his dispatches to London. In the rush, huge quantities of supplies were abandoned. The Kent-Delord House still displays a tea chest left by an officer who was quartered there. Prevost even left some of his wounded to Macomb's care in the Dunham house that still stands in the center of the city. Prevost's generals were disgusted, and two of them were reported to have given up their swords, refusing to serve in Canada while he remained there. General Robinson said that the retreat was conducted "in the most precipitate and disgraceful manner. . . . I am sick at heart, everything I see and hear is discouraging. This is no field for a military man above the rank of a Colonel of Riflemen."[9]

The British army's failure at Plattsburgh is not easily explained. Prevost and Downie approached the battle with differing understandings of the meaning of a cooperative attack. Downie believed that it meant the huge British army would capture the forts early in the battle and then turn their guns on Macdonough's fleet. At the least this might cripple some of Macdonough's ships; at the most it might drive him out of the bay altogether.

Prevost, on the other hand, thought that the defeat of the fleet should

The Charles Dunham House in Plattsburgh prior to enlargement c. 1940. The British used the basement as a hospital and left some of their wounded there when they retreated.

come first, after which, presumably, the forts could be taken. The storming of the forts by a direct crossing of the river was a part of his plan, but he shrank from the loss of life it would entail, once he had seen it attempted. Throughout the war, he had shuddered at the "further effusion of blood." A humane man, he was not offensive minded and was not originally sent to Canada to wage a war. Once it came, he probably should have been replaced, although as long as it remained a defensive operation he performed skilfully. His superiors in London were expecting too much of him, after two years of defending Canada, that he would be suddenly able to reorient his aims to offensive operations.

Once the British fleet surrendered, it is easier to trace his thinking in ordering a retreat, although perhaps not such a hasty and disorderly one. Uppermost in his mind was the futility of further effort without British control of the lake; in this view he was later indirectly supported by the Duke of Wel-

lington. He was also obsessed with the fear that troops from New England
would cut his supply line to Canada which, with the British naval defeat,
now had to be entirely by land.

The routes of the retreat included the Ashley, State, and Lake Shore
roads. At Plattsburgh the cart and oxen of Gideon Rugar were impressed to
carry the wounded, together with a member of the family to drive; he managed to get back from Chazy with the oxen. At Chazy Landing, British troops
impressed the oxen of William Lawrence. He sent his thirteen-year-old son,
Putnam, in a successful venture to reclaim them. The retreating army arrested Dr. Nathan Carver and two other Chazy men and held them in Montreal for several weeks.[10]

At Chazy, officers again moved in on the Hubbells, and also used his law
office. They burned fence rails for fuel in the fireplace at the office, but Mrs.
Hubbell saved the building after their departure when she discovered the
floor was on fire. The British left some of their wounded at Dewey's Tavern,
and those who died were buried in the family cemetery. The retreat did not
go completely unchallenged, however. A small cavalry detachment of twenty
men from Orwell, Vermont, followed the British to Chazy and surprised the
rear guard, capturing seven dragoons and the contents of two baggage
wagons. Major Wool wanted to mount a pursuit with regulars but Macomb,
suspecting a British trap, waited until later in the morning. By that time, according to Macomb, "A continual fall of rain and a violent storm prevented
further pursuit," although he hoped, between deserters and captives, that at
least a third of the British army would be destroyed.[11]

This is Macomb's only word on the subject, but it is an insufficient explanation of his failure to pursue a disorganized foe. If fear of a ruse deterred
him on the night of the battle, by morning he could reason that they had a
long lead on him. Yet the storm would have been no more detrimental to
him than to his quarry, which did indeed get bogged down in mud. It is possible that Macomb, after so many days of waiting to be attacked, found it difficult to shift gears and order an attack of his own, even if he could have pulled
his disparate units together. More likely, he assessed his chances of success
and found them wanting with a force largely made up of militia and volunteers which he had had no time to forge into an army.

Nevertheless, accounts abound about attempted and successful British
desertions. Gideon Rugar remembered a British soldier, wounded in battle,
being cared for by the women of his family. At the time of the retreat the
troops took him with them, although he wanted the Rugars to conceal him so
he would not have to go. Mrs. Moses Shute Mooers was a girl at her father's
home near Cooperville and saw deserters near by. According to her, one of
them said they had been told they were going to fight the "heathen

Yankees," but instead "they found that we talked just as they did. They said we were their own brothers and sisters."[12]

All along the line of retreat, individuals and groups deserted as opportunity allowed. John Watts led his entire platoon into the woods and, by family tradition, concealed himself in a hollow tree. He settled in Mooers Forks and started a branch of the family which a descendant still calls "The Hollow-Tree Wattses."[13] By the time of the next army report, made in Odelltown on the 15th, 234 desertions had occurred since the previous week. Outpost duty still claimed 460 men, chiefly because a brigade under Major General Power remained in Champlain until the 25th.

A few days later the *Montreal Herald* had difficulty in finding something to celebrate: "History produces nothing superior to the valor and gallantry of the officers and crew of the *Confiance;* suffice it to say that she was literally fought to the water's edge. . . . Would that a veil could be drawn over the scene on shore! but it must afford a sad tale in the page of British history."[14]

Gradually the people of Plattsburgh came back and the village began to return to normal. People like Mrs. Delord could recover the family silver concealed in a well. A son born to Tom Haynes, Plattsburgh's negro barber, and his wife "Black Maria" was named "Sir George Prevost." The militia were disbanded, and the Vermont volunteers started for home on the 12th, except for the St. Albans contingent, which was delayed until the 14th for lack of transportation. Aiken's company was also dismissed with thanks from Macomb, who gave each boy a rifle to show his appreciation. His quartermaster probably reminded him that he would be personally accountable and so he asked Aiken to get them back, promising at the same time to refer his commitment to Congress. After twelve years Congress provided that each boy (now a man) receive a rifle inscribed with his name.

When the Plattsburgh jail caught fire, the British released the prisoners: a father and son, arrested for murder; another for stabbing, another for counterfeiting and four for larceny and other crimes. The father and son, who were French, were pursued into Canada and the son was recaptured. He was tried and sentenced to be hanged, but he killed himself in jail. The sheriff, not to be denied his fee, hanged the dead body.[15]

The two fleets in the bay were shattered; not a sail in either squadron was functioning. The *Confiance* was almost foundering and the *Linnet* had a foot of water above her lower deck. The pumps were kept busy while gunboats towed them into shallow water. Macdonough paroled forty-seven of the severely wounded British and sent them to the hospital at Isle-aux-Noix. The slightly wounded he added to his 367 prisoners. The wounded and dead of both fleets and the army were put under the care of Dr. Mann on Crab

Island. He reported more than thirty amputations within four days. Simeon Doty described the two long plank hospitals, the wounded laid in two rows "groaning and taking on terribly and calling for the doctor." British and American dead were buried together in trenches without coffins.[16]

The casualties among the officers received more ceremonious treatment. On the 14th, the American dead were placed in one of the *Saratoga's* boats and covered with the flag of their vessel. The boat was followed to the *Confiance* by Macdonough and his officers. The British dead and living joined the procession. On shore they were met by a large escort of military personnel and civilians, and all marched to Riverside Cemetery. Against the backdrop of minute guns from the forts, the dead were solemnly lowered into adjoining graves which form an irregular cluster. In 1818 a marble monument for Downie arrived and was installed with the inscription "Erected by his affectionate Sister-in-law, Mary Downie." In 1819 a ceremonial reburial of the remains of Lieutenant Colonel James Wellington and Ensign John Chapman was made from their original resting places in East Beekmantown. In 1843 the hitherto unmarked graves were identified with the marble markers that appear today. The enclosure became complete in 1844 with the reburial from Isaac Platt's garden of the remains of Lieutenant Robert Kingsbury. However, no stone marks his grave site.[17]

In his reports Macdonough assessed the actions of individuals. Of the moving of the *Preble* during the battle he said: "Lt. Budd acted with propriety in getting under way with the *Preble*. He would otherwise have been boarded by the enemy's galleys." But he believed that the *Eagle* should not have been moved because her killed and wounded did not justify it, and the action exposed the *Saratoga* to galling fire from the *Linnet* when she already faced the *Confiance*. Lieutenant Henley of the *Eagle* made his own report to the secretary of the navy in which he indicated that he had not been given sufficient acknowledgement from Macdonough, on which Macdonough commented that "His statement is unquestionably very erroneous and will, I fear, ultimately be injurious to himself."[18] But the future was kind to Henley — he received a vote of thanks and a gold medal from Congress, and was made master commandant and much later, captain.

Macdonough paroled the surviving British officers a few days after the battle. On the 12th, Pring made a detailed report of the action to his superior, Yeo on Lake Ontario. But from Isle-aux-Noix on the 17th, he dwelt on the Prevost-Downie dispute, describing "the want of the promised cooperation of the land forces, to which I attribute the cause of our failure." Unmistakeably pinpointing Prevost as the villain, "It may not be improper to remark that had the enemy's works been stormed, even after the action had been terminated, our squadron might have been preserved from falling into their hands by running under cover of the batteries, as the enemy's force was for some considerable time unequal to take possession of us."[19]

Before they departed, the officers of the *Linnet* and the *Confiance* separately wrote letters of appreciation to Macdonough for their "honorable treatment" and for his "unbounded liberality and humane attention." This was gratifying, as were the honors heaped upon both Macdonough and Macomb. Each received promotions back dated to the day of the battle. Each was voted gold medals and resolutions of thanks from Congress. They received swords, had portraits painted, and were given keys to various cities. Macdonough's wife in Connecticut gave birth to their first baby the day after the news reached Middletown. Even the governor of Vermont praised the victors, urged that political differences ought to be laid aside, and ordered that the militia be made ready to march at a moment's warning! Perhaps in recognition of his change of perspective, Vermonters reelected Chittenden that fall.

The citizens of Plattsburgh honored Macdonough and Macomb at a civic dinner on the 23rd. A procession was formed at the Mooers house which Macomb had used as headquarters, and marched to Israel Green's Inn. There a repast, with "segars" and a variety of beverages, was consumed. Seventeen formal toasts were drunk. Not to be outdone, Burlington entertained them with a splendid dinner and ball on the 26th. Twenty one toasts were made!

An attempt to honor Vergennes' favorite son, General Samuel Strong, who had led the Vermont volunteers at Plattsburgh, almost ended in a riot. Pliny Moore's son witnessed the event and described it in this way:

> Last Wednesday a sword was presented to General Strong by a committee from the State of New York. There was a great concourse of people assembled, a great part of the inhabitants. . . . Col. Smith of Plats'g presented the sword after which Gen. Strong treated the populace to as much as they could drink. Many got drunk and fought, the mayor ordered the Sherif to exercise his authority he rushed in the middle of the crowd and was caught by five or six of them who began to beat him but several civil officers went to his assistance and after a short scuffle rescued him the troop was then ordered out to quiet the disturbance and populace ordered to disperse on penalty of the law. The troop and civil officers secured all the ring leaders and committed them to jail. I saw three put in jail and was since told that there were a number of others. It was a complet mob as ever was.[20]

12

AFTERMATH

The battle of Plattsburgh, decisive as it was, still left many tangled threads to unravel. Smugglers continued to ply their trade on Lake Champlain, and Collector Sailly had difficulty holding good assistants until he promised to back them fully in all suits. One of the most serious confrontations with smugglers occurred in November 1814, when a rowboat containing $8,000 in merchandise eluded revenue officers at Rouses Point. Sailly sent a cutter and five men in pursuit. They found the goods concealed at Whitehall, but the owners and armed citizens recaptured them, severely injuring two of the revenue men in the process. Naval officers stationed nearby refused to help, and even struck one of the inspectors with a musket.[1]

Meanwhile, Macdonough faced the problem of winter quarters for the two fleets under his control. He and his officers expected a renewed land attack by the huge British army whose primary object would be to capture or destroy the fleets. Thus Macdonough decided to make winter quarters at the south end of the lake, as far removed from the scene of anticipated trouble as possible. He repaired both fleets at Plattsburgh and on October 2 sent the *Saratoga*, *Confiance*, *Ticonderoga*, and *Linnet* to Whitehall. As the *Saratoga* passed Burlington, she fired a salute which Macdonough's grandson believes was "the last gun, probably, she ever fired."[2] Macdonough kept the brig *Eagle*, *Preble*, *Montgomery*, the ten galleys, and the sloops *Growler* and *Eagle* (he quickly gave them back their original names) as provision vessels and living quarters for the men attached to the galleys.

Early in November Macdonough recovered six tons of nine-inch shells which the British, expecting to return, had hidden in the waters off Chazy Landing. Then he raised the British sloop loaded with naval stores which had sunk off Isle La Motte during the retreat. From it he retrieved thousands of pounds of ammunition.[3]

Macdonough took the rest of his fleet to Whitehall on November 18, and turned over his command to Lieutenant Charles Budd of the *Preble*. He stayed in the area for another three weeks, however, with quarters on the *Confiance*. The fleet was moored stern to stern at the elbow below Taft's Island. Macdonough warned Budd to keep the ships in good shape and to watch for incendiaries. If he patrolled down the lake, he ought not go beyond Point au Fer, and he should return before the lake froze over. He should later be on the alert for a British attack over the ice.

Early in December, Macdonough went to his home in Middletown on the first stage of travels that were supposed to take him to Washington. Rumors of a British attack on Whitehall kept surfacing, however, and early in January he was ordered back to the lake. He talked to Budd and went on to see the military commanders at Burlington and Plattsburgh. He came to the conclusion that no imminent attack was being planned, but that large-scale shipbuilding was going on at Isle-aux-Noix. If that were true, Americans would need to build also, but he asked for relief from his responsibilities on the lake, chiefly for the sake of his health. The reports he picked up concerning British ship construction included twelve large galleys on the stocks and three ships with their keels already laid.

Macdonough was not relieved of command and spent the rest of the winter at Whitehall, but the arrival of a definitive peace treaty and its ratification by the Senate made a new naval race unnecessary. His fleet remained moored in its original location for about three years and was dismantled, probably in 1818. In that year all ships of war on Lake Champlain and the Great Lakes were outlawed by the Rush-Bagot Agreement with Great Britain. In 1825 the vessels at Whitehall were sold at public auction. The buyers sold off the materials and probably moved the ships into East Bay. There they finally sank near the mouth of the Poultney River.

The military commanders at Plattsburgh and Burlington continued to expect a new British attack in force. Reports even appeared in the newspapers about the thousand sleighs and ten thousand buffalo robes as well as the massing of men and cannon at Isle-aux-Noix. The armies on both sides of the lake were on the alert, as were Mooers's and Strong's militia. Macomb began the construction of two new forts, Tompkins and Gaines, to protect the southern approaches to the existing three at Plattsburgh.

Prevost did indeed dally with the idea of trying to capture the fleet at Whitehall, but he discarded it because of the distance and the temptation it would offer his troops to desert. But the British navy was in no mood to give up; naval construction at Isle-aux-Noix was to be extensive enough to regain control of Lake Champlain. This would put Americans to great expense, make them keep a large force there, and prevent them from bolstering their resources at Sackets Harbor.

Lake Ontario, which was Yeo's primary concern, was also the scene of determined preparations for the next season's warfare. Yeo controlled the lake
in October with the launching of his monstrous three-deck *St. Lawrence* of
100 guns. Both he and Chauncey planned to build ships all winter, but Yeo
had a head start. In November, he received a supplement of 250 shipwrights
and carpenters and started a ship at Kingston. Macdonough was ordered to
send Chauncey some of his seamen; 219 started out, but some deserted or fell
sick and were left on the way. Forty-five of them refused to go beyond
Brownville until they had been paid for their service on Lake Champlain, and
Chauncey sent marines to bring them in. Eventually, 203 arrived. Chauncey
had three new ships in mind, and he actually started two before the peace
treaty put an end to both his and Yeo's feverish exertions. Yeo's valedictory
on the war contained these conclusions:

> The experience of two years' active service has served to convince me that
> tho' much has been done by the mutual exertions of *both services*, we also
> owe as much, if not more, to the perverse stupidity of the enemy; the impol-
> icy of their plans; the disunion of their commanders, and lastly, between
> *them* and their *Ministers* of *War* the fatal, and, *fortunate for us, mistaken*
> confidence they placed in the *attachment of the Canadians to their cause*,
> was another delusion highly favorable to *ours*, which they are now con-
> vinced of.[4]

The war was not technically at an end during the fall, and organized disaffection reached its climax with the meeting of the Hartford Convention.
On October 17, the Massachusetts legislature invited the New England states
to a conference to formulate their grievances. The Republican legislatures of
New Hampshire and Vermont failed to authorize delegates but twenty-six
were chosen from Federalist Massachusetts, Rhode Island, and Connecticut.
The Massachusetts delegation included only one extremist, and the convention itself, when it opened at Hartford on December 15, quickly came under
the control of the moderates. It consisted, wrote Henry Adams, of "mostly
cautious and elderly men, who detested democracy, but disliked enthusiasm
almost as much."[5]
  If it had been held earlier, its disruptive effects would undoubtedly have
been great. But it was content to adopt a series of resolutions not directly related to the war, which all could see was nearly at an end. The resolutions and
several proposed constitutional amendments, although far-ranging, fell far
short of the secessionist threats that had been made by the extremists who
did not attend. They were an expression of New England's political and commercial fears for its future in the Union. Yet before the impact of the convention could be fully felt, word was received of Jackson's success in repelling the

British at New Orleans. It was followed shortly by news of the peace treaty that had been signed while the convention was in session. Interest in the Hartford resolutions disappeared overnight, and even the constitutional amendments were lost in the general rejoicing over the end of hostilities.

By the time of the Hartford Convention, a peace conference had already been sitting for four months at Ghent, in what is now Belgium. The conclave had finally come about after many months of sparring between Great Britain and the United States over the time and place for serious talks. The process had started in the first winter of the war with the Russian czar's offer of mediation, and Madison's appointment of Gallatin and Bayard to join the American minister in St. Petersburg, John Quincy Adams.

Owing to the preoccupation of both the Russian and British governments with the war, as well as a breakdown in communications, the Americans in Russia did not learn for months that the British had rejected mediation. Eventually the British, in no hurry for negotiations to start, proposed bilateral talks between the United States and Great Britain. Madison accepted the suggestion early in 1814 and supplemented the old commission with two additional members — Henry Clay and Jonathan Russell. Negotiations over the time and place of the conference consumed several more months.

On August 8, 1814, the peace talks finally got under way, but both sides approached the table with unrealistic agenda. The American delegation, in addition to demanding restitution and compensation for past grievances, was even supposed to work for a cession of all of Canada and under no condition to agree to disarm the lakes or to cede any American territory — the principal of the *status quo ante bellum.*

The British wanted to create an "Indian territory" north of the Ohio River and to acquire large cessions of land west of Lake Superior, in the Champlain Valley, and in Maine based upon the principal of *uti possidetis* (possession of territory already occupied). Their demands amounted to a cession of nearly one-third of all the United States. Freed from their war in Europe by the defeat of Napoleon in the spring, they planned four major campaigns in North America, carefully designed to reinforce their demands at the peace table. They expected to occupy New Orleans, attack in the Chesapeake, and occupy segments of the Champlain Valley and Maine. At the conference they waited for word from the fronts before making any commitments.

News of the conquests in Maine and the burning of Washington encouraged the British to demand peace on their own terms, while the Americans used the subsequent repulse of the British at Baltimore and Plattsburgh to hold out against any cession of territory.[6] Their hand thus strengthened by

Plattsburgh, their chief advantage was now the absolute control of Lakes Erie and Champlain, which offset British military preponderance all along the rest of the border. Most of the weaknesses of the American war effort remained, however, and the divisions in the country were even then being advertised at the Hartford Convention.

With the deadlock of both military and diplomatic undertakings, the prime minister, Lord Liverpool, in November wrote to the Duke of Wellington in Paris, offering him full powers to continue the war until peace could be made under favorable conditions. But Europe was seething with a profound unrest during this period between the first exile of Napoleon and his return to continue the struggle. Wellington declared that his going to America would suggest that the situation was much worse than it really was. What was needed was not another general, but naval superiority on the lakes; without it the peace might as well be signed at Ghent. "Why stipulate for the *uti possidetis*?" he scolded his government; "you can get no territory; indeed, the state of your military operations, however creditable, does not entitle you to demand any."[7]

A further setback to British hopes came in November. For the first time London newspapers, copying from the American press, revealed to the British people the scope of their government's demands. Weary and heavily taxed for a twenty-year war against France, the British public was aghast at the belligerent nature of their government's diplomacy, and the Whigs pressed for an early peace. At a crucial cabinet meeting on November 18, the government abandoned its plans for territorial gains, opening the way to a break in the long deadlock.

Probably the British were more readily persuaded to come to terms because of the continuing instability of Europe than for military considerations in North America. Lord Liverpool underlined this point to Foreign Secretary Castlereagh at Vienna:

> I think we have determined, if all other points can be satisfactorily settled, not to continue the war for the purpose of obtaining, or securing any acquisition of territory. We have been led to this determination by the consideration of the unsatisfactory state of the negotiations at Vienna, and by that of the alarming situation of the interior of France. . . . Under such circumstances, it has appeared to us desirable to bring the American war, if possible, to a conclusion.[8]

The negotiations now proceeded rapidly. Both sides bargained, then retreated a step. The Americans had long since given up their demand for an outlawing of impressment. One by one they dropped their demands on the blockade, prewar spoliations, contraband, neutral trading rights, and compensation for wartime destruction. The British had earlier dropped all their much-publicized efforts in behalf of their Indian allies; they now relinquished their expectations of border changes and of exclusive armament on the Great Lakes. The resulting treaty of Christmas Eve had to be anemic to be signed at all. It adopted the American policy of the *status quo* for all territories, the restoration of prisoners and the return of or restitution for Negro slaves carried off by the British forces, and the termination of all hostilities with the Indians, returning them to the situation that existed in 1811. The uncertainties in the old boundary line of 1783 were referred to three mixed commissions to whom were assigned sections of the entire boundary from the Atlantic Ocean to the Lake of the Woods. If these two-man commissions could not agree, a "final and conclusive" decision was to be reached by the arbitration of a friendly sovereign or state.

The main achievement of the treaty was the mere cessation of hostilities, because the omissions are striking. Among them were impressment, which the British never renounced, and neutral rights, which were nowhere defined. Such a treaty does not represent a triumph for anyone. Both sides were tired of war and realized that a victory would cost more than either was willing to pay. Furthermore, the British, at the peak of their influence in Europe, were nevertheless dealing with an explosive situation. The return of Napoleon to resume the war in the spring of 1815 required their utmost energies and culminated with his final defeat at Waterloo in June. From first to last, except for a brief period in 1814, the American War of 1812 was a secondary theatre of operations for the British. The most noteworthy fact about it was their ability to maintain their North American possessions intact.

The war also had a significant impact upon the United States. Some historians like to call it the Second American Revolution, fought to preserve the ideals of the first. The country emerged from the war with a new sense of nationality; for many years it turned inward, focussing on internal growth and development. The war marked the end of an era when American policy and politics were largely determined by events outside the United States, yet relations with Great Britain improved after the war and a series of long-range treaties were negotiated on single issues.

It also produced a few warriors who, tested in the struggle, emerged to lead the nation's military establishment for many years: Macomb, Brown, Wool, Snelling, and Totten. Two war heroes, Jackson and Harrison, became presidents and another, Scott, was a candidate; Jackson's fame, however, rested on the battle of New Orleans, fought *after* the peace treaty had been signed, while Harrison's grew out of the Indian skirmish at Tippecanoe which took place *before* the war. Moreover, a parallel list shows lives compromised or ruined by the war: Hull, Dearborn, Wilkinson, and Hampton.

The career of Alexander Macomb demonstrates the subsequent usefulness of one of the notable personalities of the war. He remained in command of about three thousand men at Plattsburgh throughout the winter, but in the spring was ordered to Washington to join five other generals in reorganizing the army. It was to be reduced to a peacetime establishment of 10,000 men, which meant that only 39 of 216 field officers and 450 of 2,055 regimental officers could be retained. A place was found for Macomb, and by 1828 he was the commanding general.

The reduction in the size of the army was based upon the generally held view that the militia was "the only force that can be tolerated with safety by a free people, in times of peace." Macomb, mellowed by his experience with the militia during the war, wrote a long "Memoir" in which he called them the country's "great natural arm," indispensable to its survival, and preferable to either an armed state, anarchy, or despotism. His participation in a decade of debates was made with a full awareness of the weaknesses in the militia structure and training. As commanding general he was able to get some reforms adopted, but his biggest contribution was a manual he produced to give uniformity to the regulations for militia and volunteers.[9]

The postwar life of Governor General Sir George Prevost is, on the contrary, one of the tragedies of the time. His downfall, however, had been long in preparation. Throughout the war years, his deliberate courting of the French majority aroused deep resentment among his British subjects, who were convinced that his policies were betraying his imperial trust. By 1813, he had accumulated an array of powerful and vocal enemies, not the least of which were the British fur merchants, who accused him of forbearance toward the enemy.

The ringleader of his opposition continued to be the Anglican bishop of Quebec, who showered the colonial secretary, Lord Bathurst, with his grievances. He objected to Prevost's evident determination to leave the patronage of the church in the hands of the clergy. He was particularly agitated over Bathurst's formal bestowal of bishopric upon the head of the Catholic Church, in effect establishing "a religion which every man of unfettered judgment admits to be equally unfavourable to morality, to industry, and to improvement." Meanwhile, his own church "languishes in neglect and decline."[10]

In countering this onslaught, Prevost described Bishop Mountain as possessing "far more disposition for politics than theology;" and as "tainting every act by a fixed prejudice." Prevost declared that the great mass of the people "were to be soothed to my purposes, not offended on the very subject of their dearest interests."[11]

From his seat on the Executive Council, Bishop Mountain was also able to work from within the government. The Executive and Legislative councils, still with British majorities, turned savagely against the French Assembly. Prevost assumed that the attacks upon the Assembly were partly efforts to discredit him. Letters to London charged him with courting popularity, subverting the constitution, and neglecting the best interests of the empire, and they contained the hope for a new governor who would not "be terrified by the clamours of the ignorant, nor appalled by the projects of the vicious." The Executive Council petitioned Bathurst to ask Parliament for a change in the constitution of Canada. The councillors denounced the Assembly as containing few members of "any respectable class in society," and "destined by nature and trained by custom to the humble and laborious occupations of life," and they thought the people's "attachment to His Majesty's Government is palsied to the heart."[12]

The Assembly countered with its own grievances. Maintaining that its members had no alternative to passing the proposals of the minority except to be treated as rebels, they depicted the struggle as "le parti Anglais du Gouvernement d' un côté, et la masse du peuple de l'autre." Avowing their affection and loyalty, they warned that some day the colony might have to be held by force rather than remaining a dependency attached by its own happiness — a strong hint of troubles ahead.[13]

Bathurst would probably have been able to sustain Prevost if complaints had come only from the tiny British minority in Quebec. But Prevost's retreat from Plattsburgh raised a new enemy against him — the British navy. Yeo charged him with exerting undue pressure upon the commander on Lake Champlain, Captain George Downie, to commit his fleet prematurely to battle, and then of failing to carry out his agreement to seize the forts and turn them on the American fleet.

This ugly dispute was continued in England for a year and a half. Yeo was ordered home to formulate the charges against Prevost, and the commanders of the fleet at Plattsburgh were directed to attend a naval court-martial. Prevost was ordered home to face charges by the army, as was usual for a defeated commander; his trial promised to be more serious, however, because of the navy's accusations. He had the satisfaction before he left Canada of receiving from the French Assembly an unprecedented resolution of "the highest veneration and respect," praising his administration for "energy, wisdom and ability," and crediting him with rescuing them from enemy subjugation. It voted him a service of plate not to cost more than £5,000.[14]

In August 1815, the court-martial of Captain Pring and the other commanders was held in Portsmouth, England. The testimony filled more than 300 pages and included not only the correspondence between Prevost and

Downie just before the battle, but lengthy testimony of each commander about the behavior of his ship. The court easily acquitted all the officers except Lieutenant McGhie of the *Chub*, who had deserted as soon as he reached Canada after the battle. "The British Navy succeeded in exonerating its own personnel while at the same time fastening the major responsibility for the disaster at Plattsburgh upon the British Army," concludes a recent student of the proceedings.[15]

The court-martial shed no light on the reasons for the British fleet's unreadiness to carry out a London-ordered campaign. It sought no explanation for Downie's allowing himself to be drawn into close engagement when his long-range guns might have won the battle from a distance. Prevost also had the correspondence with which to prove that he had carefully refrained from suggesting how the navy should conduct its battle.

One-sided as was the decision, it remained unrefuted. Prevost, unafraid of the "strictest investigation," left for England in April 1815. For the rest of his life he became a pawn in a match between the army and navy. He pressed for his own trial, only to have the date deferred several times, while his reputation was being compromised by the widely publicized naval court-martial. The date was finally set for February 5, 1816, but Sir George died one month earlier at forty-eight years of age, and the army never held a court-martial to put its own version on the record. Consequently, his accusers, the British in Quebec and the admiralty in London, had the last word in public. His reputation has been distorted ever since.

Lady Prevost spent the next several years trying to get some sign of royal vindication of her husband's character. She asked for a peerage without money; a formal statement of the prince regent's approbation, and changes in the family escutcheon. Only the third request was granted. The family coat of arms was redesigned to contain new supporters — two grenadiers with flags, one flowing toward the inscription "West Indies," the other toward "Canada" — and the new motto was to be *Servatum cineri* (preserver from ruin). In this very restrained manner, Prevost's government posthumously recognized his services to the empire.

Prevost was not the only one to suffer from the war. After June 1814, the troops at Plattsburgh received no pay and by the following March Dr. Beaumont said they had not been paid for ten months.[16] At first Dr. Mann rejoiced over this state of affairs. He found that during the fall of 1814, soldiers were not being attacked by fevers as in previous seasons. He attributed it to the fact that, without pay, the men could not buy alcohol: "This embarrassment, which was considered a national calamity, proved a blessing to the soldier." An enemy of the liquor ration for troops, he found that British deserters, who had never had spiritous rations, were in far better health than

Americans. Yet by early November, even Mann had doubts, and he wrote to Vice President Elbridge Gerry about the hardships of men going unpaid or being discharged without pay.[17]

The worst civilian sufferers in this situation were the business partners Henry Delord and William Bailey of Plattsburgh. At Macomb's importunities they began in August to grant credit to servicemen at their Red Store. The army's accounting procedures invited fraud until a printed permission slip was adopted. Great quantities of goods passed from the store to officers and men under this system, for which the partners received certificates and repeated assurances that the debts were as good as gold.

By February 1815, Bailey and Delord had nearly exhausted their resources, and they notified Macomb of their inability to continue. The general again applied pressure, pointing out that there was still danger of mutiny from unpaid troops. With his apparently iron-clad guarantee of repayment, the partners continued to sell to the men on credit, and when their own means ran dry they borrowed heavily in order to keep going; they even loaned money to other merchants so that they too could sell to servicemen.

Portents of disaster appeared in the spring after the battle when Macomb was transferred to Washington. The troops at Plattsburgh were also moved out, still unpaid, while Bailey and Delord stood helplessly by. In the reorganization of the army, soldiers who had enlisted for the war were discharged, and the rest were reassigned to military posts all over the country. Although finally paid, they were now inaccessible to their creditors in Plattsburgh.

At first the partners thought they could pursue their individual debtors, but Delord's health broke down, and the burden in the early months rested on Bailey alone. They also employed collectors at a percentage of their collections, but the results were minimal. To make matters worse, some of the collectors never returned the certificates. Many more of them were lost when Bailey's house burned in 1822. Long before that, however, the firm had gone bankrupt, and the partners were the subject of a series of suits by their own creditors. Sheriff's seizures of the property of both men were made in 1815 and 1819 to satisfy the claims, and a final levy on Delord's possessions was made immediately after his death in 1825. In the seizure of 1815, Delord lost his home and three-acre estate, but friends purchased it and restored it to his wife and daughter.

Discouraged by the failure to collect the $20,000 from individual servicemen, the partners began to seek help from Washington. Their appeals were handicapped by their inability to produce many of the certificates, and by fears in official Washington of the consequences if the private debts of servicemen were assumed by the government, even if Macomb and his officers had authorized them. After Delord's death, his widow and Bailey continued

to petition for redress. Periodically during the 1830s and as late as 1841, bills
were debated in committee or on the floor, but they came to nothing. Not
even the few certificates that survived were ever redeemed.[18]

A few comments need to be made about the final resting place of local
casualties of the war. Mention has been made of the reburial in Riverside
Cemetery of the three British officers who were killed on the Beekmantown
Road, also of the multiple burials near Pike's Cantonment which have disappeared from view, as has the site of the many interments on Crab Island. In
1868, during the laying of a railroad, the remains of ninety-one soldiers were
uncovered near the lake shore at the wharf in Plattsburgh. They were re-
buried ceremonially in the military cemetery on the army post. So were the
twenty-five skeletons which were uncovered in 1892 when Fort Moreau was
graded to make a parade ground on the post.

The North Country has shown repeatedly that it is prepared to honor its
war dead. Since the 1890s, permanent monuments have marked the sites of
the skirmishes at Culver Hill and Halsey's Corners. Metal markers denote the
remains of Fort Brown and of several houses in the county that played some
part in the War of 1812. The war struck closer to the inhabitants of the Champlain Valley than any other they have engaged in, and its reminders can be
seen everywhere that interested people care to look.

APPENDIX

THE FLEETS AT THE BATTLE OF PLATTSBURGH*

American

	Tons	Crew	Guns	
Ship *Saratoga*	734	210	26	8 long 24s, 6 42-lb. carr., 12 32-lb. carr.
Brig *Eagle*	480	120	20	8 long 18s, 12 32-lb. carr.
Schooner *Ticonderoga*	350	110	17	8 long 12s, 4 long 18s, 5 32-lb. carr.
Sloop *Preble*	80	30	7	7 long 9s
Six gunboats	420	246	12	1 long 24, 1 18-lb. columbiad each
Four gunboats	160	104	4	1 long 12 each
Total	2,224	820	86	

British

	Tons	Crew	Guns	
Frigate *Confiance*	1,200	300	37	27 long 24s, 4 32-lb. carr., 6 24-lb. carr.
Brig *Linnet*	350	120	16	16 long 12s
Sloop *Chub*	112	40	11	10 18-lb. carr., 1 long 6
Sloop *Finch*	110	40	11	6 18-lb. carr., 4 long 6s, 1 18-lb. columbiad
Three gunboats	210		6	1 long 24, 1 32-lb. carr. each
One gunboat	70		2	1 long 18, 1 32-lb. carr. each
One gunboat	70	417	2	1 long 18, 1 18-lb. carr.
Four gunboats	160		4	1 32-lb. carr. each
Three gunboats	120		3	1 long 18 each
Total	2,402	917	92	

*From Rodney Macdonough, *Life of Commodore Thomas Macdonough, U.S. Navy* (Boston: Fort Hill Press, 1909), pp. 165, 169.

NOTES

Abbreviations

ASPIA — American State Papers, Indian Affairs
ASPMA — American State Papers, Military Affairs
AUS — Archives of the United States
CO — Colonial Office
MG — Manuscript group
PAC — Public Archives of Canada
RG — Record Group

1 — Settlement of the Champlain Valley

1. *The Bulletin of the Fort Ticonderoga Museum,* 12 (December 1969):358–64.

2. The best account of these events is Oscar Bredenberg, *Military Activities in the Champlain Valley after 1777* (Champlain, N.Y.: Moorsfield Press, 1962).

3. Walter Hill Crockett, *Vermont, the Green Mountain State,* 4 vols. (New York: Century History, 1921), 2:336–44; Charles A. Jellison, *Ethan Allen, Frontier Rebel* (Syracuse: Syracuse University Press, 1969), p. 285. The most thorough scholar of the negotiations is Professor Ian Pemberton of the University of Windsor, Windsor, Ontario, who has not yet published his findings.

4. Rev. Nathan Perkins, *A Narrative of a Tour through the State of Vermont* (Rutland, Vt., C. E. Tuttle, 1964); and Rev. Timothy Dwight, *Travels in New-England and New-York,* 4 vols. (New Haven, Conn.: T. Dwight, 1821–22).

5. Abby M. Hemenway, *The Vermont Historical Gazetteer,* 5 vols. (1867–91), 2 (Burlington, Vt.: Miss A. M. Hemenway, 1871): 521–22.

6. H. N. Muller III, *The Commercial History of the Lake Champlain-Richelieu River Route, 1760–1815,* Ph.D. diss., University of Rochester, N.Y., 1968), p. 164.

7. Ibid., p. 172.

2 — A Postponed War

1. Eli F. Hecksher, *The Continental System: An Economic Interpretation* (Gloucester, Mass.: P. Smith, 1964), p. 324.

2. *National Intelligencer*, July 3, 1807.

3. Ibid., Feb. 15 and Nov. 30, 1808.

4. Hecksher, *Continental System*, p. 245.

5. William Bailey to Benjamin Mooers, Dec. 1807, Bailey Collection, Special Collections, Feinberg Library, State University College, Plattsburgh, N.Y.

6. *Moorsfield Antiquarian* (Champlain, N.Y.), May 1937, pp. 53–67.

7. *Vermont Centinel* (Burlington), April 15, 1808.

8. Richard P. Casey, "North Country Nemesis: The Potash Rebellion and the Embargo of 1807–1809," *The New York Historical Society Quarterly* (January 1980) p. 40.

9. Ibid.

10. H. N. Muller III, *The Commercial History of the Lake Champlain-Richelieu River Route, 1760–1815*. (Ph.D. diss., University of Rochester, N.Y., 1968), pp. 218, 232–36, 247, 276–77.

11. Ray W. Irwin, *Daniel D. Tompkins* (New York: New York Historical Society, 1968), p. 72.

12. Casey, "North Country Nemesis," p. 37. Material for this section also comes from Walter Hill Crockett *Vermont, the Green Mountain State*, 4 vols. (New York: Century History, 1921), 3: 6–15 and Abby M. Hemenway, *The Vermont Historical Gazetteer*, 5 vols. (1867–91), 2 (Burlington, Vt.: Miss A. M. Hemenway, 1871): 495.

13. Turreau to Talleyrand, quoted in E. A. Cruickshank, "A Study of Disaffection in Upper Canada in 1812–15," *Proceedings and Transactions of the Royal Society of Canada* 6, sec. 2 (1912): 12.

14. Henry to Craig, Feb. 14 and March 18, 1809. All the letters are quoted in Douglas Brymner, ed., *Report on Canadian Archives, 1896* (Ottawa: S. E. Dawson, 1897).

15. James D. Richardson, ed., *Messages and Papers of the Presidents*, 10 vols. (Washington, D.C.: Government Printing Office, 1896–99), 2: 473, 77.

16. *The Weekly Register* (Baltimore), 1: 371.

17. Jefferson to John Adams, Jan. 21, 1812, and same to James Maury, April 25, 1812, Adrienne Koch and William Peden, eds., *The Life and Selected Writings of Thomas Jefferson* (New York: Modern Library, 1944), pp. 617, 620; Henry Clay, *The Papers of Henry Clay*, James F. Hopkins, ed., 5 vols. (Lexington: University of Kentucky Press, 1959–73), 1: 602–609; Clay to Congress, Dec. 31, 1811, *The Weekly Register*, 1: 333.

18. *Annals of the Congress of the United States*, Twelfth Congress, First Session, Part II, 1811–12, 1397.

19. *National Intelligencer*, June 13, 1812.

20. Clay to Congress, Jan. 11, 1812, Clay, *The Papers of Henry Clay*, 1: 613–15.

21. Colonial Secretary to Prevost, May 15, 1812, PAC, CO 42, Vol. 146.

22. Richardson, *Messages and Papers*, 2: 482–87.

23. Norman K. Risjord, "1812: Conservatives, War Hawks, and the Nation's Honor," *William and Mary Quarterly* (April 1961), pp. 196–210.

24. J. C. A. Stagg, "James Madison and the 'Malcontents': The Political Origins of the War of 1812," *William and Mary Quarterly* (October 1976), pp. 557–85.

25. Roger H. Brown, *The Republic in Peril: 1812* (New York: Columbia University Press, 1964), p. 88.

26. *The Times* (London), Feb. 19, 1813.

3—The Eve of the War—The Northeast

1. See, for example, Helen Taft Manning, *The Revolt of French Canada, 1800–1835* (New York: St. Martin's, 1962); and Mason Wade, *The French Canadians, 1760–1945* (Toronto: Macmillan, 1955).

2. C. W. C. Oman, "How General Isaac Brock Saved Canada," *Blackwood's Magazine,* Dec. 1912, p. 738; Lady Edgar, *General Brock* (Toronto: Oxford University Press, 1926); James Hannay, *How Canada Was Held for the Empire* (London: T. C. & E. C. Jack, 1905), p. 24; William C. H. Wood, ed., *Select British Documents of the Canadian War of 1812*, 3 vols. (Toronto: The Champlain Society, 1920), 1: 4; C. S. Forester, "Victory on Lake Champlain," *American Heritage,* Dec. 1963, pp. 6–7.

3. Prevost to Colonial Secretary, March 3, 1812, PAC, CO 42, Vol. 146.

4. Ibid.

5. Prevost to Brock, Sept. 14, 1812, PAC, MG 24, A1.

6. De Salaberry to Prevost, June 18, 1812, PAC, RG 8, Vol. 796.

7. Prevost to Brock, March 31, 1812, PAC, CO 42, Vol. 136.

8. Prevost to Brock, Dec. 24, 1811, Ferdinand Brock Tupper, *The Life and Correspondence of Major-General Sir Isaac Brock, K. B.* (London: Simpkin, Marshall, 1847), p. 135.

9. J. Mackay Hitsman, *The Incredible War of 1812, A Military History* (Toronto: University of Toronto Press, 1965), pp. 28, 39.

10. Walter R. Nursey, *The Story of Isaac Brock* (Toronto: William Briggs, 1908), p. 131.

11. Walter Hill Crockett, *Vermont, the Green Mountain State,* 4 vols. (New York: Century History, 1921), 3: 4.

12. Royal Corbin to Pliny Moore, Nov. 12, 1810, and Nov. 11, 1811, McLellan Collection, Charles W. McLellan, Champlain, N.Y.

13. John Freligh to Dr. Michael Freligh, Nov. 27, 1808, Freligh Collection, Special Collections, Feinberg Library, State University College, Plattsburgh, N.Y.

14. Ibid., May 19, 1812.

15. The new structure was outlined in General Orders, June 18, 1812, in Daniel D. Tompkins, *The Public Papers of Daniel D. Tompkins,* 3 vols. (Albany: State of New York, 1898), 1: 336–42.

16. Ibid., pp. 349–50.

17. Zadock Thompson, *History of Vermont* (Burlington, Vt.: C. Goodrich, 1842), pp. 209–211.

4—War Comes

1. John to Michael Freligh, July 8, 1812, Freligh Collection, Special Collections, Feinberg Library, State University College, Plattsburgh, N.Y.

2. Foster to Castlereagh, April 21, 1812, PAC, CO 42, Vol. 148.

3. Harry L. Coles, *The War of 1812* (Chicago: University of Chicago Press, 1965), p. 109.

4. Griswold Proclamation, Aug. 6, 1812, AUS, RG 107, mic. 221, roll 44.

5. John to Michael Freligh, Aug. 11, 1812, Freligh Collection.

6. Ibid., Sept. 9, 1812.

7. Abraham Per Lee to his father, May 26, 1812, Nell J. B. Sullivan and David K. Martin, *A History of the Town of Chazy* (Burlington, Vt.: George Little Press, 1970), p. 97.

8. Mooers to Tompkins, June 27, July 4 and Sept. 25, 1812, Bailey Collection, Special Collections, Feinberg Library, State University College, Plattsburgh, N.Y.

9. Champlain Committee of Safety to Mooers, July 8, 1812, ibid.; same to Bloomfield, Sept. 22, 1812, McLellan Collection, Charles W. McLellan, Champlain, N.Y.

10. Daniel Robinson to Mooers, July 8 and 10, 1812, Bailey Collection.

11. Prevost to Brock, July 10, 1812, PAC, MG 24, A1.

12. Caleb Nichols to Secretary of War, June 23, 1814, AUS, RG 107, mic. 222, roll 13.

13. Report of Baynes enclosed in Baynes to Prevost, Aug. 12, 1812, PAC, RG 8, Vol. 677.

14. Mooers to Noble, July 18, 1812, Bailey Collection.

15. Mooers to Smith, July 13, 1812, ibid.

16. NacNeil to Noble, Sept. 9 and Oct. 1, 1812, Frederick J. Seaver, *Historical Sketches of Franklin County* (Albany: J. B. Lyon, 1918), p. 619.

17. Mooers to Tompkins, Aug. 1, 1812, Bailey Collection.

18. Battalion Orders, n.d., "Notebooks," 3, Kellogg Papers, Special Collections, Feinberg Library, State University College, Plattsburgh, N.Y.

19. Division Orders, Aug. 25, 1812, Bailey Collection.

20. Division Orders, Aug. 27, 3, and 21, 1812, ibid.

21. *Plattsburgh* (N.Y.) *Republican*, March 16, 1872.

22. Ibid.

23. Baynes's report to Prevost, Aug. 12, 1812, PAC, RG 8, Vol. 677.

24. Henry Adams, *The Formative Years*, Herbert Agar, ed., 2 vols. (Boston: Houghton, Mifflin, 1947), 2: 739.

25. Prevost to Colonial Secretary, Aug. 24, 1812, PAC, CO 42, Vol. 147.

26. Dearborn to Prevost, Aug. 26, 1812, PAC, RG 8, Vol. 677.

27. Prevost to Colonial Secretary, Aug. 17, 1812, PAC, CO 42, Vol. 147.

28. Pike to Armstrong, Aug. 5, 1812, AUS, RG 94, mic. 566, roll 1; John to Michael Freligh, Sept. 9, 1812, Freligh Collection.

29. *The Weekly Register* (Baltimore), Oct. 31, 1812.

30. Tompkins to Mooers and to Bloomfield, Sept. 14, 1812, Daniel D. Tompkins, *The Public Papers of Daniel D. Tompkins, Governor of New York, 1807–1817*, 3 vols. (Albany: State of New York, 1898–1902), 3: 125–27.

31. Bloomfield to Eustis, Nov. 5, 1812, RG 107, mic. 221, roll 42.

32. Jesse S. Myer, *Life and Letters of Dr. William Beaumont* (St. Louis: C. V. Mosby, 1912), p. 29.

33. Eustis to Dearborn, Sept. 28, 1812, AUS, RG 107, mic. 221, roll 6.

34. Rodney Macdonough, *Life of Commodore Thomas Macdonough, U.S. Navy* (Boston: Fort Hill Press, 1909), pp. 109–111.

5 — Indians, Furs, and Prisoners of War

1. William Henry Harrison, *Messages and Letters of William Henry Harrison*, Logan Esarey, ed., 2 vols. (Indianapolis: Indiana Historical Commission, 1922), 1: 417–19.

2. Memorandum of John Norton, Aug. 10, 1808, PAC, CO 42, Vol. 140.

3. Granger to Secretary of War, May 30, 1812, ASPIA, 1: 807.

4. Elliot to Daniel Claus, Oct. 16, 1810, PAC, RG 10, Vol. 27; Craig to Lieutenant Governor Francis Gore, Feb. 2, 1811, enclosed in Craig to Colonial Secretary, March 29, 1811, PAC, CO 42, Vol. 143.

5. Brock to Prevost, Dec. 3, 1811, Douglas Brymner, ed., *Report on Canadian Archives, 1896* (Ottawa: S. E. Dawson, 1897), p. 65; "Philalethes" in *Quebec Mercury*, Jan. 18, 1812.

6. Clay to John Parker, Dec. 7, 1811, Henry Clay, *The Papers of Henry Clay*, James F. Hopkins, ed., 5 vols. (Lexington: University of Kentucky Press, 1959–73), 1: 599.

7. James D. Richardson, ed., *Messages and Papers of the President*, 10 vols. (Washington, D.C.: Government Printing Office, 1896–99), 1:525.

8. Much of the correspondence involving Mooers and the Indians is to be found in the Bailey Collection, Special Collections, Feinberg Library, State University College, Plattsburgh, N.Y.

9. For Williams' activities, see his journal in the *Plattsburgh* (N.Y.) *Republican*, Dec. 11 and 18, 1886, Jan. 1 and 15, Feb. 5 and 12, March 5, 19, and 26, and April 2, 1887.

10. Dearborn to Williams, Aug. 5, and Dearborn to Mooers, Aug. 6, 1812, Bailey Collection.

11. Dearborn to Mooers, Nov. 26, 1812, AUS, RG 107, mic. 221, roll 54.

12. Hastings to Mooers, March 31, 1813; Mooers to Erwin, April 10, 1813, and Erwin to Mooers, Sept. 23, 1813, Bailey Collection.

13. Erwin to Mooers, Sept. 5, 1813, ibid.

14. Pay increase in Williams' journal, *Plattsburgh Republican*, Jan. 1, 1887; Williams' bill, Aug. 24, 1813, and Mooers to Inspector General, May 31, 1814, Bailey Collection.

15. *Plattsburgh Republican*, Dec. 18, 1886.

16. A detailed description of these arrangements is found in Kenneth W. Porter, *John Jacob Astor, Business Man*, 2 vols. (Cambridge, Mass.: Harvard University Press, 1931), 1.

17. Captain A. Gray to Prevost, Jan. 13, 1812, PAC, RG 8, Vol. 676.

18. Astor to Eustis and to Gallatin, June 8, 1812, AUS, RG 107, mic. 221, roll 42; Astor to Pliny Moore, Oct. 13 and 17, 1812, Feb. 3 and March 17, 1813, *Moorsfield Antiquarian* (Champlain, N.Y.: 1937–39) Nov. 1937, pp. 191–99.

19. Sailly Memoirs, *Plattsburgh Republican*, March 16, 1872.

20. Astor to Secretary of the Treasury, May 31, 1817, Porter, *John Jacob Astor*, 1: 263–65.

21. Monroe to Astor, May 16, 1814, ibid., p 269.

22. Sinclair to Secretary of the Navy Jones, Sept. 11, 1814, AUS, RG 45, roll 39.

23. See the discussion in Anthony G. Dietz, *The Prisoner of War in the United States during the War of 1812* (Ph.D. diss., American University, Washington, D.C., 1964), p. 371.

24. Prevost to Colonial Secretary, Sept. 22, 1812, PAC, CO 42, Vol. 147.

25. Report of Brigade Major Shekleton, Nov. 4, 1813, William C. H. Wood, ed., *Select British Documents of the Canadian War of 1812*, 3 vols. (Toronto: The Champlain Society, 1920), 2: 814–15.

26. Prevost to Colonial Secretary, Nov. 30, 1814, PAC, CO 42, Vol. 157.

27. *The Weekly Register* (Baltimore), 8: 129.

28. Beasley to Mason, March 1, 1814, AUS, RG 98, Vol. 141.

29. Dietz, *Prisoners of War*, p. 107.

30. Colonial Secretary to Prevost, Aug. 12, 1813, PAC, CO 42, Vol. 150.

31. Barclay to Prevost, Dec. 19, 1813, Wood, *Select British Documents*, 2: 828–29.

32. Dietz, *Prisoners of War*, p. 375.

33. *North Country Notes* (Plattsburgh, N.Y.: Clinton County Historical Association), April 1975.

34. *Montreal Herald*, July 23, 1814.

35. Dietz, *Prisoners of War*, p. 350.

6 — The Tragic First Winter

1. Henry Adams, *The Formative Years, A History of the United States during the Administrations of Jefferson and Madison*, Herbert Agar, ed., 2 vols. (Boston: Houghton, Mifflin, 1947), 2:747.

2. Letter from Plattsburgh to a friend in Utica, *Political and Commercial Register* (Philadelphia), Dec. 8, 1812.

3. *The Weekly Register* (Baltimore), Nov. 14, 1812.

4. Ibid., Oct. 24, 1812.

5. Winter to Pliny Moore, June 2, 1813; Moore to Winter, June 16, 1813; Shepherd to Moore, March 14, 1814, McLellan Collection, Charles W. McLellan, Champlain, N.Y.

6. *Federal Republican and Commercial Gazette* (Georgetown, Washington, D.C.), Nov. 25, 1812.

7. Moore to Astor, March 26, 1813, *Moorsfield Antiquarian* (Champlain, N.Y.), Nov. 1937, p. 199.

8. General Orders, Nov. 19, 1812, *The Weekly Register*, Dec. 12, 1812.

9. Eustis to Mooers, Dec. 18, 1812, AUS, RG 107, mic. 22, roll 6.

10. Rodney Macdonough, *Life of Commodore Thomas Macdonough, U. S. Navy* (Boston: Fort Hill Press, 1949), p. 113.

11. Beaumont to Samuel Beaumont from Camp Seranac, Feb. 26, 1813, Beaumont Papers, Yale Medical Library, New Haven, Conn.

12. Inspector General to Pike, n.d., AUS, RG 94, mic. 566, roll 1.

13. *The Weekly Register*, Jan. 23, 1813.

14. *Plattsburgh* (N.Y.) *Republican*, Jan. 15, 1813.

15. Pike and Richards to Secretary of War, Feb. 15 and March 21, 1813, AUS, RG 107, mic. 221, roll 5.

16. Journal of Pliny Moore, Dec. 5, 1812, McLellan Collection.

17. The medical sections are based upon James Mann, *Medical Sketches of the Campaigns of 1812, 13, 14* (Dedham, Mass.: H. Mann, 1816). For the Burlington statistics, see pp. 199–200.

18. Jesse S. Myer, *Life and Letters of Dr. William Beaumont* (St. Louis: C. V. Mosby, 1912), pp. 48–53.

19. Beaumont to his parents, Feb. 26, 1813, Beaumont Papers.

20. Mann, *Medical Sketches,* p. ix.

21. Ibid., pp. 35–36.

22. Ibid., pp. 109–110.

23. Harry L. Coles, *The War of 1812* (Chicago: University of Chicago Press, 1965), p. 109.

24. Nell J. B. Sullivan and David K. Martin, *A History of the Town of Chazy, Clinton County, New York* (Burlington, Vt.: George Little Press, 1970), p. 98.

7 — A Summer of Setbacks: 1813

1. Jesse S. Myer, *Life and Letters of Dr. William Beaumont* (St. Louis: C. V. Mosby, 1912), p. 44.

2. Lewis to Armstrong, June 4, 1813, *Montreal Herald,* July 10, 1813.

3. Armstrong to Dearborn, June 19, 1813, AUS, RG 107, mic. 221, roll 6.

4. Porter to Armstrong, July 27, 1813, ibid., mic. 222, roll 9.

5. Robert Christie, *Memoirs of the Administration of the Colonial Government of Lower-Canada* (Quebec, 1818), p. 78.

6. Harrison to Armstrong, March 17, 1813, AUS, RG 107, mic. 221, roll 53.

7. Perry to Secretary of the Navy, AUS, RG 45, mic. 125, roll 31.

8. *Moorsfield Antiquarian* (Champlain, N.Y.), May 1938, pp. 37–38; Mooers to Clark, June 4, 1813, Bailey Collection, Special Collections, Feinberg Library, State University College, Plattsburgh, N.Y.

9. Erwin to Mooers, Sept. 5, 1813, ibid.

10. Macdonough to Jones, Jan. 22, 1813, E. A. Cruikshank, "A Study of Military Operations," *Proceedings and Transactions of the Royal Society of Canada,* 3rd ser., 8 (Ottawa, 1915): 45.

11. Ibid., p. 47; Rodney Macdonough, *Life of Commodore Thomas Macdonough, U. S. Navy* (Boston: Fort Hill Press, 1909), pp. 116–17; Lt. Macdonough to Chauncey, March 10, 1815, ibid., p. 117.

12. James Mann, *Medical Sketches of the Campaigns of 1812, 13, 14* (Dedham, Mass.: H. Mann, 1816), p. 265.

13. *The Weekly Register* (Baltimore), Dec. 11, 1813; *Plattsburgh* (N.Y.) *Republican,* May 4, 1872.

14. *The Weekly Register,* July 10, 1813.

15. Jones to Macdonough, June 17, 1813, Cruikshank, "Military Operations," p. 52.

16. Walter Hill Crockett, *Vermont, the Green Mountain State,* 4 vols. (New York: Century History, 1921), 3:62.

17. Hampton to Madison, Nov. 10, 1812, AUS, RG 107, mic. 222, roll 5.

18. Both letters are found in *Moorsfield Antiquarian,* May 1938, pp. 40–41.

19. Hampton to Mooers, Aug. 29, 1813, Bailey Collection.

20. Williams' Journal, *Plattsburgh Republican,* Jan. 1, 1887.

21. Clark to Armstrong, June 4, 1813, AUS, RG 107, mic. 222, roll 7.

22. All penalties are found in *Moorsfield Antiquarian,* Aug. 1938, pp. 81–89.

23. "Return of the Regimental Courts Martial," PAC, RG 8, Vol. 165.

24. Colonial Secretary to Prevost, Aug. 10, 1812, PAC, CO 42, Vol. 147; Prince Regent to Prevost, Oct. 7, 1812, PAC, RG 8, Vol. 677.

25. Prevost to Colonial Secretary, Sept. 15 and Nov. 15, 1813, and May 10, 1814, PAC, CO 42, Vols. 151, 152 and 156.

26. Adams, John Quincy, *The Diary of John Quincy Adams, 1794-1845*, Allan Nevins, ed. (New York: Scribner's, 1951), p. 131.

27. Cruikshank, "Military Operations," p. 51.

28. Citizens to Mooers, July 31, 1813, Bailey Collection.

29. William C. H. Wood, ed., *Select British Documents of the Canadian War of 1812*, 3 vols. (Toronto: The Champlain Society, 1920), 3, pt. 2, pp. 850-52, 855-60.

30. Sailly's Memoirs, *Plattsburgh Republican*, March 23, 1872; Henry to Julia Delord, May 14, 1820, Kent-Delord Collection, Special Collections, Feinberg Library, State University College, Plattsburgh, N.Y.

31. *The Weekly Register*, Aug. 14, 1813; Morgan to Commandant, Aug. 22, 1813, Bredenberg Collection, Bixby Memorial Library, Vergennes, Vt.

32. Ritter to Moore, March 10, 1814, George S. Bixby, *Peter Sailly* (Albany: University of the State of New York, 1919), p. 82; Sailly to Mrs. Delord, Oct. 10, 1814, Kent-Delord Collection.

8 — The Hampton-Wilkinson Fiasco

1. James R. Jacobs, *Tarnished Warrior* (New York: Macmillan, 1938), pp. 115-16.

2. *The Weekly Register* (Baltimore), 1:469-74.

3. William A. Ganoe, *The History of the United States Army* (New York: D. Appleton, 1924), p. 132.

4. Jacobs, *Tarnished Warrior*, p. 289.

5. Wilkinson to Hampton, Aug. 13, 1813, AUS, RG 107, mic. 222, roll 7; Wilkinson to Armstrong, Aug. 30, 1813, E. A. Cruikshank, "A Study of Military Operations," *Proceedings and Transactions of the Royal Society of Canada*, 3rd ser., 8 (Ottawa, 1915): 65.

6. Hampton to Armstrong, Aug. 22, 1813, AUS, RG 107, mic. 222, roll 7.

7. Hampton to Armstrong, Sept. 7, 1813, ibid.

8. Ibid.

9. Mooers to Tompkins, Sept. 17, 1813, Bailey Collection, Special Collections, Feinberg Library, State University College, Plattsburgh, N.Y.; John to Michael Freligh, Sept. 17 and 22, 1813, Freligh Collection, Special Collections, Feinberg Library, State University College, Plattsburgh, N.Y.

10. Hampton to Armstrong, Sept. 15, 1813, *Message from the President*, pt. 1 (Albany: Websters and Skinners, and H. C. Southwick, 1814), p. 72.

11. Hampton to Armstrong, Sept. 22, 1813, ibid., pp. 72-74.

12. Abby M. Hemenway, *The Vermont Historical Gazetteer*, 5 vols. (1867-91), 2 (Burlington, Vt.: Miss A. M. Hemenway, 1871): 294-95.

13. *The Weekly Register*, Oct. 30, 1813.

14. Hampton to Armstrong, Oct. 4, 1813, Peter S. Palmer, *History of Lake Champlain* (Plattsburgh: J. W. Tuttle, 1853), p. 172.

15. Journal of Pliny Moore, McLellan Collection, Charles W. McLellan, Champlain, N.Y.

16. Moore to Parker, Nov. 2, 1813, ibid.

17. Thurber to Mooers, Nov. 3, 1813, Bailey Collection.

18. *The Weekly Register,* Nov. 3, 1813; Chittenden's Proclamation, Nov. 10, 1813, Hemenway, 1 (Burlington, Vt.: Miss A. M. Hemenway): 671.

19. Ibid., pp. 671–72.

20. Armstrong to Hampton, Sept. 25, 1813, *Message from the President,* 1: 74–75.

21. The most thorough study of the campaign is Victor J. H. Suthren, "The Battle of Chateaugay," in *Canadian Historic Sites: Occasional Papers in Archeology and History,* no. 11 (Ottawa: National Historic Sites Service, 1974), pp. 95–150.

22. Purdy to Wilkinson, n.d., *Message from the President,* 1: 63.

23. Suthren, "The Battle of Chateaugay," p. 135.

24. Wilkinson to Armstrong, Nov. 1, 1813, ASPMA, 1:473; Hampton to Armstrong, Nov. 1, 1813, AUS, RG 107, mic. 222, roll 7; same, Nov. 4, 1813, ibid.

25. Wilkinson to Armstrong, Nov. 3, 1813, ibid.; Wilkinson to Hampton, Nov. 6, 1813, ibid., roll 9; Hampton to Armstrong, Nov. 8, 1813, *Message from the President,* 1:86; Hampton to Wilkinson, Nov. 8, 1813, AUS, RG 107, mic. 222, roll 7.

26. Winter to Moore, Jan. 11, 1814, McLellan Collection.

27. Hampton to Armstrong, Nov. 12, 1813, *Message from the President,* 1: 86–87; same, Nov. 13, 1813, AUS, RG 107, mic. 222, roll 7.

28. Hampton to Armstrong, Nov. 15, 1813, ibid.; Wilkinson to Armstrong, Nov. 15 and 17, 1813, *Message from the President,* 2:42–47, 57.

29. Wilkinson to Armstrong, Nov. 26, 1813, AUS, RG 107, mic. 222, roll 9.

30. Williams' journal, *Plattsburgh* (N.Y.) *Republican,* Feb. 5, 1887; Duane to Parker, Jan. 24, 1814, Jacobs, *Tarnished Warrior,* p. 300.

31. Memorial of Moore and Platt to Congress, Jan. 1815, McLellan Collection.

32. Wilkinson to Armstrong, Nov. 24, 1813, AUS, RG 107, mic. 221, roll 58; Izard to Wilkinson, Dec. 3, 1813, ibid., mic. 222, roll 9.

33. Wilkinson to Armstrong, Dec. 8, 1813, Jacobs, *Tarnished Warrior,* p. 300; Wilkinson to Citizens of Plattsburgh, Jan. 5, 1814, *The Weekly Register,* Feb. 3, 1814; Wilkinson to Armstrong, Jan. 7, 1814, James Wilkinson, *Memoirs of My Own Times,* 3 vols. (Philadelphia: Abraham Small, 1816), 3: App. xlviii.

34. James Mann, *Medical Sketches of the Campaigns of 1812, 13, 14* (Dedham, Mass.: H. Mann, 1816), p. 116.

35. Ibid., pp. 119, 126–27, 144.

36. Information from Herbert McCoy of Plattsburgh, N.Y. a descendant of Gates Hoit.

37. Mann, *Medical Sketches,* p. 144.

38. *The Weekly Register,* Jan. 29, 1814.

9—The Third Tense Summer: 1814

1. Walter Hill Crockett, *Vermont, The Green State,* 4 vols. (New York: Century History 1921), 3:77.

2. Wilkinson to Armstrong, Jan. 7, 1814, James Wilkinson, *Memoirs of My Own Times,* 3 vols. (Philadelphia: Abraham Small, 1816), 3: App. xlviii; same, Jan. 16, 1814, AUS, RG 107, mic. 222, roll 14; same, Jan. 18, 1814, ibid. mic. 221, roll 58.

3. Shepherd to Moore, March 14, 1814, McLellan Collection, Charles W. McLellan, Champlain, N.Y.

4. Williams' Journal, *Plattsburgh* (N.Y.) *Republican,* Feb. 5, 1887.

5. *The Weekly Register* (Baltimore), April 23, 1814.

6. Ibid., May 7, 1814.

7. Macomb to Armstrong, April 28 and May 24, 1814, AUS, RG, 107, mic. 221, roll 55.

8. Armstrong to Izard, May 25, 1814, and Izard to Armstrong, July 12, 1814, ibid., rolls 7 and 62.

9. Izard to Armstrong, May 9 and July 3, 1814, ibid., rolls 54 and 62.

10. Macomb to Izard enclosed in Izard to Armstrong, May 24, 1814, ibid., roll 62; General Orders, July 16, 1814, *The Weekly Register,* Aug. 6, 1814; Armstrong to Izard, Aug. 11, 1814, AUS, RG 107, mic. 221, roll 7.

11. *Plattsburgh Republican,* May 14, 1814.

12. Fenwick to Delord, Aug. 6, 1814, Kent-Delord Collection, Special Collections, Feinberg Library, State University College, Plattsburgh, N.Y.

13. *Plattsburgh Republican,* March 26, 1872.

14. Abby M. Hemenway, *The Vermont Historical Gazetteer,* 5 vols. (1867–91), 1 (Burlington, Vt.: Miss A. M. Hemenway, 1867):106.

15. Jones to Macdonough, Jan. 28, 1814, Walter Hill Crockett, *Vermont, the Green Mountain State,* 4 vols. (New York: Century History, 1921), 3:87–88.

16. Henry P. Smith, ed., *History of Addison County, Vermont* (Syracuse: D. Mason, 1886), p. 231.

17. Armstrong to Izard, May 25, 1814, AUS, RG 107, mic. 221, roll 7.

18. Izard to Armstrong, June 10, 1814, ibid., roll 62.

19. Izard to Armstrong, May 24, 1814, ibid.

20. Izard to Armstrong, May 17, 1814, *The Weekly Register,* June 4, 1814.

21. Henry Harmon Noble, "The Battle of the Bouquet River," *Twentieth Annual Report of the American Scenic and Historic Society* (Albany, 1915), pp. 589–98; Sailly to Moore, June 8, 1814, McLellan Collection.

22. Izard to Armstrong, July 31, 1814, AUS, RG 107, mic. 221, roll 62.

23. *Plattsburgh Republican,* April 6, 1872.

24. Wm. Renwick Riddell, *Addresses by Wm. Renwick Riddell* (privately printed, n.d.), p. 7.

25. Freligh to Winter, Jan. 29, 1814, enclosed in Prevost to Colonial Secretary, March 27, 1814, PAC, CO 42, Vol. 156.

26. Baynes to Prevost, May 1, 1814, enclosed in Prevost to Colonial Secretary, May 17, 1814, ibid.

27. Izard to Armstrong, July 3, 1814, AUS, RG 107, mic. 221, roll 62.

28. Izard to Armstrong, June 29, 1814, with enclosure from Brigadier General Thomas A. Smith, ibid.; Richard Patterson, "Lieutenant Colonel Benjamin Forsyth," *North Country Notes* (Plattsburgh, N.Y.: Clinton County Historical Association), Nov. 1974.

29. Ibid.

30. Izard to Armstrong, July 12, 1814, AUS, RG 107, mic. 221, roll 62.

31. Macdonough to Secretary of the Navy, Aug. 12, 1814, AUS, RG 45, roll 39.

32. Bathurst to Prevost, June 3, 1814, PAC, CO 42, Vol. 23.

33. Charles P. Lucas, *The Canadian War of 1812* (Oxford: Clarendon Press, 1906), p. 197.

34. Prevost to Bathurst, Aug. 27, 1814, PAC, CO 42, Vol. 157.

35. Same, Aug. 5, 1814, ibid.

36. Izard to Armstrong, Aug. 11, 1814, AUS, RG 107, mic. 221, roll 62.

37. Same, Aug. 20, 1814, ibid.

38. The exchange is found in *The Weekly Register*, Oct. 27, 1814.

10 — The British Occupation of Plattsburgh

1. Macomb to Secretary of War, Aug. 31, 1814, AUS, RG 107, mic. 221, roll 64.

2. Journal of Pliny Moore and Moore to Brisbane, Aug. 29, 1814, McLellan Collection, Charles W. McLellan, Champlain, N.Y.; Hubbell reminiscences, *Plattsburgh* (N.Y.) *Republican*, Feb. 1, 1879.

3. *The Weekly Register* (Baltimore), Oct. 1, 1814.

4. Beaumont to his brother, Sept. 1, 1814, Beaumont Papers, Yale Medical Library, New Haven, Conn.

5. Macomb to Mooers, Aug. 31, 1814 and Division Orders, Sept. 4, 1814, Bailey Collection, Special Collections, Feinberg Library, State University College, Plattsburgh, N.Y.

6. *North Countryman*, (Rouses Point, N.Y.), March 25, 1937.

7. General Orders, Sept. 5, 1814, *Plattsburgh Republican*, Sept. 24, 1814.

8. Ibid.

9. James Mann, *Medical Sketches of the Campaigns of 1812, 13, 14* (Dedham, Mass.: H. Mann, 1816), p. 150.

10. These dispositions are fully described in Rodney Macdonough, *Life of Commodore Thomas Macdonough, U.S. Navy*, 2 vols. (Boston: Fort Hill Press, 1909).

11. Bathurst to Prevost, June 3, 1814, PAC, CO 42, Vol. 23.

12. Macomb to Secretary of War, Sept. 18, 1814, AUS, RG 107, mic. 221, roll 62.

13. A. L. Burt, *The United States, Great Britain and British North America* (New Haven, Conn.: Yale University Press, 1940), p. 342; Charles P. Lucas, *The Canadian War of 1812* (Oxford: Clarendon Press, 1906), p. 200; William C. H. Wood, ed., *Select British Documents of the Canadian War of 1812*, 3 vols. (Toronto: The Champlain Society, 1920), 1:117.

14. Enclosed in Prevost to Colonial Secretary, April 1, 1815, PAC, CO 42, Vol. 161.

15. Abby M. Hemenway, *The Vermont Historical Gazetteer*, 5 vols. (1867–91), 2 (Burlington, Vt.: Miss A. M. Hemenway, 1871): 491–92.

16. Ernest Thompson Seton, *Rolf in the Woods* (New York: Grosset & Dunlap, 1911), pp. 385–86.

17. Allan S. Everest, ed., *Recollections of Clinton County and the Battle of Plattsburgh* (Plattsburgh, N.Y.: Clinton County Historical Association, 1964), pp. 25–26.

18. *Plattsburgh Republican,* March 26, 1887.

19. Everest, *Recollections,* p. 39.

20. Ibid., pp. 39–40.

21. Macomb to Secretary of War, Sept. 8, 1814, AUS, RG 107, mic. 221, roll 64.

22. Told by a descendant, Miss Greta Howes, to Addie Shields, Clinton County (N.Y.) Historian.

23. *Plattsburgh* (N.Y.) *Sentinel,* Jan. 24, 1873.

24. Mooers to Tompkins, Sept. 6, 1814, Bailey Collection; Division Orders, Sept. 18, 1814, *The Weekly Register,* Oct. 15, 1814; Macomb to Secretary of War, Sept. 15, 1814, AUS, RG 107, mic. 221, roll 64.

25. *Plattsburg Republican,* April 4, 1935.

26. Major John Sinclair of the Royal Artillery to Baynes, March 20, 1815, enclosed in Prevost to Colonial Secretary, April 2, 1815, PAC, CO 42, Vol. 161.

27. Hemenway, *Historical Gazetteer,* 2:296–97.

28. Ibid., pp. 53–54.

29. Dr. David S. Kellogg, "The Invasion of 1814," a lecture delivered in 1888, Kellogg Papers, Special Collections, Feinberg Library, State University College, Plattsburgh, N.Y.

30. Macomb to Mooers, Sept. 10, 1814, Bailey Collection.

31. Williams' journal, *Plattsburgh Republican,* March 19 and 27, 1887.

32. George H. Richards, *Memoir of Alexander Macomb* (New York: M'Elrath, Bangs, 1833), pp. 92–94.

11 — The Battle of Plattsburgh

1. Nell J. B. Sullivan and David K. Martin, *A History of the Town of Chazy, Clinton County, New York* (Burlington, Vt.: George Little Press, 1970), p. 102.

2. The exchange of letters is found in PAC, CO 42, Vol. 158.

3. Macdonough to Secretary of the Navy, Sept. 11, 1814, AUS, RG 45, roll 39.

4. *Plattsburgh* (N.Y.) *Republican,* Feb. 1, 1879.

5. For Robinson's detailed account of the engagement, see Robinson to Merry (unidentified) from Chambly, Sept. 22, 1814, Public Archives of Ontario, Ottawa.

6. Macomb to Secretary of War, Sept. 15, 1814, AUS, RG 107, mic. 221.

7. William C. H. Wood, ed., *Select British Documents of the Canadian War of 1812,* 3 vols. (Toronto: The Champlain Society, 1920), 3:352.

8. Sinclair to Baynes, March 20, 1815, *North Countryman* (Rouses Point, N.Y.), Feb. 26, 1926.

9. Robinson to Merry, Sept. 22, 1814, Public Archives of Ontario.

10. Sullivan and Martin, *Town of Chazy,* p. 103.

11. Macomb to Secretary of War, Sept. 15, 1814, AUS, RG 107, mic. 221, roll 64.

12. Allan S. Everest, ed., *Recollections of Clinton County and the Battle of Plattsburgh* (Plattsburgh, N.Y.: Clinton County Historical Association, 1964), pp. 32, 26.

13. *North Country Notes* (Plattsburgh, N.Y.: Clinton County Historical Association), May 1976.

14. *Montreal Herald,* Sept. 17, 1814.

15. *The Weekly Register* (Baltimore), Oct. 15, 1814.

16. Everest, *Recollections,* p. 49.

17. The American army officer buried in Riverside Cemetery was Lt. George Runk; the navy contributed Lt. Peter Gamble, Acting Midshipman James Baldwin and Pilot Joseph Barron, all of the *Saratoga,* Lt. John Stansbury of the *Ticonderoga,* and Acting Sailing Master Rogers Carter of the *Preble.* The British navy lost Capt. George Downie, Lt. William Gunn, Lt. William Paul, Capt. Alexander Anderson of the Marines, and Boatswain Charles Jackson. From their army, in addition to Wellington, Chapman, and Kingsbury, Capt. John Purchase of the Seventy-sixth Regiment rests there.

18. Walter Hill Crockett, *Vermont, the Green Mountain State,* 4 vols. (New York: Century History, 1921), 3:191–92.

19. Oscar Bredenberg, *The Battle of Plattsburgh Bay, The British Navy's View* (Plattsburgh, (N.Y.: Clinton County Historical Association, 1978), pp. 19–20.

20. Amasa to Pliny Moore, June 30, 1814, McLellan Collection, Charles W. McLellan, Champlain, N.Y.

12 — Aftermath

1. *Plattsburgh* (N.Y.) *Republican,* May 25, 1844.

2. Rodney Macdonough, *Life of Commodore Thomas Macdonough, U. S. Navy* (Boston: Fort Hill Press, 1909), p. 200.

3. Macdonough to Secretary of the Navy, Nov. 6, 1814, AUS, RG 45, roll 40.

4. Yeo to Viscount Melailee, May 30, 1815, PAC, MG 12, Adm. 1, Vol. 2738.

5. Henry Adams, *The Formative Years, A History of the United States during the Administrations of Jefferson and Madison,* Herbert Agar, ed., 2 vols. (Boston: Houghton, Mifflin, 1947), 2:936.

6. The most detailed account of the conference is Fred L. Engleman, *The Peace of Christmas Eve* (New York: Harcourt, Brace, 1962).

7. Wellington's Supplementary Dispatches, A. L. Burt, *The United States, Great Britain and British North America* (New Haven, Conn.: Yale University Press, 1940), p. 362.

8. Samuel Flagg Bemis, *A Diplomatic History of the United States* (New York: H. Holt, 1942), p. 167.

9. *The Weekly Register* (Baltimore), 13: 273–74; ASPMA, 3:458–600.

10. Anglican Bishop to Bathurst, June 3, 1813, PAC, CO 42, Vol. 153.

11. Prevost to Bathurst, July 23, 1814, ibid., Vol. 157.

12. "A Brief Review of the Political Scene of the Province of Lower Canada during the last seven years," May 12, 1814, ibid., Vol. 159; Executive Council to Bathurst, July 14, 1814, ibid.

13. Assembly Committee to Bathurst, Nov. 19, 1814, ibid.

14. Prevost to Bathurst, March 29, 1814, ibid., Vol. 161.

15. Oscar Bredenberg, *The Battle of Plattsburgh Bay, The British Navy's View* (Plattsburgh, N.Y.: Clinton County Historical Association, 1978), p. 20.

16. Beaumont to his brother, Jan. 9, Feb. 25, and Mar. 25, 1815, Beaumont Papers, Yale Medical Library, New Haven, Conn.

17. James Mann, *Medical Sketches of the Campaigns of 1812, 13, 14* (Dedham, Mass.: H. Mann, 1816), pp. 37, 272–74.

18. See 66.7a, boxes 4 and 6, Kent-Delord Collection, Special Collections, Feinberg Library, State University College, Plattsburgh, N.Y.

BIBLIOGRAPHY

For readers interested in more information on the broader aspects of the War of 1812, the most recent comprehensive treatment is John K. Mahon, *The War of 1812* (Gainesville: University of Florida Press, 1972). A briefer but excellent coverage is Harry L. Coles, *The War of 1812* (Chicago: University of Chicago Press, 1965). The best treatment from the Canadian point of view is J. Mackay Hitsman, *The Incredible War of 1812, A Military History* (Toronto: University of Toronto Press, 1965). Benson J. Lossing, *Pictorial Field-Book of the War of 1812* (New York: Harper & Brothers, 1868), although not always accurate, is still unsurpassed for the wealth of detail and illustrations.

For more specialized aspects of the conflict, the best chronicle of events leading up to war is Bradford Perkins, *Prologue to War: England and the United States, 1805–1812* (Berkeley: University of California Press, 1961). The causes of the war are treated in Reginald Horsman, *The Causes of the War of 1812* (Philadelphia: University of Pennsylvania Press, 1962) and, from a more specific point of view, Roger H. Brown, *The Republic in Peril: 1812* (New York: Columbia University Press, 1964).

The best analysis of the naval war is still Alfred Mahan, *Sea Power in Its Relation to the War of 1812*, 2 vols. (Boston: Little, Brown, 1905). Fred L. Engelman, *The Peace of Christmas Eve* (New York: Harcourt, Brace, 1962) is the most complete coverage of the peace conference. The following bibliography lists only those sources that were specifically helpful in writing this account of one of the major theatres of the war.

Unpublished Sources

Bailey Collection. Special Collections, Feinberg Library, State University of New York, Plattsburgh.

Beaumont Papers, Yale Medical Library, New Haven, Conn.

Bredenberg Collection. Bixby Memorial Library, Vergennes, Vt.

Freligh Collection. Special Collections, Feinberg Library, State University of New York, Plattsburgh.

Kellogg Papers. Special Collections, Feinberg Library, State University of New York, Plattsburgh.

Kent-Delord Collection. Special Collections, Feinberg Library, State University of New York, Plattsburgh.

McLellan Collection. Charles W. McLellan, Champlain, N.Y.

Manuscript Group 11, Colonial Office 42 — Colonial Office Papers. Public Archives of Canada, Ottawa.

Manuscript Group 24 — Nineteenth Century Pre-Confederation Papers. Public Archives of Canada, Ottawa.

Public Archives of Ontario, Ottawa.

Record Group 8 — British Military and Naval Records. Public Archives of Canada, Ottawa.

Record Group 10 — Indian Affairs. Public Archives of Canada, Ottawa.

Record Group 45 — Naval Records Collection of the Office of Naval Records and Library (Letters Received by the Secretary of the Navy, Captains' Letters, 1805–1885). Microcopy 125. Archives of the United States, Washington, D.C.

Record Group 94 — Letters Received by the Office of the Adjutant General, 1805–1821. Microcopy 566. Archives of the United States, Washington, D.C.

Record Group 98 — Records of the Army Command: Post-Revolutionary War Period 1792–1826). Archives of the United States, Washington, D.C.

Record Group 107 — War Department, Secretary's Office: Archives of the United States, Washington, D.C.:

> Letters Received by the Secretary of War, Regular Series, 1801–1860. Microcopy 221.
>
> Letters Sent by the Secretary of War, Military Affairs. Microcopy 221.
>
> Letters Received by the Secretary of War, Unregistered Series, 1789–1860. Microcopy 222.

Published Sources

American State Papers. Documents, Legislative and Executive, of the Congress of the United States: Foreign Relations. 38 vols. Washington, D.C.: Gales and Seaton, 1832–34.

American State Papers. Documents, Legislative and Executive, of the Congress of the United States: Indian Affairs. 2 vols. Washington D.C.: Gales and Seaton, 1832–34.

American State Papers. Documents, Legislative and Executive, of the Congress of the

United States: Military Affairs. 7 vols. Washington, D.C.: Gales and Seaton, 1832–61.

Annals of the Congress of the United States, 1789–1824. 42 vols. Washington, D.C.: Gales and Seaton, 1834–56.

Brymner, Douglas, ed. *Report on Canadian Archives, 1896.* Ottawa: S. E. Dawson, 1897.

Clay, Henry. *The Papers of Henry Clay.* James F. Hopkins, ed. 5 vols. Lexington: University of Kentucky Press, 1959–73.

Harrison, William Henry. *Messages and Letters of William Henry Harrison.* Logan Esarey, ed., 2 vols. Indianapolis: Indiana Historical Commission, 1922.

Johnson, Herbert T., ed. *Roster of Soldiers in the War of 1812–14.* St. Albans, Vt.: Messenger Press, 1933.

Koch, Adrienne, and Peden, William, eds. *The Life and Selected Writings of Thomas Jefferson.* New York: Modern Library, 1944.

Message from the President of the United States, transmitting a Letter from the Secretary of War with Sundry Documents. Albany: Websters and Skinners, and H. C. Southwick, 1814.

Myer, Jesse S. *Life and Letters of Dr. William Beaumont.* St. Louis: C. V. Mosby, 1912.

Richardson, James D., ed. *Messages and Papers of the Presidents.* 10 vols. Washington, D.C.: Government Printing Office, 1896–99.

Tompkins, Daniel D. *The Public Papers of Daniel D. Tompkins, Governor of New York, 1807–1817.* 3 vols. Albany: State of New York, 1898–1902.

Wood, William C. H., ed. *Select British Documents of the Canadian War of 1812.* 3 vols. Toronto: The Champlain Society, 1920.

Secondary Works

Adams, Henry. *The Formative Years, A History of the United States during the Administrations of Jefferson and Madison.* Herbert Agar, ed. 2 vols. Boston: Houghton, Mifflin, 1947.

Adams, John Quincy. *The Diary of John Quincy Adams, 1794–1845.* Allan Nevins, ed. New York: Scribner's, 1951.

Bemis, Samuel Flagg. *A Diplomatic History of the United States.* New York: H. Holt, 1942.

Bixby, George S. *Peter Sailly, 1754–1826.* Albany: University of the State of New York, 1919.

Brown, Roger H. *The Republic in Peril: 1812.* New York: Columbia University Press, 1964.

Burt, A. L. *The United States, Great Britain and British North America.* New Haven, Conn.: Yale University Press, 1940.

Chapelle, Howard I. *The History of the American Sailing Navy; the Ships and Their Development.* New York: Norton, 1949.

Christie, Robert. *Memoirs of the Administration of the Colonial Goernment of Lower-Canada, by Sir James Henry Craig and Sir George Prevost.* Quebec, 1818.

Clark, Byron N., ed. *A List of Pensioners of the War of 1812.* Boston: Research Publication, 1904.

Coles, Harry L. *The War of 1812.* Chicago: University of Chicago Press, 1965.

Crockett, Walter Hill. *Vermont, the Green Mountain State.* 4 vols. New York: Century History, 1921.

Dietz, Anthony G. *The Prisoners of War in the United States during the War of 1812.* Ph.D. dissertation, American University, Washington, D.C., 1964.

Dwight, Rev. Timothy. *Travels in New-England and New-York.* 4 vols. New Haven: T. Dwight, 1821–22.

Engelman, Fred L. *The Peace of Christmas Eve.* New York: Harcourt, Brace, 1962.

Everest, Allan S., ed. *Recollections of Clinton County and the Battle of Plattsburgh, 1800–1840.* Plattsburgh, N.Y.: Clinton County Historical Association, 1964.

Ganoe, William A. *The History of the United States Army.* New York: D. Appleton, 1924.

Hannay, James. *How Canada Was Held for the Empire.* London: T. C. & E. C. Jack, 1905.

Hecksher, Eli F. *The Continental System: An Economic Interpretation.* Gloucester, Mass.: P. Smith, 1964.

Hemenway, Abby M. *The Vermont Historical Gazetteer.* 5 vols. Vols. I and II, Burlington, Vt.: Miss A. M. Hemenway, 1867, 1871; Vol. III, Claremont, N.H.: Claremont Manufacturing, 1877; Vol. IV, Montpelier, Vt.: Watchman & State Journal Press, 1882; Vol. V, Brandon, Vt.: Mrs. Carrie E. H. Page, 1891.

Hitsman, J. Mackay. *The Incredible War of 1812, A Military History.* Toronto: University of Toronto Press, 1965.

Horsman, Reginald. *The Causes of the War of 1812.* Philadelphia: University of Pennsylvania Press, 1962.

Hurd, Duane, ed. *History of Clinton and Franklin Counties, New York.* Philadelphia: J. W. Lewis, 1880.

Irwin, Ray W. *Daniel D. Tompkins, Governor of New York and Vice President of the United States.* New York: New York Historical Society, 1968.

Jacobs, James R. *Tarnished Warrior, Major-General James Wilkinson.* New York: Macmillan, 1938.

Jellison, Charles A. *Ethan Allen, Frontier Rebel.* Syracuse: Syracuse University Press, 1969.

Lady Edgar. *General Brock.* Toronto: Oxford University Press, 1926.

Lossing, Benson J. *Pictorial Field-Book of the War of 1812.* New York: Harper & Brothers, 1868.

Lucas, Charles P. *The Canadian War of 1812.* Oxford: Clarendon Press, 1906.

Macdonough, Rodney. *Life of Commodore Thomas Macdonough, U.S. Navy.* Boston: Fort Hill Press, 1909.

Mahan, Alfred. *Sea Power in Its Relation to the War of 1812.* 2 vols. Boston: Little, Brown, 1905.

Mahon, John K. *The War of 1812.* Gainesville: University of Florida Press, 1972.

Mann, James. *Medical Sketches of the Campaigns of 1812, 13, 14.* Dedham, Mass.: H. Mann, 1816.

Manning, Helen Taft. *The Revolt of French Canada, 1800-1835.* New York: St. Martin's, 1962.

Nursey, Walter R. *The Story of Isaac Brock.* Toronto: William Briggs, 1908.

Palmer, Peter S. *History of Lake Champlain.* Plattsburgh: J. W. Tuttle, 1853.

Perkins, Bradford, *Prologue to War: England and the United States, 1805-1812.* Berkeley: University of California Press, 1961.

Perkins, Rev. Nathan. *A Narrative of a Tour through the State of Vermont from April 27 to June 12, 1789.* Rutland, Vt.: C. E. Tuttle, 1964.

Porter, Kenneth W. *John Jacob Astor, Business Man.* 2 vols. Cambridge, Mass.: Harvard University Press, 1931.

Proceedings of the New York State Historical Association, Vol. XIV. New York: New York State Historical Association, 1915.

Richards, George H. *Memoir of Alexander Macomb, The Major General Commanding the Army of the United States.* New York: M'Elrath, Bangs, 1833.

Seaver, Frederick J. *Historical Sketches of Franklin County and Its Several Towns.* Albany: J. B. Lyon, 1918.

Seton, Ernest Thompson. *Rolf in the Woods.* New York: Grosset & Dunlap, 1911.

Smith, Henry P., ed. *History of Addison County, Vermont.* Syracuse: D. Mason, 1886.

Stanley, George F. G. *Canada's Soldiers, 1604-1954; The Military History of an Unmilitary People.* Toronto: Macmillan, 1954.

Stephen, James. *War in Disguise; or the Frauds of the Neutral Flags.* New York: Hopkins & Seymour, 1806.

Sullivan, Nell Jane Barnett, and Martin, David Kendall. *A History of the Town of Chazy, Clinton County, New York.* Burlington, Vt.: George Little Press, 1970.

Thompson, Zadock. *History of Vermont, Natural, Civil, and Statistical.* Burlington, Vt.: C. Goodrich, 1842.

Tupper, Ferdinand Brock. *The Life and Correspondence of Major-General Sir Isaac Brock, K. B.* London: Simpkin, Marshall, 1847.

Wade, Mason, *The French Canadians, 1760-1945.* Toronto: Macmillan, 1955.

Wilkinson, James. *Memoirs of My Own Times.* 3 vols. Philadelphia: Abraham Small, 1816.

Pamphlets, Journals, and Newspapers

Bredenberg, Oscar. *The Battle of Plattsburgh Bay, The British Navy's View.* Platts-burgh, N.Y.: Clinton County Historical Association, 1978.

_____. *Military Activities in the Champlain Valley after 1777.* Champlain, N.Y.: Moorsfield Press, 1962.

Broadwell, Andrew S. *The Dewey Tavern, A Historic Landmark.* Rouses Point, N.Y., 1965.

Casey, Richard P. "North Country Nemesis: The Potash Rebellion and the Embargo of 1807–09." *The New York Historical Society Quarterly,* January 1980.

Cruikshank, E. A. "A Study of Disaffection in Upper Canada in 1812–15." *Proceedings and Transactions of the Royal Society of Canada* 6, sec. II (1912), Ottawa, 1913.

_____. "A Study of Military Operations on the Frontier of Lower Canada in 1812 and 1813." *Proceedings of the Royal Society of Canada,* 3rd ser., 8. Ottawa, 1915.

Federal Republican and Commercial Gazette (Georgetown, Washington, D.C.).

Forester, C. S. "Victory on Lake Champlain." *American Heritage,* December 1963.

Montreal Herald.

Moore, Amasa C. *An Address on the Battle of Plattsburgh Delivered at the Celebration of the Anniversary, Sept. 11th, 1843.* Plattsburgh: J. W. Tuttle, 1844.

Moorsfield Antiquarian. 1 and 2 (1937–39). Champlain, N.Y.

Morton, Doris B. *Whitehall in the War of 1812.* Whitehall, N.Y.: Washington County Historical Society, 1964.

National Intelligencer.

Noble, Henry Harmon. "The Battle of the Boquet River." *Twentieth Annual Report of the American Scenic and Historic Society.* Albany, 1915.

North Countryman (Rouses Point, N.Y.).

North Country Notes. Monthly publication of the Clinton County Historical Association, Plattsburgh.

Oman, C. W. C. "How General Isaac Brock Saved Canada." *Blackwood's Magazine,* December 1912.

Patterson, Richard. "Lieutenant Colonel Benjamin Forsyth." *North Country Notes,* November 1974.

Plattsburgh (N.Y.) *Republican.*

Plattsburgh (N.Y.) *Sentinel.*

Political and Commercial Register (Philadelphia).

Quebec Mercury.

Riddell, Wm. Renwick. *Addresses by Wm. Renwick Riddell.* Privately printed, n.d.

Risjord, Norman K. "1812: Conservatives, War Hawks, and the Nation's Honor." *William and Mary Quarterly,* April 1961.

Stagg, J. C. A. "James Madison and the 'Malcontents': The Political Origins of the War of 1812." *William and Mary Quarterly,* October 1976.

Suthren, Victor J. H. "The Battle of Chateaugay." *Canadian Historic Sites: Occasional Papers in Archeology and History,* no. 11. Ottawa: National Historic Sites Service, 1974.

The Times (London).

Vermont Centinel (Burlington).

The Weekly Register (Baltimore).

INDEX

THE WAR OF 1812 IN THE CHAMPLAIN VALLEY

was composed in 10-point Compugraphic Garamond and leaded two points
by Metricomp Studios;
with display type in Mergenthaler VIP Garamond
by DIX Typesetting Co. Inc.;
printed by sheet-fed offset on 50-pound acid-free Glatfelter Antique Cream paper,
Smythe-sewn, and bound over 70-point binder's boards in Joanna Kennett MV500 series,
also adhesive-bound with 10-point Carolina laminated covers,
by Maple-Vail Book Manufacturing Group, Inc.;
and published by

SYRACUSE UNIVERSITY PRESS
SYRACUSE, NEW YORK 13210